BEST-EVER
Recipes

VOLUME III

EDITORIAL

EDITORIAL DIRECTOR, FAMILY CIRCLE BOOKS: Carol A. Guasti
ASSOCIATE EDITOR: Kim E. Gayton
PROJECT EDITOR: David Ricketts
COPY EDITOR: Laura Crocker
BOOK DESIGN: Karen Benson
DESIGN DIRECTION: MBS + K
COVER PHOTO: Jerry Simpson
ILLUSTRATIONS: Lauren Jarrett
EDITORIAL PRODUCTION COORDINATOR: Celeste Bantz
EDITORIAL ASSISTANT: Sherieann Holder
EDITORIAL INTERNS: K. Keith Warren, Adam A. Hicks
SENIOR TYPESETTER: Alison Chandler
TYPESETTING: Maureen Harrington, Cheryl Aden
INDEXER: Candace Gylgayton

MARKETING

DIRECTOR, FAMILY CIRCLE BOOKS & LICENSING: Margaret Chan-Yip
ASSOCIATE BUSINESS MANAGER: Carrie Meyerhoff
ADMINISTRATIVE ASSISTANT: Laura Berkowitz

Published by The Family Circle, Inc.
110 Fifth Avenue, New York, NY 10011

Manufactured in the United States of America

10 9 8 7 6 5 4 3 2 1

Library of Congress Cataloging in Publication Data
Main entry under title:

Family circle best-ever recipes volume iii.
Includes index.
1. Cookery.
I. Family Circle, Inc.   II. best-ever recipes.

1992   91-649509

ISBN 0-933585-25-X
ISSN 1052-6633

OTHER BOOKS BY FAMILY CIRCLE

To order **FamilyCircle** books, write to Family Circle Books,
110 Fifth Avenue, New York, NY 10011.

To order **FamilyCircle** magazine, write to Family Circle Subscriptions,
110 Fifth Avenue, New York, NY 10011.

*T*able *of Contents*

*I*ntroduction

Buzzwords for life in the 90's — cocooning, nesting, stress-busting — all reflect our desire to create a family sanctuary amidst the clamor of daily living. To help lessen your kitchen load and put the joy back in cooking, the Editors of Family Circle have gathered together a collection of tempting and time-smart recipes for *Best-Ever Recipes, Volume III*.

Weekday meals present the cook's biggest dilemma: creating healthful dinners that the whole family enjoys and that don't take hours to prepare. We provide you with over 50 entrée recipes using poultry, beef, pork, seafood, pasta, vegetables and legumes — all of which can be ready in record time. *Plus*, each and every recipe comes with a suggested menu to make your meal planning a breeze. To help with the rest of the day, we also offer sections on beat-the-clock breakfasts and make-ahead lunches.

Weekends and holidays offer more time and inspiration for a cook to shoot for star-quality meals. There's something for every occasion in Chapter 2, from easy entertaining for a relaxing weekend, to feasts that tantalize the tastebuds *and* feed the spirit. And we don't forget the holidays: Thanksgiving, Christmas — even a New England-style Fourth of July clambake!

Frequently a meal needs just the right accent to be complete. Our potpourri of soups, salads and side dishes will brighten any meal. You'll also find a chapter devoted to that miracle of modern living: the microwave oven. And, last but definitely not least, no meal is quite complete without dessert. Our last chapter overflows with sweet endings, from light and luscious sherbets to freshly baked delicacies — there's something to please everyone's palate.

The recipes in this volume emphasize fresh ingredients, great taste and ease of preparation. To help keep your family meals well balanced, we've flagged recipes that are low-calorie, low-sodium, low-cholesterol and/or low-fat.

CRITERIA FOR LOW-CALORIE, LOW-SODIUM, LOW-CHOLESTEROL AND LOW-FAT DISHES

The limit for these guidelines goes up to and includes the number.

Low-Calorie	Low-Sodium	Low-Cholesterol
Main dish . 350 cal.	Main dish . 140 mg	Main dish . . . 75 mg
Side dish . . 100 cal.	Side dish . . 100 mg	Side dish . . . . 15 mg
Snack . . . . . 100 cal.	Snack . . . . 65 mg	Snack . . . . 7 mg
Condiment . 25 cal.	Condiment . . 50 mg	Condiment . . . 5 mg
Dessert . . . 150 cal.	Dessert . . . . . 50 mg	Dessert . . . . . 25 mg

Low-Fat No more than 30% of the calories in a dish should be attributable to fat. To calculate this, apply the following: Grams of fat in the recipe x 9 calories (9 calories in 1 milligram fat) divided by total calories in dish x 100 = percentage of calories attributable to fat.

RECOMMENDED DIETARY ALLOWANCES (RDA)

RECOMMENDED DIETARY ALLOWANCES (RDA) The Committee on Dietary Allowances of the National Academy of Sciences/National Research Council publishes and frequently revises the Recommended Dietary Allowances (RDA) which set standards for the daily nutritional needs of healthy males and females at various stages in their lives. Consult the chart below for recommended dietary guidelines.

CALORIES What *is* a calorie? The term "calorie" is used to describe the *measure of energy* derived from the foods we eat. When the number of calories consumed exceeds the amount needed by the body, the excess calories are transformed into fat. Stored fat may be used by the body during times of stress, but an overabundance of fat just sits in the body. In a well-balanced diet, about 8% to 12% of the calorie count should come from protein, no more than 30% from fat (primarily poly- or mono-unsaturated), and the rest should come from complex carbohydrates.

PROTEIN How much protein is needed in a healthy diet? Nutritionists seem to agree that a diet high in complex carbohydrates, low in fats and with moderate consumption of protein is the ideal diet both for weight control *and* for good health.

A "protein" is a long chain of amino acids. Protein is a component of all body cells, antibodies and enzymes, and is essential for the growth, repair and maintenance of healthy cells. Proteins from most animal sources — meat, fish, eggs, poultry and dairy products — usually are "complete," meaning they have a complete chain of the amino acids needed for a healthy diet. Proteins from plant sources usually are incomplete and must be paired with complementary proteins to provide all the necessary amino acids — i.e., rice with beans or peanut butter with milk.

FAT Despite negative press, not all fat is bad. Fat provides energy, helps the body maintain its heat and assists in the absorption of fat-soluble vitamins, such as vitamin E. However, fat has more calories than a similar amount of either carbohydrates or protein, so a little goes a long way.

Fat is made up of three types of linked fatty acids: saturated, polyunsaturated and monounsaturated. Saturated fat is found primarily in animal sources, but also is present in some plant sources, such as palm and coconut oils — these are the high-cholesterol fats. Polyunsaturated fat is found primarily in vegetable sources and some fish sources such as herring, salmon and mackerel. Monounsaturated fat also is primarily from plant sources and is found in olive and peanut oils, for example.

What does all this mean? Evidence seems to suggest that polyunsaturated fats may help to reduce the amount of cholesterol by increasing the ratio of HDLs (high density lipoproteins) in the blood. These cholesterol-carrying particles actually help sweep excess cholesterol out of the bloodstream. Saturated fats, on the other hand, may increase the ratio of LDLs (low density lipoproteins) in the blood. These LDLs deposit excess cholesterol in the arteries, which may result in plaque on blood vessel walls, subsequent hardening of the arteries and cardiovascular disease. Monounsaturated fats also seem to have a beneficial effect on cholesterol levels. Recent studies of Mediterranean populations, where use of olive oil is common, show the incidence of cardiovascular disease is very low in this region.

CARBOHYDRATES Let's hear it for carbohydrates! They provide efficient energy, are comparatively low in calories and leave you with a satisfied "full" feeling — great news for dieters.

All carbohydrates are composed of sugars, arranged in various combinations. Simple carbohydrates are made of three simple sugars: glucose, fructose and galactose, found in fruits and cane sugars, or in combinations of two single sugars.

Complex carbohydrates are combinations of simple sugars arranged in long and intricate chains. They fall into three categories: starch, which is broken down by the body to use as its chief source of energy; glycogen, which is excess glucose that is stored in the liver; and cellulose, the woody, stringy part of plants known as fiber (essential to the proper functioning of the digestive tract). Potatoes, whole-grain breads and cereals, rice, pasta, legumes, fruits and vegetables are all good sources of "complex" carbohydrates.

There are no recommended levels of daily intake for carbohydrates. But it is believed that an increase of complex carbohydrates and moderation of simple sugars (such as honey and table sugar) is beneficial to the diet.

DAILY NUTRITION COUNTDOWN CHART

Refer to the nutrient value listings on each of our recipes and then use the following guidelines to ensure a well-balanced, healthful diet.

Average Healthy Adult

	Women	Men
Calories[1]	2,000	2,700
Protein[2]	50 g (200 cal)	63 g (252 cal)
Fat[3]	66 g (594 cal)	90 g (810 cal)
Sodium[4]	1,100-3,300 mg	1,100-3,300 mg
Cholesterol[5]	300 mg	300 mg

Calories that do not come from protein or fat should be derived from complex carbohydrates found in whole grains, fresh fruits, vegetables, pasta, etc.

[1]RDA [2](8%-12% of calories) RDA [3](30% of calories) Amer. Heart Assoc. and Nat'l Acad. of Science [4]USDA [5]Amer. Heart Assoc.

SODIUM All animals need salt, and humans are no exception. Sodium, which makes up 40% of the salt molecule, is a major component of the fluid surrounding the cells in the body. Sodium is necessary to regulate the balance of water in body tissues and is active in muscle contraction. It touches off the heartbeat and controls its rhythm. But as crucial as sodium is, we need surprisingly little of it to function.

Excess sodium in the diet is considered to be a contributing cause of high blood pressure, heart disease, hypertension (a risk factor in strokes) and kidney failure. Processed foods generally contain high levels of sodium and many people oversalt food both while cooking and at the table. With sodium, as with most minerals, moderation is the key.

The U.S. Dept. of Agriculture (USDA) recommends 1,100 to 3,300 milligrams (1.1 to 3.3 grams) of sodium a day for both the average healthy adult male and female.

CHOLESTEROL Cholesterol seems to be the buzzword of late; many people are concerned with its adverse effects. It may surprise you to learn that most of the cholesterol in your body is produced by your liver. Cholesterol is an essential part of cell membranes, is used in building nerve sheaths and is the raw material for manufacturing hormones.

According to Harvard Medical School research, the body is capable of producing all the cholesterol it needs — without getting it from food sources. Excess levels of cholesterol in the blood have been linked with the increased likelihood of heart disease, atherosclerosis (clogged arteries) and stroke. The most concentrated form of cholesterol is the egg yolk, as well as organ meats — liver, kidney and brains. Also, any whole-milk dairy product, most red meats and some seafood are culpable.

The American Heart Association recommends no more than 300 milligrams daily for both the average healthy adult female and male.

GUIDELINES FOR GOOD EATING How do you balance all of this nutritional information? In addition to the RDA, the USDA and the U.S. Dept. of Health and Human Services have suggested several guidelines for a sensible eating plan. But as research continues, these guidelines, as well as the RDA, are subject to change. The best defense is a well-informed attack: keep up-to-date on the latest medical and nutritional findings. If you have specific dietary problems, or are taking any prescription medication, consult a physician first before planning your diet.

Eat a wide variety of foods. Plan meals around basic food groups: breads, cereals, rice and pasta; meat, poultry, fish, beans and peas, eggs and nuts; milk and milk products; fruits and vegetables. Vary the selection to ensure you're receiving all the necessary nutrients.

Maintain a healthy weight. Consult your physician to decide upon your optimum weight. If you need to lose weight, avoid extreme approaches which promise a rapid weight loss and severely restrict the variety of foods or calories allowed. Such radical changes in weight can be dangerous. Instead, aim for a ½ to 1 pound loss per week. Set a reasonable weight goal and strive to obtain permanent results through better habits of eating and exercise.

Choose a diet low in fat, saturated fat, and cholesterol. It is recommended that no more than 30% of the day's total calories come from fat. High levels of fat, especially saturated fat, and cholesterol in the diet have been linked to an increased risk for heart disease. Choose lean meats, fish and poultry without the skin, and explore methods of cooking that add little or no extra fats. Remember that legumes are an excellent, low fat source of protein, especially when combined with other foods, such as rice, which complete the protein.

To balance your diet, increase your consumption of fruits, vegetables and grains. Milk and milk products are important for their calcium content, but use lowfat, nonfat and skim varieties. Use your judgment with egg consumption: the cholesterol is almost entirely in the yolk, so substitute 2 egg whites for 1 whole egg whenever possible.

Try to avoid overuse of prepackaged, processed foods. You'll be saving yourself from extra sugars, salt, cholesterol and fats.

Choose a diet with plenty of vegetables, fruits, and grain products. Foods high in complex carbohydrates, such as whole-grain breads, cereals, vegetables, fruits and legumes are an excellent source of vitamins, minerals and fiber. They also are low in fat and the fiber adds bulk to help you feel full.

Use sugars only in moderation. Any necessary sugars are easily obtained by eating fresh fruit. Excess sugar increases risk of tooth decay and calorie overload.

Use salt and sodium only in moderation. Processed foods, cheeses, cured meats, baking soda, baking powder and table salt all contain sodium. Salt added during cooking often is unnecessary (except when baking) and can be replaced with herbs and spices. High blood pressure is more prevalent in persons who consume excessive amounts of salt and sodium.

If you drink alcoholic beverages, do so in moderation. Alcohol is high in calories and has little or no nutritional benefit.

CHAPTER 1

Easy Weekday Meals & Menus

Every day our list of tasks, errands, and obligations seems to grow longer until our free time just disappears. In the midst of this schedule madness, dinnertime has become a welcome release, a time to catch up with the family while enjoying good food. But how do you prepare a great dinner without chaining yourself to the kitchen? Try the Family Circle solution: cooking fast and easy with fresh ingredients!

This chapter will help you create complete meals that are simple to prepare and cook quickly. For instance, cuts of meat such as boneless chicken breasts can be sautéed or stir-fried with other fresh ingredients in just minutes to create a great one-dish meal like our Chicken Teriyaki with Rice. Fresh fish fillets, pork chops and beef steaks, like our Minute Steaks Moutarde, also can deliver convenient, lean-n'-mean meals in 10 minutes or less!

With a few simple twists, leftovers can be transformed into fabulous main-dish salads. And, by adding a little of this and that, the pasta possibilities basically are endless.

And that's not all. To give you a head start on your race against suppertime, each recipe comes with a suggested menu to help you create healthy, well balanced and great tasting meals. Enjoy!

Chicken, Green Bean & Potato Salad with Herb Yogurt Dressing (recipe, page 8) is the perfect choice for a light, luscious midweek summer supper.

Poultry

Chicken and turkey are so versatile — and delicious! There's no limit to the wonderful ways you can use them.

Chicken Teriyaki with Rice

LOW-CHOLESTEROL
Makes 4 servings.
Nutrient Value Per Serving: 507 calories, 36 g protein, 18 g fat, 49 g carbohydrate, 539 mg sodium, 74 mg cholesterol.

4	boned, skinless chicken breast halves (about 18 ounces)	½	teaspoon ground ginger
		½	cup walnuts, chopped
½	cup plus 3 tablespoons low-sodium teriyaki sauce	1	cup long-grain rice, cooked according to package directions, salt optional
2	tablespoons peanut oil	1	orange, peeled and sectioned
½	teaspoon sesame seeds	½	lemon, sliced

TOKYO CHICKEN STIR-FRY

Chicken Teriyaki with Rice

Cantaloupe & Honeydew Melon Chunks

o ❖ o

OPEN SESAME!

An aromatic, herbaceous plant, sesame grows to a height of 2 to 4 feet in tropical and subtropical areas. Native to India, the plant is cultivated in China as well. The tiny creamy white or black seeds are used whole, toasted, ground, or pressed to extract the fragrant, flavorful oil.
● White sesame seeds are widely available; black sesame seeds are sold in specialty food stores. Sprinkle sesame seeds over salads to add crunch, or use them to make candies and breads.

Orange and lemon add a subtle spark of citrus to Chicken Teriyaki with Rice.

1. Combine the chicken with ½ cup of the teriyaki sauce in a medium-size bowl. Cover the bowl, and marinate the chicken in the refrigerator for 1 to 2 hours.

2. Drain the chicken, and discard the marinade. Slice the chicken into thin strips. Heat the oil in a wok or large skillet over medium-high heat. Add the chicken and stir-fry for 5 minutes, or until the chicken is cooked through. Add the sesame seeds, ginger, chopped walnuts, remaining 3 tablespoons of teriyaki sauce and the rice, and stir-fry to heat the ingredients through. Add the orange and the lemon, and serve immediately.

Chicken Florentine

LOW-CALORIE
Bake at 375° for 20 minutes.
Makes 4 servings.
Nutrient Value Per Serving: 276 calories, 38 g protein, 11 g fat, 6 g carbohydrate, 494 mg sodium, 110 mg cholesterol.

1 **bag (10 ounces) fresh spinach, rinsed well and stemmed**	1 **tablespoon all-purpose flour**
	½ **cup milk**
4 **boned, skinless chicken breast halves (5 ounces each)**	⅛ **teaspoon ground nutmeg**
	⅛ **teaspoon freshly ground pepper**
½ **teaspoon salt**	¼ **cup shredded Fontina cheese**
2 **tablespoons unsalted butter**	

1. Preheat the oven to moderate (375°). Lightly grease 4 individual baking dishes, or 1 large, shallow baking dish.

2. Cook the spinach in a small amount of boiling water in a covered saucepan just until the spinach is tender. Drain the spinach, and squeeze it to remove most of the liquid. Chop the spinach coarsely.

3. Sprinkle the chicken with ¼ teaspoon of the salt. Heat 1 tablespoon of the butter in a large skillet. Add the chicken, and brown it on both sides over medium heat. Remove the chicken, and set it aside.

4. Add the remaining tablespoon of butter to the skillet. Stir in the flour until it is smooth. Add the milk, remaining ¼ teaspoon of salt, the nutmeg and pepper, and cook over medium heat, stirring constantly, until the sauce is thickened and bubbly. Remove the skillet from the heat. Reserve about 2 tablespoons of the sauce. Mix the spinach into the sauce remaining in the skillet.

5. Divide the spinach among the individual baking dishes, or spread it on the bottom of the large baking dish. Top the spinach with the chicken. Spread the reserved sauce over the chicken.

6. Bake in the preheated moderate oven (375°) for 10 minutes, or until lightly golden and bubbly on top. Sprinkle with the Fontina cheese. Bake for 10 minutes more.

POULTRY PERFECT!

Chicken Florentine

Zucchini Sauté
(recipe, page 153)

Herbed Italian Bread
(recipe, page 160)

Fresh or Canned Pear Halves

o ❖ o

*"*N*ext to eating good dinners, a healthy man with a benevolent turn of mind, must like, I think, to read about them.*"*
— *William Makepeace Thackeray*

Chicken, Green Bean & Potato Salad with Herb Yogurt Dressing

LOW-CALORIE • LOW-SODIUM • LOW-FAT

Makes 4 servings.

Nutrient Value Per Serving: 336 calories, 35 g protein, 9 g fat, 28 g carbohydrate, 128 mg sodium, 82 mg cholesterol.

- **1 container (8 ounces) plain lowfat yogurt**
- **2 tablespoons Basil Dressing (recipe, page 90) OR: bottled vinaigrette dressing**
- **1 pound new potatoes, scrubbed**
- **½ pound green beans, trimmed**
- **4 roasted chicken breast halves (1½ pounds), skinned, boned and sliced (about 13 ounces)**
- **Lettuce leaves, torn, washed and dried (optional)**

1. Combine the yogurt with the Basil Dressing or bottled vinaigrette in a small bowl, and set aside the dressing.

2. If the potatoes are large, halve or quarter them. Simmer the potatoes in a large pot of water for 15 minutes. Add the green beans and simmer for 5 minutes more, or until the vegetables are tender. Drain the vegetables.

3. Arrange the chicken, potatoes and green beans on a large serving platter, over a bed of lettuce leaves if you wish. Drizzle the salad with the dressing.

CHILL OUT CHICKEN SALAD

Chicken, Green Bean & Potato Salad with Herb Yogurt Dressing

Italian Bread

Lemon Sherbet

Mustard Chicken Stir-Fry

LOW-CALORIE • LOW-CHOLESTEROL

Makes 4 servings.

Nutrient Value Per Serving: 206 calories, 22 g protein, 9 g fat, 10 g carbohydrate, 857 mg sodium, 49 mg cholesterol.

- **1 tablespoon sugar**
- **1 teaspoon all-purpose flour**
- **1 teaspoon ground ginger**
- **½ teaspoon salt**
- **½ cup water**
- **2 tablespoons Dijon-style mustard**
- **2 tablespoons reduced-sodium soy sauce**
- **1 tablespoon rice wine vinegar**
- **1 clove garlic, finely chopped**
- **¾ pound boned, skinless chicken breast halves, cut crosswise into ½-inch-thick slices**
- **2 tablespoons vegetable oil**
- **5 green onions, trimmed, halved lengthwise, and cut into 2-inch pieces**
- **¼ pound fresh snow peas, stringed**
- **1 medium-size sweet red OR: yellow pepper, cored, seeded, and cut lengthwise into thin strips**

ORIENT EXPRESS

Mustard Chicken Stir-Fry

Hot Cooked Rice

Tossed Green Salad

Peachy Buttermilk Shake
(recipe, page 210)

1. Combine the sugar, flour, ginger, salt, water, mustard, soy sauce, vinegar and garlic in a small bowl. Add the chicken, and stir until it is well coated with the marinade. Cover the bowl, and marinate the chicken in the refrigerator for 30 minutes.

2. Heat 1 tablespoon of the oil in a large skillet or wok over medium-high heat. Remove the chicken from the bowl to the skillet with a slotted spoon; reserve the marinade. Stir-fry the chicken for 3 minutes, or just until the chicken is cooked through. Remove the chicken to a plate, and keep it warm. Wipe out the skillet with paper toweling.

3. Heat the remaining tablespoon of oil in the skillet over medium heat. Add the green onion, and stir-fry for 1 minute. Add the snow peas and the red or yellow pepper, and stir-fry for 3 minutes. Pour the reserved marinade into the skillet. Bring the mixture to boiling. Add the chicken to the skillet and cook, stirring, for 2 minutes, or until the sauce is bubbly and thickened. Serve immediately.

The marinade is the scrumptious secret of Mustard Chicken Stir-Fry — a combination of ginger, soy sauce, rice wine vinegar, garlic and Dijon-style mustard.

Chicken Rice Pilaf

LOW-CHOLESTEROL · LOW-FAT

Makes 4 servings.

Nutrient Value Per Serving: 494 calories, 30 g protein, 10 g fat, 68 g carbohydrate, 665 mg sodium, 64 mg cholesterol.

1	tablespoon vegetable oil	1½	cups one-third-less-salt chicken broth
1	large onion, finely chopped (1 cup)	½	teaspoon salt
1	tablespoon curry powder	⅛	teaspoon freshly ground pepper
½	teaspoon ground cumin	1½	cups uncooked instant converted rice
2	cups cubed cooked chicken	½	cup plain lowfat yogurt
1	cup frozen peas, thawed		

1. Heat the oil in a large skillet over medium heat. Add the onion, curry powder and cumin, and sauté for 3 minutes. Add the chicken, peas, broth, salt and pepper. Bring the mixture to boiling. Reduce the heat to medium-low and simmer, uncovered, for 5 minutes.

2. Stir in the rice. Bring the rice mixture to boiling, and boil for 1 minute. Cover the skillet, and remove it from the heat. Let the rice mixture stand for 7 minutes, or until the rice is tender. Stir in the yogurt, and serve the pilaf at once.

Southern Fried Chicken Strips

LOW-CHOLESTEROL

Makes 4 servings.

Nutrient Value Per Serving: 360 calories, 31 g protein, 16 g fat, 21 g carbohydrate, 375 mg sodium, 70 mg cholesterol.

¼	cup milk	½	teaspoon salt
½	cup plain lowfat yogurt	½	teaspoon freshly ground black pepper
1	pound boned, skinless chicken breasts, cut into about 3 x ½ x ½-inch strips	¼	teaspoon ground hot red pepper
¾	cup all-purpose flour		Vegetable oil
¾	teaspoon dried thyme, crumbled		

1. Combine the milk with the yogurt in a medium-size bowl. Add the chicken strips, and toss to mix the ingredients.

2. Combine the flour, thyme, salt, black pepper and ground hot red pepper on a piece of wax paper, and stir to mix the ingredients.

3. Pour ¼ inch of oil into a heavy skillet. Heat the oil over medium-high heat until it is hot (about 325°).

4. Meanwhile, toss the chicken strips, a few at a time, in the flour mixture to coat them evenly.

5. Working in batches, fry the chicken strips in the hot oil in the skillet for 3 to 5 minutes, or until the strips are browned on both sides and cooked through. Remove the chicken strips to paper toweling to drain. Serve the chicken strips hot.

A TASTE OF THE MIDDLE EAST

Chicken Rice Pilaf

Steamed Carrots

Apple Berry Whirl
(recipe, page 204)

SOUTHERN LIVING

Southern Fried Chicken Strips

Steamed Green Beans

Mashed Potatoes

Vanilla Ice Milk with Raspberries

○ ❖ ○

SAFETY FIRST

- Always wash your hands before preparing foods, and after handling raw poultry, fish or meat.
- Be sure children wash their hands before and after eating.
- Use only clean utensils and bowls to mix foods.
- Thaw frozen foods in the refrigerator, not at room temperature, or use a microwave oven and carefully follow the directions for defrosting.
- If you are preparing foods in advance, remember to refrigerate meat, fish, egg and poultry dishes as soon as possible after cooking them.
- Pack lunches in insulated bags, and chill the bagged lunches overnight so they retain the optimum temperature.
- For lunch foods that should be served hot, reheat them and pack them in insulated bags or thermoses just before leaving the house.
- Refrigerate hard-cooked eggs soon after cooking, and use them within 1 week. Unrefrigerated hard-cooked eggs are safe for no more than 2 hours.
- Any questions? Call the toll-free USDA Meat and Poultry Hotline for information on the safe handling and storage of meat and poultry. Dial 1-800-535-4555 weekdays, 10 a.m. to 4 p.m., E.S.T. (in metropolitan Washington, D.C., dial 202-447-3333).

Chicken Burgers with Sweet Red Pepper Sauce

LOW-CHOLESTEROL

Makes 4 servings.

Nutrient Value Per Serving: 419 calories, 23 g protein, 29 g fat, 16 g carbohydrate, 765 mg sodium, 66 mg cholesterol.

¾	**pound sweet red peppers, cored, seeded and coarsely chopped**
5	**tablespoons olive oil**
1	**clove garlic, finely chopped**
½	**cup chicken broth**
1	**medium-size onion, finely chopped (½ cup)**
½	**cup finely chopped sweet green pepper**
1	**pound ground chicken**
1	**cup fresh bread crumbs (2 slices bread)**
2	**egg whites OR: 1 whole egg, slightly beaten**
2	**tablespoons Dijon-style mustard**
1	**teaspoon dried tarragon, crumbled**
½	**teaspoon salt**
¼	**teaspoon freshly ground pepper**
2	**tablespoons all-purpose flour**

1. Cook the red peppers in 2 tablespoons of the oil in a large saucepan over medium-high heat for 5 minutes. Add the garlic, and cook for 5 minutes. Reduce the heat to medium and cook until the red peppers are tender, for about 10 minutes. Add the broth to the skillet. Bring the mixture to boiling and cook, covered, for 5 minutes. Transfer the mixture to the container of a food processor or electric blender. Whirl until the mixture is puréed. If you wish the sauce to have a thinner consistency, add more broth. Keep the sauce warm.

2. Cook the onion and the green pepper in 1 tablespoon of the oil in a large, nonstick skillet for 3 to 5 minutes, or just until the vegetables are tender. Transfer the vegetables to a large bowl. Wipe out the skillet.

3. Add the chicken, bread crumbs, egg whites or beaten egg, mustard, tarragon, salt and black pepper to the bowl, and mix the ingredients gently to combine them. Shape the mixture into four equal ½-inch-thick patties. Sprinkle both sides of the patties with the flour.

4. Cook the patties in the remaining 2 tablespoons of oil in the skillet for 2 to 4 minutes on each side, or until the patties are lightly browned; turn over the patties carefully. Serve the patties with the warm sauce.

Whole Wheat Breaded Drumsticks

Removing the skin from the chicken and using an egg white in the coating helps to reduce the fat in this delicious alternative to fried chicken.

LOW-CALORIE

Bake at 375° for 35 minutes.

Makes 4 servings.

Nutrient Value Per Serving: 271 calories, 29 g protein, 11 g fat, 13 g carbohydrate, 840 mg sodium, 85 mg cholesterol.

Butter OR: nonstick vegetable cooking spray	1 teaspoon lemon juice
8 chicken drumsticks (2 pounds)	1 cup whole wheat bread crumbs (4 slices stale whole wheat bread)
⅓ cup country-style Dijon mustard	½ teaspoon dried basil, crumbled
1 egg white	1 tablespoon olive oil

1. Preheat the oven to moderate (375°). Lightly grease a 15 x 10 x 1½-inch jelly-roll pan, or spray it with nonstick vegetable cooking spray.

2. Remove the skin from the drumsticks, and pat the drumsticks dry with paper toweling.

CHICKEN WITH A CRUNCH

Whole Wheat Breaded Drumsticks

Mashed Potatoes

Sautéed Sugar Snap Peas

Lemon Sponge Cake with Strawberry Sauce
(recipe, page 198)

∘ ❖ ∘

CHICKEN BITS

● Trying to cut down on fat? Remove the skin from chicken, and you'll cut both fat and calories. A 3-ounce portion of skinless roasted chicken breast has only 116 calories.

● In a hurry? Cut chicken grilling or broiling time in half by first partially cooking the chicken in the microwave.

● Love stuffing? Double the recipe, and bake the extra stuffing in a separate pan, or spoon it underneath the skin of the bird.

● Unexpected guests? Keep purchased chicken tenders or strips on hand. These morsels of breast meat sauté or stir-fry in minutes.

● Need to cut down your cholesterol intake? Dip skinless chicken pieces in either honey mustard, or an egg white mixed with 1 teaspoon of water, then coat the chicken with bread crumbs. Bake the chicken pieces in a baking pan sprayed with nonstick vegetable cooking spray.

Whole Wheat Breaded Drumsticks are "fried" in the oven, the low-calorie way to add crunch.

3. Combine the mustard, egg white and lemon juice in a pie plate or shallow dish. Combine the bread crumbs with the basil on a piece of wax paper. Dip the drumsticks in the mustard mixture, turning to coat them evenly. Then dip the drumsticks in the bread crumb mixture, coating them evenly. Place the drumsticks in the prepared pan, and drizzle them evenly with the oil.

4. Bake the drumsticks in the preheated moderate oven (375°) for 35 minutes, or until the drumsticks are golden brown and cooked through.

o ❖ o

"Cuisine is when things taste like themselves. "

— *Curnonsky*

Chicken Breasts with Green Mole Sauce

LOW-CALORIE
Broil chicken for 6 minutes.
Makes 4 servings.
Nutrient Value Per Serving: 259 calories, 36 g protein, 10 g fat, 5 g carbohydrate, 453 mg sodium, 82 mg cholesterol.

1	tablespoon vegetable oil	1	cup chicken broth (from 13¾-ounce can)
½	cup coarsely chopped onion (1 medium-size onion)	½	cup water
1	clove garlic, crushed	2	teaspoons lime juice
⅛	teaspoon ground cumin	4	boned, skinless chicken breast halves (about 5 ounces each)
1	mild green chili pepper (from 4-ounce can)		Sliced green onion, for garnish
⅓	cup fresh cilantro		Cherry tomatoes, for garnish
¼	cup parsley		
¼	cup shelled sunflower seeds		

1. Preheat the broiler. Lightly grease the broiler-pan rack.

2. Heat the oil in a medium-size skillet over medium heat. Add the onion, garlic and cumin, and cook until the onion is tender, for about 3 minutes. Place the onion mixture in the container of a food processor or electric blender along with the chili pepper, cilantro, parsley, sunflower seeds, broth and water. Whirl until the onion-chili pepper mixture is puréed; it will be slightly grainy. Return the onion-chili pepper mixture to the skillet and simmer, stirring occasionally, for 20 minutes, or until the mixture is thickened. Stir in the lime juice. Set aside the mole sauce.

3. Broil the chicken breasts 6 inches from the heat source for 3 minutes on each side, or just until the chicken is cooked through. Garnish the chicken with the green onion and the cherry tomatoes. Serve the chicken breasts with the mole sauce.

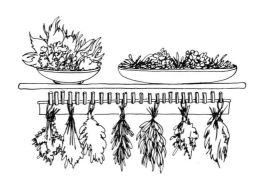

Adobe Chicken Stew

LOW-CALORIE · LOW-CHOLESTEROL
Makes 4 servings.
Nutrient Value Per Serving: 245 calories, 23 g protein, 9 g fat,
18 g carbohydrate, 493 mg sodium, 62 mg cholesterol.

1	tablespoon vegetable oil	1	cup thawed frozen corn
1	large onion, finely chopped (1 cup)	1	teaspoon ground cinnamon
1	clove garlic, finely chopped	¾	teaspoon salt
2	cans (10 ounces each) no-salt-added tomatoes, undrained	¼	teaspoon ground cloves
		¼	teaspoon ground cumin
2	cups cubed cooked chicken	⅛	teaspoon freshly ground pepper

1. Heat the oil in a medium-size saucepan over medium heat. Add the onion and sauté for 3 minutes, or until the onion is softened. Add the garlic and sauté for 1 minute, or until fragrant.

2. Add the tomatoes with their liquid, the chicken, corn, cinnamon, salt, cloves, cumin and pepper to the saucepan. Bring the stew to boiling over medium-high heat. Reduce the heat to medium-low. Simmer the stew, uncovered, for 20 minutes, or until the ingredients are heated through and the flavors have mingled.

Mexican Rice Tart

LOW-CALORIE · LOW-CHOLESTEROL · LOW-FAT
Bake at 350° for 30 to 35 minutes.
Makes 6 servings.
Nutrient Value Per Serving: 226 calories, 13 g protein, 4 g fat,
34 g carbohydrate, 292 mg sodium, 26 mg cholesterol.

Rice Crust:

1¼	cups long-grain white rice	2	tablespoons sliced green onion
2	egg whites	2	tablespoons sliced canned ripe black olives
2	tablespoons sliced canned ripe black olives	⅔	cup bottled picante sauce
2	tablespoons sliced green onion		Dairy sour cream, for garnish (optional)
	Nonstick vegetable cooking spray		Additional chopped mild green chili peppers, for garnish (optional)

Filling:

⅓	cup shredded Monterey Jack cheese		Additional sliced black olives, for garnish (optional)
1	cup shredded cooked chicken breast (5 ounces)		Additional bottled picante sauce (optional)
2	tablespoons chopped mild green chili peppers		

A NIGHT IN NEW MEXICO

Bean Nachos
(see Tip, page 15)

Adobe Chicken Stew

Orange Onion Salad
(recipe, page 139)

Vanilla Ice Milk with Raspberries

o ❖ o

ONE DISH FIESTA

Mexican Rice Tart

Tossed Green Salad

Chocolate Pudding with Raspberry Purée

o ❖ o

BEAN NACHOS

A low-cholesterol, low-fat side dish or snack to tempt any palate.

● Preheat the oven to hot (400°).

● Combine 1 can (16 ounces) of drained and rinsed red kidney beans with ½ cup of prepared mild chili salsa in the container of a food processor or electric blender. Pulse until the bean mixture is almost puréed. Spread the bean mixture evenly over 4 flour tortillas.

● Bake the tortillas in the preheated hot oven (400°) for about 5 minutes, or just until the tortillas and bean mixture are warmed through. Scatter 1 cup of coarsely chopped pimiento-stuffed olives over the tops of the tortillas. Cut the tortillas into quarters. Serve the nachos warm, with a dollop of plain lowfat yogurt on each if you wish. Makes 4 servings.

1. Prepare the Rice Crust: Cook the rice following the package directions, adding salt if you wish. Drain the rice to remove any excess liquid. Cool the rice slightly. Lightly beat the egg whites in a small bowl. Stir in the olives and the green onion. Stir the egg white mixture into the rice.

2. Coat the inside of a 10-inch tart pan with a removable bottom with nonstick vegetable cooking spray. Spoon the rice mixture into the pan to cover the bottom evenly and make a high rim.

3. Preheat the oven to moderate (350°).

4. Prepare the Filling: Scatter half the Monterey Jack cheese over the rice crust. Combine the chicken, chili peppers, green onion, olives and picante sauce in a medium-size bowl. Spread the filling evenly in the crust.

5. Bake the tart in the preheated moderate oven (350°) for 20 minutes. Scatter the remaining Monterey Jack cheese over the top of the tart. Bake for 10 to 15 minutes more, or until the cheese is melted. Let the tart stand for 10 minutes. Remove the side of the pan, and place the tart on a serving plate. Cut the tart into wedges. If you wish, garnish the tart with dairy sour cream, additional chopped mild green chili peppers, and additional sliced black olives. Serve the tart with additional picante sauce, if you wish.

A colorful meal-in-a-dish: Mexican Rice Tart.

Chicken & Broccoli Quiche

A light and luscious variation on a traditional quiche, this main dish pie is baked without a crust.

LOW-CALORIE

Bake at 350° for 30 to 45 minutes.
Makes 4 dinner, or 6 lunch servings.

Nutrient Value Per Dinner Serving: 327 calories, 32 g protein, 15 g fat, 14 g carbohydrate, 629 mg sodium, 115 mg cholesterol.

Nonstick vegetable cooking spray	**½ cup plain lowfat yogurt**
1½ cups diced cooked chicken (4 to 5 ounces)	**1 whole egg**
1 box (10 ounces) frozen chopped broccoli, thawed and well drained	**1 egg white**
	¼ cup all-purpose flour
	½ teaspoon baking powder
1 cup part-skim ricotta cheese	**½ teaspoon salt**
¼ cup grated Parmesan cheese	**2 tablespoons margarine, melted**

1. Preheat the oven to moderate (350°).

2. Lightly spray a 9-inch pie plate with nonstick vegetable cooking spray. Combine half the chicken with half the broccoli in the pie plate.

3. Combine the ricotta and Parmesan cheeses with the yogurt, egg, egg white, flour, baking powder, salt and margarine in the container of an electric blender. Whirl until the mixture is puréed. Pour the mixture over the chicken and broccoli in the pie plate. Scatter the remaining chicken and broccoli over the top.

4. Bake the quiche in the preheated moderate oven (350°) for 30 to 45 minutes, or until a wooden pick inserted in the center comes out clean. Let the quiche stand for 10 minutes before slicing it.

A PIECE OF PIE FOR SUPPER

Chicken & Broccoli Quiche

Cherry Tomatoes

Breadsticks

Angel Food Cake with Sliced Apricots

○ ❖ ○

PICKIN' CHICKEN

● Grade A chicken is meatier and generally better looking than grade B or C chicken.

● The chicken's diet affects its skin tone, which can vary from bright yellow to almost white; both colors are acceptable.

● Avoid packages with bruised-looking chicken, as well as those with an "off" odor. A package with accumulated liquid generally indicates that the chicken has been sitting there for a while.

● Purchased chicken parts are just as economical as a whole chicken, and certainly save preparation time. The percentage of edible meat per chicken part is 50% of the wings, 53% of the legs and thighs, and 63% of the breasts. In comparison, 51% of a whole bird is edible (42% with the fat and skin eliminated).

● For every 4-ounce serving, buy 8 ounces of chicken with the bone in, or 5 to 6 ounces of boned parts.

**STEW FOR SUPPER,
ITALIAN-STYLE**

Mediterranean Chicken Stew
Orzo Pasta
Sliced Oranges with
Toasted Coconut

o ⋅❖⋅ o

*"It is not really
an exaggeration
to say that peace and
happiness begin,
geographically,
where garlic is used
in cooking.*"

— *Marcel Boulestin*

Mediterranean Chicken Stew

LOW-CALORIE

Makes 4 servings.

Nutrient Value Per Serving: 348 calories, 33 g protein, 19 g fat,
12 g carbohydrate, 941 mg sodium, 127 mg cholesterol.

1	**pound boned chicken thighs, cut into 1½-inch chunks**
¼	**cup white wine**
1	**tablespoon cornstarch**
½	**teaspoon dried basil, crumbled**
¼	**teaspoon dried oregano, crumbled**
½	**pound Italian sausage**
½	**pound eggplant, cut into 1-inch cubes (2 cups)**
⅓	**cup water**
2	**teaspoons olive oil**

1 **sweet green pepper, cored, seeded, and cut into ¼-inch strips**

½ **medium-size onion, cut into thin slices**

1 **clove garlic, finely chopped**

1 **can (14 ounces) Italian-style plum tomatoes, undrained and coarsely chopped**

¼ **cup oil-cured black olives, pitted**

Lettuce leaves, torn, washed and dried

1. Combine the chicken with the wine, cornstarch, basil and oregano in a medium-size bowl. Cover the bowl with plastic wrap, and marinate the chicken in the refrigerator for 30 minutes.

2. Remove the casings from the sausage. Cook the sausage in a large, nonstick skillet over medium-high heat, breaking the meat into smaller pieces with a wooden spoon. When the sausage is almost cooked, remove the chicken from the bowl to the skillet with a slotted spoon; discard the marinade remaining in the bowl. Cook, stirring, for 8 minutes, or until the chicken is cooked through. Remove the chicken and sausage with a slotted spoon to a colander to drain any excess oil.

3. Add the eggplant and the water to the skillet. Cover the skillet and cook over medium-high heat for 5 minutes, or until the eggplant is tender. Remove the eggplant with a slotted spoon to the colander with the chicken and sausage. Add the oil to the skillet, and reduce the heat to medium. Add the green pepper, onion and garlic, and cook, stirring, for 5 minutes, or until the vegetables are soft. Add the tomatoes with their liquid and the olives. Return the chicken, sausage and eggplant to the skillet. Bring the mixture to boiling over medium-high heat. Lower the heat and simmer, stirring occasionally, for about 5 minutes, or until the sauce is thickened.

4. Serve the stew on a bed of lettuce leaves.

Thai Chicken & Noodles in Peanut Sauce

Makes 4 servings.

Nutrient Value Per Serving: 531 calories, 34 g protein, 23 g fat, 49 g carbohydrate, 921 mg sodium, 117 mg cholesterol.

8	ounces fine egg noodles	¼	cup water **OR:** chicken broth
2	tablespoons Oriental sesame **OR:** vegetable oil	¼	cup smooth peanut butter
½	cooked chicken, skinned and shredded	3	tablespoons soy sauce
3	green onions, trimmed	3	tablespoons cider vinegar
1	clove garlic	1	tablespoon sugar
½	inch peeled fresh ginger **OR:** ¼ teaspoon ground ginger		

1. Bring at least 12 cups of water to boiling in a large pot. Place the noodles in a very large, shallow, heat-proof serving bowl. Add the boiling water to the bowl to cover the noodles. Cover the bowl with plastic wrap, and let the noodles stand for 6 minutes. Drain the noodles, and return them to the bowl. Add 1 tablespoon of the Oriental sesame or vegetable oil to the noodles along with the chicken. Toss to coat the ingredients.

2. Cut the green ends from the onions, and cut the ends into 3-inch pieces. Slice the pieces lengthwise into slivers. Set aside the slivered green onion.

3. Combine the white parts of the green onion with the garlic and the ginger in the container of a food processor or electric blender. Whirl until the ingredients are chopped. Add the water or broth, the peanut butter, soy sauce, vinegar, sugar and remaining tablespoon of oil. Whirl until the peanut sauce is smooth.

4. Toss half the peanut sauce with the chicken/noodle mixture in the bowl. Serve the chicken/noodle mixture warm, garnished with the slivered green onion. Pass the remaining peanut sauce. Or chill the chicken/noodle mixture for up to 1 day, and serve it cold or at room temperature.

A TASTE OF THAI

Thai Chicken & Noodles in Peanut Sauce

Oriental Zucchini Carrot Slaw
(recipe, page 145)

Sliced Oranges with Honey Orange Sauce
(recipe, page 202)

○ ❖ ○

THE COLD FACTS: STORING CHICKEN

● Store fresh chicken in the coldest part of the refrigerator for up to 2 days. There's no need to rewrap the chicken if the packaging is in good condition.

● To freeze chicken, rinse it under cold running water and pat it dry. Rewrap the chicken, and freeze it for up to 2 months.

o ◆◆ o

CREAMY POLENTA

● Combine 5 cups of water with 1 teaspoon of salt in a large saucepan, and bring the mixture to simmering. Very gradually whisk in 1¼ cups of cornmeal, adding it in a thin stream. Cook the cornmeal until it is very thick and leaves the side of the pan, for about 20 minutes.

● Add 5 tablespoons of unsalted butter to the saucepan, and stir to incorporate the butter into the polenta. Serve half the polenta with Turkey Cutlets Milano (recipe, at right). Reserve the other half for another meal.

Makes 8 servings.

Turkey Cutlets Milano

LOW-CALORIE · LOW-CHOLESTEROL

Makes 4 servings.

Nutrient Value Per Serving: 281 calories, 29 g protein, 12 g fat, 14 g carbohydrate, 593 mg sodium, 70 mg cholesterol.

3	tablespoons all-purpose flour
¾	teaspoon salt
¼	teaspoon freshly ground pepper
1	pound turkey cutlets
2	to 3 tablespoons olive oil
¼	pound mushrooms, sliced
1	small clove garlic, finely chopped
1	can (14½ ounces) no-salt-added stewed tomatoes
¼	cup pitted black olives, sliced
¼	teaspoon dried basil, crumbled

1. Combine the flour, ½ teaspoon of the salt and the pepper on a piece of wax paper. Dredge the turkey cutlets in the flour mixture to coat both sides of the cutlets.

2. Heat 1 tablespoon of the oil in a large, nonstick skillet. Add half the cutlets, and brown them on both sides. Remove the cutlets to a plate. Add another tablespoon of oil to the skillet, if necessary, and repeat with the remaining cutlets.

3. Add 1 tablespoon of the oil to the skillet, and heat it. Add the mushrooms, and sauté for 3 minutes. Add the garlic, and sauté for 30 seconds. Add the tomatoes, olives, basil and remaining ¼ teaspoon of salt. Simmer the sauce, uncovered, over high heat to reduce it slightly. Return the cutlets to the skillet. Lower the heat, cover the skillet, and simmer for 5 minutes to cook the cutlets through. Serve the cutlets with the sauce.

A quick dish for a cold night: Turkey Cutlets Milano with cauliflower and polenta.

Turkey & Chicken Loaf with Salsa

LOW-CALORIE
Bake at 350° for 45 minutes.
Makes 4 servings.
Nutrient Value Per Serving: 239 calories, 22 g protein, 12 g fat, 10 g carbohydrate, 568 mg sodium, 128 mg cholesterol.

- **½ pound ground turkey**
- **½ pound ground chicken**
- **1 large onion, chopped (1 cup)**
- **1 cup fresh bread crumbs (2 to 2½ slices bread)**
- **½ cup coarsely chopped sweet green pepper**
- **½ cup coarsely chopped sweet red pepper**
- **2 cloves garlic, finely chopped**
- **¼ cup chopped fresh cilantro**
- **1 egg**
- **1 teaspoon ground cumin**
- **¾ teaspoon salt**
- **¼ teaspoon freshly ground black pepper**
- **Bottled salsa, heated (optional)**

1. Preheat the oven to moderate (350°). Lightly grease an 8½ x 4½ x 2⅝-inch loaf pan, and set it aside.

2. Combine the turkey, chicken, onion, bread crumbs, green and red peppers, garlic, cilantro, egg, cumin, salt and pepper in a large bowl. Mix the ingredients well. Press the mixture gently into the prepared pan.

3. Bake the loaf in the preheated moderate oven (350°) for 45 minutes, or until the loaf is firm. Cool the loaf in the pan for 10 minutes. Unmold the loaf onto a serving platter, and slice the loaf. Serve the loaf with heated bottled salsa, if you wish.

TWO BIRD COMBO

Turkey & Chicken Loaf with Salsa
Corn Niblets
Citrus Salad with Lime Vinaigrette
(recipe, page 139)
Raspberry Sherbet
(recipe, page 208)

Turkey Meatball Soup

These meatballs also are delicious in a tomato sauce over pasta, or speared with wooden picks and served as an appetizer.

Makes 4 servings.
Nutrient Value Per Serving: 410 calories, 28 g protein, 19 g fat, 32 g carbohydrate, 869 mg sodium, 120 mg cholesterol.

- **¾ pound fresh ground turkey**
- **¼ cup grated Parmesan cheese**
- **1 egg**
- **2 tablespoons lowfat milk**
- **2 tablespoons chopped parsley**
- **1 tablespoon plain bread crumbs**
- **¾ teaspoon salt**
- **¼ teaspoon rubbed sage**
- **⅛ teaspoon freshly ground pepper**
- **2 medium-size onions, chopped (1 cup)**
- **2 tablespoons olive oil**
- **3 cloves garlic, finely chopped**
- **1 carrot, peeled, halved lengthwise, and thinly sliced crosswise (½ cup)**
- **1 can (13⅓ ounces) tomatoes in juice, undrained and chopped**
- **4 cans (10½ ounces each) reduced-sodium chicken broth**
- **¼ to ½ teaspoon liquid red pepper seasoning**
- **3 ounces uncooked wagon wheel pasta (1⅓ cups)**
- **2 cups (5 ounces) broccoli flowerets**

LET'S TALK TURKEY SOUP

Turkey Meatball Soup
Hot Bread with Seasoned Butter
(recipe, page 161)
Melon Wedges

1. Combine the turkey, Parmesan cheese, egg, milk, parsley, bread crumbs, ¼ teaspoon of the salt, the sage and pepper in a medium-size bowl. Shape a heaping teaspoonful of the turkey mixture into a small meatball. Repeat to make 40 meatballs. Refrigerate the meatballs.

2. Cook the onion in the oil in a large saucepan over low heat until the onion is softened, for about 7 minutes. Add the garlic and the carrot, and cook until the carrot is softened, for about 5 minutes.

3. Add the tomatoes with their liquid, the broth, remaining ½ teaspoon of salt and the liquid red pepper seasoning. Bring the tomato mixture to boiling. Lower the heat and simmer, covered, for 10 minutes. Add the pasta and cook, covered, for 8 minutes, or until the pasta is almost tender.

4. Add the meatballs and the broccoli to the saucepan. Simmer, covered, for 4 minutes, or until the meatballs are cooked through and the broccoli is tender.

**ON A ROLL
TURKEY DINNER**

Stuffed Turkey Rolls

Baked Shredded Sweet Potatoes
(recipe, page 152)

Brussels Sprouts

Apples and Cheese with Crackers

o ❖ o

"*A*ppetite
*comes
with eating.*"
—*François Rabelais*

Stuffed Turkey Rolls

LOW-CALORIE ▪ MICROWAVE

Bake at 375° for 20 to 25 minutes; or microwave at full power for 8 to 9 minutes.

Makes 4 servings.

Nutrient Value Per Serving: 312 calories, 29 g protein, 13 g fat, 17 g carbohydrate, 318 mg sodium, 94 mg cholesterol.

Half 6-ounce package cornbread stuffing mix (about 1 cup)	2 tablespoons chopped parsley
Half stuffing mix seasoning packet (about 1 tablespoon)	2 tablespoons chopped pecans
3 tablespoons unsalted butter	⅔ cup very hot water
	1 pound turkey breast cutlets
	¼ teaspoon paprika

1. Preheat the oven to moderate (375°). Grease a 9 x 9 x 2-inch square baking dish, and set the dish aside.

2. Combine the stuffing mix with the seasoning, 2 tablespoons of the butter, the parsley and chopped pecans in a medium-size bowl. Stir in the hot water to melt the butter. Spread the stuffing mixture on the turkey cutlets, and roll up the cutlets. Place the turkey rolls, seam side down and not touching, in the prepared dish. Sprinkle the rolls with the paprika. Dot the rolls with the remaining tablespoon of butter.

3. Bake the turkey rolls in the preheated moderate oven (375°) for 20 to 25 minutes. Remove the rolls to a cutting board, and slice them. Place the slices on a serving platter, and spoon the pan juices over them.

Microwave Instructions

(for a 650-watt variable power microwave oven)

Ingredient Changes: Reduce the butter to 2 tablespoons.
Directions: Assemble the stuffed turkey rolls following the directions in Step 2 above, using all the butter. Place the rolls, seam side down and not touching, in an 11 x 7 x 2-inch microwave-safe dish. Sprinkle the rolls with the paprika. Cover the dish with wax paper. Microwave at full power for 8 to 9 minutes, or until the rolls are cooked, rotating the dish one half turn halfway through the cooking time. Let the rolls stand, covered, for 2 minutes. Slice the rolls, and serve.

Turkey-Stuffed Peppers

A leaner version of an old favorite.

Bake at 375° for 30 minutes.
Makes 4 servings.

Nutrient Value Per Serving: 352 calories, 24 g protein, 17 g fat,
26 g carbohydrate, 712 mg sodium, 77 mg cholesterol.

2	large sweet red peppers	1	tablespoon fresh sage, chopped OR: ¾ teaspoon rubbed sage
2	large sweet green peppers	1	pound ground turkey
1	tablespoon olive oil	¼	cup parsley, chopped
1	large onion, chopped (1 cup)	½	cup dry bread crumbs
1	clove garlic, finely chopped	1	cup barbecue sauce
1	tablespoon fresh thyme, chopped OR: ¾ teaspoon dried thyme, crumbled		

1. Preheat the oven to moderate (375°). Halve the red and green peppers lengthwise, and remove the seeds. Blanch the pepper halves in a large pot of boiling water for 5 minutes. Drain the pepper halves, cut side down, on paper toweling.

2. Heat the oil in a medium-size skillet. Add the onion and the garlic and cook over low heat, stirring occasionally, for 5 minutes, or until the onion is translucent. Stir in the thyme and the sage, and cook for 30 seconds more.

3. Combine the onion mixture with the turkey, parsley and bread crumbs in a small bowl. Arrange the pepper halves, cut side up, in a 13 x 9 x 2-inch glass baking dish. Spoon the stuffing into the pepper halves. Spoon the barbecue sauce over the stuffed peppers.

4. Bake the stuffed peppers, uncovered, in the preheated moderate oven (375°) for 30 minutes, or until the stuffing is cooked through; the juices will run clear when the stuffing is pierced with a fork.

SAVORY STUFFED PEPPERS

Turkey-Stuffed Peppers
Tossed Salad
Corn on the Cob
Chocolate Pudding

◦ ❖ ◦

THYME

With its pungent flavor and gentle aroma of mint and lemon peel, thyme (pronounced "time") is related to the mint family. Its tiny leaves are slightly sweet in taste. There are several varieties of thyme, some of which are used for ornamental ground cover. The variety most often used in cooking is called, appropriately enough, "common" thyme. A perennial plant, thyme can easily be grown from seeds indoors or outdoors; just make sure the plants have direct sunlight.

● Thyme can be bought fresh, or dried in leaf or ground form. It is delicious on roasted meats. Use it also in stews, soups, poultry stuffings, clam and fish chowders, fish sauces, and with tomatoes.

A taste of things to come: healthier Turkey-Stuffed Peppers in place of the fattier beef-stuffed variety.

Beef & Pork

The best of beef and most perfect pork recipes—all guaranteed to please your family's palates.

Taco Salad

Frozen chili makes this salad quick and easy to put together.

Makes 4 servings.

Nutrient Value Per Serving: 686 calories, 24 g protein, 43 g fat, 56 g carbohydrate, 1,155 mg sodium, cholesterol data unavailable.

2	packages (8¾ ounces each) frozen chili con carne with beans
	Salsa Dressing (see Tip, at right)
6	cups coarsely shredded iceberg lettuce
8	ounces no-salt-added tortilla chips, coarsely crumbled
4	ounces Monterey Jack cheese, shredded (1 cup)
1	large tomato, cored and diced
1	avocado, pitted, peeled and diced

SALAD OLÉ!

Taco Salad
Mocha Banana Split
(recipe, page 209)

○ ❖ ○

SALSA DRESSING

Stir together ½ cup of mild or medium salsa, 2 tablespoons of mayonnaise, 2 tablespoons of yogurt, and 4 thinly sliced green onions in a small bowl until the ingredients are well blended. Cover the bowl, and refrigerate the dressing until serving time. Makes about ¾ cup.

A cinch of a spicy meal, ready in minutes: Taco Salad.

1. Heat the chili con carne following the package directions.

2. Prepare the Salsa Dressing.

3. Divide the lettuce between 4 individual dinner plates. Arrange the tortilla chips on top of the lettuce. Open the bags of hot chili carefully, and mound the chili, divided equally, on top of the tortilla chips. Top each salad with the Monterey Jack cheese, tomato and avocado.

4. Just before serving, spoon some of the dressing over each salad.

Roast Beef & Spinach Salad

LOW-CALORIE · LOW-CHOLESTEROL

Makes 4 servings.

Nutrient Value Per Serving: 305 calories, 25 g protein, 20 g fat, 6 g carbohydrate, 460 mg sodium, 71 mg cholesterol.

¼ **cup olive OR: vegetable oil**	1 **package (10 ounces) fresh spinach, cleaned and trimmed**
2 **tablespoons fresh lemon juice**	½ **container (8 ounces) cherry tomatoes, halved**
1 **tablespoon Dijon-style mustard**	¼ **red onion, cut into rings**
½ **teaspoon dried tarragon, crumbled**	8 **ounces rare roast beef, thinly sliced**
¼ **teaspoon salt**	4 **ounces Monterey Jack OR: Brie cheese, sliced**
4 **drops liquid red pepper seasoning**	

1. Combine the olive or vegetable oil with the lemon juice, mustard, tarragon, salt and liquid red pepper seasoning in a small jar or plastic container with a tight-fitting lid. Shake the jar well to combine the ingredients. If making the dressing in advance, refrigerate it until serving time. At serving time, shake the jar well.

2. Tear any large spinach leaves into bite-size pieces. Arrange the spinach on 4 individual dinner plates. Arrange the cherry tomatoes and the onion rings over the spinach. (The salads can be prepared 2 hours in advance up to this point, covered with plastic wrap, and refrigerated.)

3. Just before serving, roll up the roast beef slices, and cut them crosswise into 1½-inch pieces. Cut the Monterey Jack or brie cheese into 2 x 1-inch pieces. Divide the beef and the cheese evenly among the salads. Spoon half the dressing over the salads. Reserve the remaining dressing to use with another salad.

**BEEF TREAT
TO BEAT THE HEAT**

Roast Beef & Spinach Salad

Rye Bread and Butter

Bread Pudding
with Raspberry Sauce
(recipe, page 204)

∘ ❖ ∘

"*A man's own dinner is to himself so important that he cannot bring himself to believe that it is a matter utterly indifferent to anyone else.*"

—*Anthony Trollope*

Warm Steak & Red Pepper Salad

Use leftover steak to make this tasty salad.

LOW-CALORIE · LOW-CHOLESTEROL · LOW-SODIUM

Makes 4 servings.

Nutrient Value Per Serving: 300 calories, 23 g protein, 20 g fat, 7 g carbohydrate, 89 mg sodium, 59 mg cholesterol.

3	tablespoons olive oil	1½	tablespoons red wine vinegar
1	large onion, halved, and thinly sliced crosswise	1	teaspoon Dijon-style mustard
1	sweet red pepper, cored, seeded, and sliced ¼ inch thick	1	pound cooked round steak, cut into 4 x ½-inch slices
1	clove garlic, finely chopped	¼	cup chopped parsley
¼	teaspoon dried rosemary, crumbled	4	cups mixed lettuce leaves

1. Heat the oil in a large skillet over medium heat. Add the onion and sauté for 3 minutes, or until the onion is tender. Add the red pepper, garlic and rosemary, and sauté until the pepper is crisply tender. Stir in the vinegar and the mustard until they are mixed. Add the steak and cook just to heat it through, for about 1 minute more. Remove the skillet from the heat, and stir in the parsley.

2. Arrange the lettuce leaves on a serving platter, or on 4 individual salad plates. Top with the steak mixture. Serve the salad at once.

Warm Fajita Rice Salad

LOW-CHOLESTEROL

Broil steak for 8 to 10 minutes.

Makes 4 servings.

Nutrient Value Per Serving: 418 calories, 21 g protein, 19 g fat, 42 g carbohydrate, 486 mg sodium, 52 mg cholesterol.

¾	pound top sirloin OR: top round beef steak, 1 inch thick	1	can (2¼ ounces) ripe black olives, drained, rinsed and halved
¼	cup fresh lime juice	1	cup cherry tomatoes, halved
½	teaspoon garlic salt	¼	cup sliced red onion rings
½	teaspoon ground cumin	2	tablespoons chopped fresh cilantro
½	teaspoon freshly ground coarse black pepper		Picante Dressing (see Tip, page 27)
¾	cup long-grain white rice	½	head iceberg lettuce, shredded
1	can (8 ounces) whole kernel corn, drained and rinsed		

TWO SALAD SUPPER

Warm Steak & Red Pepper Salad

New Potato Salad

Fresh Strawberries with Lemon Yogurt

◦ ❖ ◦

SOUTHWESTERN SALAD

Warm Fajita Rice Salad

Iced Tea

Fresh Fruit Salad

◦ ❖ ◦

1. Place the steak in a self-sealing plastic bag or a shallow dish. Combine the lime juice, garlic salt, cumin and black pepper in a small bowl. Pour the lime mixture over the steak, and seal the bag or cover the dish with plastic wrap. Marinate the steak in the refrigerator for 2 to 4 hours, turning over the steak once or twice.

2. Cook the rice following the package directions, adding salt if you wish. Set aside the rice.

3. Preheat the broiler.

4. Remove the steak from the marinade, and place the steak on the broiler-pan rack. Discard the marinade.

5. Broil the steak 3 to 4 inches from the heat source, turning over the steak once, for 8 to 10 minutes for medium-rare.

6. Combine the warm rice with the corn, olives, cherry tomatoes, onion rings and 1 tablespoon of the cilantro in a medium-size bowl. Pour half the Picante Dressing over the top of the rice mixture, and toss gently to combine them. Place the lettuce on a serving platter, and top it with the rice mixture.

7. Slice the steak diagonally across the grain into thin slices. Place the slices on top of the rice mixture. Drizzle the salad with the remaining dressing, and sprinkle with the remaining tablespoon of cilantro. Serve the salad warm, or at room temperature.

Minute Steaks Moutarde

Makes 4 servings.
Nutrient Value Per Serving: 383 calories, 28 g protein, 29 g fat, 1 g carbohydrate, 444 mg sodium, 94 mg cholesterol.

4 minute steaks (5 ounces each)	½ cup chicken broth
¼ teaspoon salt	1 tablespoon Dijon-style mustard
¼ teaspoon freshly ground pepper	½ teaspoon cornstarch
1 tablespoon vegetable oil	
2 green onions, trimmed and sliced	

1. Sprinkle both sides of the steaks with the salt and the pepper. Heat ½ tablespoon of the oil in a large, nonstick skillet over medium-high heat. Add half the steaks and cook for 1 minute on each side, or until the steaks are cooked through. Remove the steaks to a serving platter, and keep them warm. Repeat with the remaining steaks.

2. Add the remaining ½ tablespoon of oil to the skillet. Lower the heat to medium. Add the green onion, and sauté for 2 minutes. Whisk together the broth, mustard and cornstarch in a small bowl until the mixture is smooth. Stir the mustard mixture into the skillet and cook, stirring constantly, until the sauce thickens and boils. Pour the mustard sauce over the steaks, and serve immediately.

Sausage-Stuffed Acorn Squash

LOW-CALORIE · LOW-CHOLESTEROL

Bake squash at 350° for 45 minutes.

Makes 4 servings.

Nutrient Value Per Serving: 314 calories, 13 g protein, 17 g fat, 30 g carbohydrate, 846 mg sodium, 45 mg cholesterol.

2	large acorn squash, halved and seeded	1	medium-size onion, finely chopped (1 cup)
¼	teaspoon salt	½	cup finely chopped sweet red pepper
⅛	teaspoon freshly ground pepper	¼	cup finely chopped celery
1	pound bulk pork OR: turkey sausage, removed from casings	1	teaspoon dried rosemary, crumbled
		1	teaspoon vegetable oil

1. Preheat the oven to moderate (350°).

2. Sprinkle the cut sides of the squash halves with the salt and the pepper. Place the squash halves, cut side down, in a shallow baking pan.

3. Bake the squash halves in the preheated moderate oven (350°) for 30 minutes. Turn over the squash halves and bake for 15 minutes more, or until the squash are fork-tender.

4. Combine the sausage, onion, red pepper, celery and rosemary in a large bowl until they are well mixed. Shape the sausage mixture into 16 equal meatballs.

5. Working in batches, cook the meatballs in the oil in a large, nonstick skillet until they are browned. Remove the browned meatballs to a plate, and keep them warm. Fill each squash half with 4 meatballs, and serve.

Peppery Steak

If there is any steak left over from this meal, you can use it to make Warm Steak & Red Pepper Salad (recipe, page 26).

LOW-CALORIE · LOW-CHOLESTEROL · LOW-SODIUM

Bake at 375° for 10 to 15 minutes.

Makes 8 servings, or 4 servings plus leftovers.

Nutrient Value Per Serving: 178 calories, 22 g protein, 9 g fat, 1 g carbohydrate, 44 mg sodium, 59 mg cholesterol.

1	tablespoon cracked or coarsely ground black pepper	2	pounds top round steak (1½ inches thick), cut into 4 pieces
		2	to 3 tablespoons olive oil

SQUASH, ANYONE?

Sausage-Stuffed Acorn Squash

Sliced Cucumbers in Yogurt
(recipe, page 148)

Hot Rolls

Frozen Fruit Juice Bars

o ❖ o

EASY STEAK SUPPER

Peppery Steak

Squash Kebabs
(recipe, page 151)

Parslied New Potatoes

Pineapple Rings

o ❖ o

1. Preheat the oven to moderate (375°). Press the black pepper into both sides of the steaks.

2. Heat 2 tablespoons of the oil in a large, heavy skillet over medium heat. Working in batches and adding more oil, if necessary, add the steaks and cook, turning once, until the steaks are well browned, for about 3 minutes on each side. Transfer the steaks to a rimmed baking sheet.

3. Bake the steaks in the preheated moderate oven (375°) for 10 to 15 minutes for medium-rare. Remove the steaks from the oven, and let them stand for 10 minutes. Cut the steaks in half, slice and serve. Refrigerate any leftover steak to use in Warm Steak & Red Pepper Salad, or for another meal.

Squash Kebabs (recipe, page 151) make a colorful accompaniment to Peppery Steak and potatoes.

Meat & Potato Roll with Onion Gravy

Bake at 350° for 45 minutes.

Makes 4 servings.

Nutrient Value Per Serving: 436 calories, 28 g protein, 28 g fat, 17 g carbohydrate, 760 mg sodium, 96 mg cholesterol.

1	pound very lean ground beef	¾	cup unseasoned mashed potatoes
¾	cup chopped onion (1 medium-size onion)	½	cup plain lowfat yogurt
¼	cup wheat germ	1	tablespoon chopped parsley
1	egg white	2	tablespoons butter or margarine
2	cloves garlic, finely chopped	1½	tablespoons all-purpose flour
½	teaspoon salt	1	cup beef broth
¼	teaspoon freshly ground pepper		

1. Preheat the oven to moderate (350°).

2. Combine the beef, ¼ cup of the onion, the wheat germ, egg white, garlic, ¼ teaspoon of the salt and ⅛ teaspoon of the black pepper in a medium-size bowl. Combine the mashed potatoes, ¼ cup of the yogurt, the parsley, remaining ¼ teaspoon of salt and remaining ⅛ teaspoon of black pepper in a small bowl.

3. Spread the beef mixture on a piece of wax paper into a 10 x 6½-inch rectangle. Spread the potato mixture over the beef mixture, leaving a ½-inch border around all the edges. Using the wax paper as a guide and starting from a long side, roll up the beef and potato mixtures. Place the roll in a 13 x 9-inch baking dish.

4. Bake the roll in the preheated moderate oven (350°) for 45 minutes.

5. Cook the remaining ½ cup of onion in the butter or margarine in a small saucepan until the onion is tender, for about 4 minutes. Whisk in the flour and cook, stirring, for 4 minutes, or until the flour mixture is thickened; it will be quite thick. Gradually stir in the broth and cook, stirring, for 4 minutes, or until the broth mixture is thickened and bubbly. Stir in the remaining ¼ cup of yogurt. Gently heat the onion gravy through without boiling it.

6. Using a spatula, remove the roll from the baking dish to a serving platter. Serve the roll with the gravy on the side.

NEW FANGLED MEAT & POTATOES

Meat & Potato Roll with Onion Gravy

Orange Carrots (recipe, page 150)

Cherry Tomatoes

Fresh Pears

○ ❖ ○

"Salt is the policeman of taste: it keeps the various flavors of a dish in order and restrains the stronger from tyranizing over the weaker."

— Malcom de Chazal

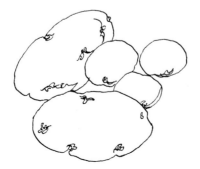

◦ ✤ ◦

BRIE

This popular French cheese is named for the province east of Paris where it originated and still is produced. Considered the cheese of kings because so many French monarchs preferred it, Brie is a creamy white, soft cheese that is mild-flavored and becomes pungent when ripe. It is made in round, flat molds; a wheel of Brie ranges from 7 to 22 inches in diameter. Brie is made from skimmed cow's milk, sometimes with added cream and has a grayish-white edible crust. Serve Brie at room temperature as an appetizer, or with fruit as dessert.

◦ ✤ ◦

Ham & Brie Triple-Deckers with Chutney Mayonnaise

LOW-CHOLESTEROL

Makes 4 servings.

Nutrient Value Per Serving: 387 calories, 22 g protein, 16 g fat, 43 g carbohydrate, 974 mg sodium, 56 mg cholesterol.

Chutney Mayonnaise:

- ¼ **cup reduced-calorie mayonnaise**
- 2 **tablespoons bottled chutney**
- 12 **slices whole wheat sandwich bread, toasted**
- 6 **ounces thinly sliced reduced-sodium baked ham**
- 1 **chunk (4 ounces) Brie OR: Monterey Jack cheese, thinly sliced**
- 4 **large lettuce leaves**
- 1 **medium-size tomato, sliced**
- ¼ **small red onion, thinly sliced**

1. Prepare the Chutney Mayonnaise: Stir together the mayonnaise and the chutney in a small bowl until they are blended.

2. Spread 8 of the toasted bread slices with the Chutney Mayonnaise. Place the ham, divided evenly, on 4 of the mayonnaise-coated toast slices. Top with the Brie or Monterey Jack cheese, divided evenly.

3. Cover each sandwich with another mayonnaise-coated toast slice, coated side up, and a lettuce leaf. Place the tomato and the onion, divided evenly, on the lettuce leaves. Top each sandwich with one of the remaining uncoated toast slices. Secure the sandwiches with wooden picks, removing the picks before eating. If you wish, cut each sandwich into quarters.

Charcuterie Salad

Makes 4 servings.

Nutrient Value Per Serving: 383 calories, 15 g protein, 30 g fat, 17 g carbohydrate, 919 mg sodium, cholesterol data unavailable.

- ¼ **cup vegetable oil**
- ¼ **cup cider vinegar**
- 1 **teaspoon sugar**
- ¼ **teaspoon caraway seeds**
- ¼ **teaspoon celery seeds**
- ⅛ **teaspoon freshly ground pepper**
- 1 **package (8 ounces) shredded cabbage**
- 1 **carrot, shredded**
- 2 **green onions, sliced**
- 4 **large romaine lettuce leaves**
- 8 **ounces fully cooked lowfat kielbasa**
- ¼ **pound thinly sliced ham**
- 1 **tart red apple, cored and cut into wedges**
- 1 **small sweet green pepper, cored, seeded, and cut into rings**

1. Whisk together the oil, vinegar, sugar, caraway seeds, celery seeds and pepper in a medium-size bowl. Add the cabbage, carrot and green onion, and toss to coat them well. Cover the bowl, and refrigerate the slaw until serving time.

2. Place the lettuce leaves on a serving platter. Top with the kielbasa, ham and apple. Add the green pepper. Lift the slaw out of the bowl with a slotted spoon, and mound it on the platter. Spoon any remaining dressing over the rest of the salad.

Ham & Cheese Omelet Roll

We used a ham and Monterey Jack cheese filling in this omelet, but you can experiment with a filling of your choice.

LOW-CALORIE

Bake at 350° for 18 minutes.

Makes 4 servings.

Nutrient Value Per Serving: 304 calories, 20 g protein, 16 g fat, 18 g carbohydrate, 599 mg sodium, 250 mg cholesterol.

Nonstick vegetable cooking spray	**½ cup shredded carrot**
4 eggs	**1 cup shredded Monterey Jack cheese (4 ounces)**
½ cup all-purpose flour	**2 tablespoons canned diced mild green chili peppers**
1 cup lowfat milk	**Additional sliced green onion, for garnish (optional)**
¼ teaspoon salt	
½ cup sliced green onion	
2 ounces thinly sliced boiled OR: baked ham, cut into 2 x ¼-inch strips	

EGG-CITING OMELET SUPPER

Ham & Cheese Omelet Roll

Tomato Wedges

Jam-Filled Pastries

(recipe, page 190)

○ ❖ ○

BREAKFAST FOODS FOR SUPPER

Surprise your family one weekday night by serving breakfast foods for dinner. Traditional breakfast foods are quick and easy to prepare, and children think it's a real treat. Some suggested menus:

● Buttermilk pancakes with applesauce and fruit yogurt.

● Scrambled eggs with cheese melted on top, home-fried potatoes with red and green peppers, and melon wedges.

● A selection of favorite cereals with sliced strawberries, peaches, bananas and fresh blueberries to make "cereal sundaes."

● English muffin halves topped with spicy mustard and slices of Canadian bacon, avocado and Monterey Jack cheese, toasted under the broiler just until the cheese melts, and served with fresh fruit compote.

Offer a taste of morning sunshine for dinner with Ham & Cheese Omelet Roll.

1. Preheat the oven to moderate (350°). Line a 15½ x 10½ x 1-inch jelly-roll pan with aluminum foil, leaving a 2-inch overhang at each short end. Generously spray the bottom and sides of the aluminum foil with nonstick vegetable cooking spray.

2. Lightly beat the eggs in a medium-size bowl. Gradually beat in the flour, milk and salt until no lumps remain. Pour the egg mixture into the prepared pan. Sprinkle on the ½ cup of green onion and the ham.

3. Bake the omelet in the preheated moderate oven (350°) for 18 minutes, or until the omelet is set and lightly browned.

4. Sprinkle the omelet immediately with the carrot, Monterey Jack cheese and chili peppers. Starting from a short end, and using the aluminum foil to lift and roll, roll up the omelet. Transfer the omelet to a serving platter. Serve the omelet hot, or at room temperature. Garnish with additional sliced green onion, if you wish.

CABBAGE PATCH CHOPS

**Pork Chops
with Red & White Cabbage**

Horseradish Applesauce
(see Tip, below)

Steamed Green Beans

Butterscotch Pudding

o ◦❖◦ o

HORSERADISH APPLESAUCE

A dish that's very low in calories and sodium, with no cholesterol or fat!
• Combine ½ cup of unsweetened applesauce, 1 tablespoon of red or white prepared horseradish and 1 teaspoon of sugar in a small bowl. Cover the bowl with plastic wrap, and refrigerate the Horseradish Applesauce until serving time. Makes about ½ cup.

Pork Chops
with Red & White Cabbage

LOW-CALORIE ▪ LOW-CHOLESTEROL
Makes 4 servings.
Nutrient Value Per Serving: 284 calories, 27 g protein, 12 g fat, 15 g carbohydrate, 848 mg sodium, 72 mg cholesterol.

1   tablespoon vegetable oil
4   center-cut pork chops (1½ pounds), trimmed
¼   teaspoon freshly ground pepper
1   bag (16 ounces) sauerkraut, drained and rinsed
1   jar (16 ounces) sweet and sour red cabbage, drained
¼   cup one-third-less-salt chicken broth

1. Heat the oil in a very large skillet over medium heat. Add the pork chops and cook, turning once, until they are browned, for about 4 minutes on each side. Drain all the fat from the skillet. Sprinkle the chops with the pepper.

2. Add the sauerkraut, red cabbage and broth to the skillet. Cover the skillet and simmer for 20 minutes, or until the chops are cooked through.

Pork Chops with Curried Pear Sauce

Bake at 375° for 35 minutes.

Makes 4 servings.

Nutrient Value Per Serving: 646 calories, 32 g protein, 43 g fat, 34 g carbohydrate, 447 mg sodium, 122 mg cholesterol.

1 firm, ripe Bosc, Bartlett OR: Anjou pear, peeled, cored, and diced	1 tablespoon vegetable oil
¼ cup (2 ounces) dried apricots, coarsely chopped	4 loin pork chops (1½ to 2 pounds), 1 inch thick
3 tablespoons dark, seedless raisins	¼ teaspoon salt
1 can (5½ ounces) pear nectar	⅛ teaspoon freshly ground pepper
¾ cup chicken broth	1 large onion, finely chopped (1 cup)
1 tablespoon lemon juice	1 clove garlic, finely chopped
1 tablespoon butter or margarine	1 tablespoon curry powder
	2 teaspoons all-purpose flour

1. Ten minutes before baking, preheat the oven to moderate (375°).

2. Combine the pear, apricots, raisins, pear nectar, broth and lemon juice in a small bowl. Set aside the pear mixture.

3. Heat the butter or margarine with the oil in a very large skillet over medium heat. Add the pork chops and cook for 3 minutes on each side, or until the chops are golden. Remove the pork chops to a 9 x 9 x 2-inch glass baking dish. Sprinkle the chops with the salt and the pepper.

4. Add the onion and the garlic to the fat remaining in the skillet, and sauté over medium heat for 2 minutes. Combine the curry powder with the flour in a small bowl. Sprinkle the curry mixture over the onion mixture and cook, stirring constantly, for 2 minutes; the onion-curry mixture will be dry. Stir in the pear mixture. Bring the sauce to boiling, stirring to loosen any browned bits from the bottom of the skillet. Lower the heat and simmer, stirring occasionally, for 2 minutes. Spoon the sauce over the pork chops in the baking dish. Cover the dish with aluminum foil.

5. Bake the pork chops in the preheated moderate oven (375°) for 20 minutes. Uncover the baking dish. Bake the pork chops for 15 minutes more, or until the pork chops are cooked through.

Pork Chops à l'Orange

Makes 4 servings.

Nutrient Value Per Serving: 632 calories, 34 g protein, 50 g fat, 9 g carbohydrate, 460 mg sodium, 145 mg cholesterol.

4 tablespoons all-purpose flour	¼ cup orange juice
¼ teaspoon salt	¼ cup water
¼ teaspoon freshly ground pepper	2 teaspoons reduced-sodium soy sauce
8 thin center-cut pork chops	½ teaspoon grated orange zest (orange part of rind only)
2 tablespoons vegetable oil	Orange slices, for garnish
1 small onion, cut into thin slivers	Parsley sprigs, for garnish
½ cup chicken broth	

WINTER EVENING DINNER

Pork Chops with Curried Pear Sauce

Steamed Peas

Endive and Watercress Salad

Mango Mint Sherbet
(recipe, page 208)

○ ❖ ○

"There is more simplicity in the man who eats caviar on impulse than in the man who eats Grape-Nuts on principle."

— G. K. Chesterton

PORK CHOPS PARISIENNE

Pork Chops à l'Orange

Zucchini Potato Pancakes
(recipe, page 152)

Applesauce

Light Ice Cream

○ ❖ ○

1. Combine 3 tablespoons of the flour with the salt and the pepper on a piece of wax paper. Coat both sides of the pork chops with the flour mixture, shaking off the excess mixture.

2. Heat 1 tablespoon of the oil in a large, nonstick skillet over medium-high heat. Placing 4 of the chops at a time in the skillet, brown the chops for 5 minutes on the first side, and 3 to 4 minutes on the other side. Remove the browned chops from the skillet, and keep them warm. Wipe the skillet clean with paper toweling.

3. Sauté the onion in the remaining tablespoon of oil in the skillet over medium heat for 2 minutes, or until the onion is slightly softened.

4. Gradually stir the broth into the remaining tablespoon of flour in a small cup until the mixture is smooth. Stir the broth mixture into the skillet along with the orange juice, water, soy sauce and orange zest. Cook, stirring, until the sauce thickens. Return the chops to the skillet. Cover the skillet, and simmer for 5 minutes. Serve the pork chops garnished with orange slices and parsley sprigs.

The perfect "comfort" meal for a hectic day: Pork Chops à l'Orange and Zucchini Potato Pancakes (recipe, page 152).

Stir-Fried Pork & Broccoli

Makes 4 servings.

Nutrient Value Per Serving: 488 calories, 25 g protein, 35 g fat, 18 g carbohydrate, 614 mg sodium, 79 mg cholesterol.

4	cups broccoli flowerets and peeled stems (10 ounces)
3½	tablespoons reduced-sodium soy sauce
2	tablespoons water
2½	teaspoons sugar
¼	teaspoon liquid red pepper seasoning
⅓	cup all-purpose flour
1	pound boneless pork loin (not tenderloin), thinly sliced, and cut into ½-inch-wide strips
3	tablespoons olive OR: vegetable oil
1	large sweet red pepper, cored, seeded, and cut into 1-inch dice
3	cloves garlic, finely chopped
2	teaspoons peeled, finely chopped fresh ginger

1. Soak the broccoli in a bowl of ice water for 30 minutes. Drain the broccoli in a colander.

2. Combine the soy sauce, water, sugar and liquid red pepper seasoning in a small bowl.

3. Place the flour on a piece of wax paper. Dredge the pork strips in the flour to coat them.

4. Working in batches if necessary, sauté the pork strips in 2 tablespoons of the olive or vegetable oil in a very large skillet over high heat for 4 minutes, or until the strips are browned and cooked through. Add the remaining oil as necessary to prevent sticking.

5. Remove the pork strips with a slotted spoon to a medium-size bowl. Lower the heat to medium. Add the red pepper, broccoli, garlic and ginger to the skillet. Cook, covered, for 4 minutes, or until the vegetables are crisply tender. Stir in the soy mixture and pork strips, and heat through.

FLASH-IN-THE-PAN PORK

Stir-Fried Pork & Broccoli

Gingered Rice
(recipe, page 157)

Orange Ice
(recipe, page 210)

○ ❖ ○

PORK

Cooked pork is delicate, tender, juicy, nutritious, and considerably leaner than the pork of our grandparents' day.

● There is wide selection of pork cuts that can add variety to your family's meals. Pork is available fresh, or cured and/or smoked. The most tender pork cuts are from the rib, loin and leg. In butcher's terms, a leg is a ham, and a fresh ham is simply one that has not been cured or smoked. Tender pork cuts require nothing more than pan-frying, or a gentle, slow roasting. Any cut of pork must be cooked thoroughly.

● Pork provides high quality proteins containing all the essential amino acids. Pork is an excellent source of thiamin, riboflavin, niacin and vitamins B_6 and B_{12}. A 3-ounce serving of lean pork has 24 grams of protein, and 206 calories.

Gingered Rice (recipe, page 157) is the perfect partner for Stir-Fried Pork & Broccoli.

Seafood

A treat for the taste buds, and good for you, too! Most seafood requires little preparation and cooks very quickly. The variety of fresh fish and shellfish available these days is amazing.

FISH FILLET DINNER

Baked Flounder Fillets

Baked Stuffed Tomatoes
(recipe, page 151)

Tossed Green Salad

Sliced Oranges with Honey Orange Sauce
(recipe, page 202)

○ ◦❖◦ ○

Baked Flounder Fillets

LOW-CALORIE ▪ LOW-FAT ▪ MICROWAVE

Bake at 425° for 10 minutes; or microwave at full power for 5 minutes.
Makes 4 servings.
Nutrient Value Per Serving: 192 calories, 32 g protein, 5 g fat,
2 g carbohydrate, 285 mg sodium, 82 mg cholesterol.

Nonstick vegetable cooking spray	1 to 2 tablespoons lime juice
4 flounder fillets (6 ounces each)	1 tablespoon olive oil
¼ teaspoon salt	1 tablespoon packaged bread crumbs
⅛ teaspoon freshly ground pepper	1 tablespoon chopped fresh cilantro OR: parsley

1. Preheat the oven to hot (425°). Coat a small baking pan with nonstick vegetable cooking spray.

2. Halve the flounder fillets crosswise, and sprinkle them with the salt and the pepper. Place the fillets in the prepared pan. Drizzle the fillets with the lime juice and the oil. Combine the bread crumbs with the cilantro or parsley in a small bowl. Sprinkle the crumb mixture over the fillets.

3. Bake the fillets in the preheated hot oven (425°) for 10 minutes, or until the fillets are cooked through.

Microwave Instructions
(for a 650-watt variable power microwave oven)

Ingredient Changes: Eliminate the nonstick vegetable cooking spray.
Directions: Sprinkle the flounder fillets with the salt and the pepper. Fold the fillets in half crosswise, and secure them with wooden picks. Place the fillets in a microwave-safe 10-inch pie plate, with the thicker parts of the fillets toward the outside of the plate. Sprinkle the fillets with the lime juice, oil, bread crumbs, and cilantro or parsley. Cover the plate with microwave-safe plastic wrap turned back at one side to vent it. Microwave the fillets at full power for 5 minutes.

Stir-Fried Asparagus, Shrimp & Rice

LOW-CALORIE · LOW-FAT

Makes 6 servings.

Nutrient Value Per Serving: 264 calories, 23 g protein, 6 g fat, 29 g carbohydrate, 367 mg sodium, 140 mg cholesterol.

1	cup long-grain white rice
1	pound fresh asparagus, trimmed
2	tablespoons margarine
1½	pounds shrimp, peeled and deveined
2	large cloves garlic, finely chopped
1	tablespoon lemon juice
½	teaspoon salt
¼	teaspoon freshly ground pepper
	Lemon wedges, for garnish (optional)

1. Cook the rice following the package directions, adding salt if you wish. Set aside the rice.

2. Slice the asparagus into 1½-inch pieces. Heat 1 tablespoon of the margarine in a large, nonstick skillet. Add the asparagus and stir-fry for 3 minutes, or until the asparagus is crisply tender. Remove the asparagus from the skillet, and set it aside.

3. Add the remaining tablespoon of margarine to the skillet, and heat. Add the shrimp and stir-fry over high heat for 2 minutes, or just until the shrimp are cooked. Stir in the garlic and stir-fry for 1 minute, or until fragrant. Stir in the lemon juice, salt and pepper.

4. Stir the asparagus and rice into the skillet, and heat to serving temperature. Garnish with lemon wedges, if you wish.

Corn & Shrimp Curry

LOW-CALORIE

Makes 4 servings.

Nutrient Value Per Serving: 346 calories, 21 g protein, 17 g fat, 29 g carbohydrate, 566 mg sodium, 151 mg cholesterol.

1	to 2 large ears corn
¼	cup (½ stick) butter or margarine
¾	pound medium-size shrimp (16 to 18), peeled and deveined
1	large onion, chopped (1 cup)
1	medium-size carrot, coarsely shredded (1 cup)
1	tablespoon curry powder
1	large clove garlic, pressed
1	teaspoon peeled, grated fresh ginger
2	tablespoons all-purpose flour
1¾	cups milk
½	teaspoon salt
3	tablespoons chopped parsley
	Cooked brown rice
	Assorted condiments, such as chutney, raisins, roasted peanuts, shredded coconut, and chopped red and green apples

FAST & FRESH STIR-FRY

Stir-Fried Asparagus, Shrimp & Rice

Steamed Baby Carrots

Raspberry Sherbet
(recipe, page 208)

A PASSAGE TO INDIA

Corn & Shrimp Curry

Toasted Pita Bread

Gingered Pineapple
Vanilla Pudding
(recipe, page 211)

1. Cut the corn kernels with a knife from the cobs into a bowl; you should have 1¾ to 2 cups of kernels.

2. Sauté the corn kernels in 1 tablespoon of the butter or margarine in a large skillet over medium heat for 3 to 5 minutes. Remove the corn from the skillet, and keep it warm. In the same skillet, sauté the shrimp in 1 tablespoon of the butter for 3 to 5 minutes, or until the shrimp are pink and curled. Remove the shrimp from the skillet, and keep them warm.

3. Melt the remaining 2 tablespoons of butter in the same skillet. Add the onion, carrot and curry powder, and sauté for 3 to 5 minutes, or until the vegetables are softened. Add the garlic and the ginger, and sauté for 1 minute. Gradually stir in the flour until the mixture is smooth. Cook, stirring constantly, for 3 to 5 minutes; the flour mixture will be very thick and dry. Gradually stir in the milk until it is well blended. Cook, stirring constantly and scraping any browned bits from the bottom of the skillet, for 3 to 5 minutes, or until the milk mixture is thickened and bubbly. Stir in the corn and shrimp, and heat them through. Stir in the salt and the parsley. Serve the curry over the brown rice, with the condiments on the side.

Shrimp Salad Calypso

LOW-CALORIE

Makes 4 servings.

Nutrient Value Per Serving: 324 calories, 31 g protein, 12 g fat, 24 g carbohydrate, 938 mg sodium, 221 mg cholesterol.

1	lime
3	tablespoons olive OR: vegetable oil
1	tablespoon cider vinegar
1	teaspoon honey
6	drops liquid red pepper seasoning
¾	teaspoon salt
2	tablespoons chopped fresh cilantro OR: parsley
1	pound cooked, shelled shrimp

1	can (15 ounces) black beans, rinsed and drained
1	small sweet green pepper, cored, seeded and diced
½	red onion, diced
2	stalks celery, sliced diagonally
½	head leafy green lettuce, thinly sliced (optional)
½	container cherry tomatoes, halved, for garnish

1. Grate the lime zest (green part of the rind only), then juice the lime. Place the lime juice and zest in a large bowl. Whisk in the olive or vegetable oil, the vinegar, honey, liquid red pepper seasoning, salt and cilantro or parsley until they are well blended.

2. Add the shrimp to the dressing in the bowl. Add the black beans, green pepper, onion and celery, and stir to coat the ingredients. Refrigerate the salad, covered, until it is chilled. (The salad can be prepared up to 1 day in advance, and refrigerated until serving time.)

3. If you wish, serve the salad on a bed of thinly sliced leaves from half a head of leafy green lettuce. Garnish the salad with the cherry tomatoes.

"The world would have been merely nothing except for life. All that lives, feeds."

—Anthelme Brillat-Savarin

ISLAND MEDLEY

Shrimp Salad Calypso

Sesame Breadsticks

Mango Mint Sherbet
(recipe, page 208)

Crispy Fillet Strips

LOW-CALORIE • LOW-CHOLESTEROL • LOW-FAT

Makes 4 servings.

Nutrient Value Per Serving: 223 calories, 22 g protein, 6 g fat, 14 g carbohydrate, 343 mg sodium, 50 mg cholesterol.

1	pound ½-inch-thick cod fillets	½	teaspoon salt
¾	cup lowfat milk	3	to 4 tablespoons olive oil
½	cup cornmeal		Chive OR: tarragon butter (optional)

1. Cut the cod fillets into 1-inch-wide strips. Place the cod strips in a shallow pan along with the milk. Soak the strips for 20 minutes. Drain the strips, and discard the milk.

2. Combine the cornmeal with the salt on a piece of wax paper. Dredge the cod strips in the cornmeal mixture to coat them.

3. Cook the cod strips in 3 tablespoons of the oil in a large, nonstick skillet over medium-high heat until the strips are golden brown on one side, for about 2 minutes. Lower the heat to medium, turn over the strips and cook them for 2 to 3 minutes more, or until the cod strips are cooked through. Work in batches and add more oil, if necessary, to prevent the cod strips from being crowded in the skillet or sticking. Serve the cod strips immediately, with chive or tarragon butter if you wish.

GONE FISHIN'

Crispy Fillet Strips

Ripe Plum Tomato Salad
(recipe, page 146)

Corn Muffins

**Oatmeal Cookies
with Applesauce**

○ ❖ ○

> " *I don't mind eels,
> Except as meals.* "
> —*Ogden Nash*

A tasty treat for the whole family: Crispy Fillet Strips with Ripe Plum Tomato Salad (recipe, page 146).

○ ❖ ○

HALIBUT

The common name of four species of flounder that are saltwater flatfish, halibut is the largest of the four. Like other flatfish that lie on the bottom of the ocean, the halibut has two eyes on one side of its head. It inhabits the deep, cold waters of the north Pacific and Atlantic Oceans.

● Halibut has firm, delicate, sweet, white flesh, and can be prepared in a variety of ways. It usually is sold as steaks or fillets.

Fish Steak Casserole

Bake at 400° for 20 to 25 minutes.
Makes 4 servings.
Nutrient Value Per Serving: 606 calories, 33 g protein, 34 g fat, 40 g carbohydrate, 745 mg sodium, 94 mg cholesterol.

½ **cup shredded carrot**	⅓ **cup all-purpose flour**
½ **cup finely chopped celery**	½ **teaspoon garlic salt**
½ **cup finely chopped onion**	¼ **teaspoon fresh dill**
1 **chicken bouillon cube**	¼ **teaspoon onion powder**
2½ **cups water**	4 **halibut OR: salmon steaks,**
¾ **cup long-grain white rice**	**½ inch thick (about**
1 **tablespoon unsalted margarine**	**1¼ pounds)**
	½ **cup mayonnaise**

1. Combine the carrot, celery, onion, bouillon cube and water in a medium-size saucepan. Bring the mixture to boiling and boil, covered, for 10 minutes. Stir in the rice and the margarine, and simmer, covered, for 20 minutes; not all the liquid will be absorbed. Remove the saucepan from the heat.

2. Preheat the oven to hot (400°).

3. Combine the flour, garlic salt, dill and onion powder on a piece of wax paper. Spread both sides of the halibut or salmon steaks with the mayonnaise. Dip each steak in the flour mixture to coat both sides. Lightly brown the steaks in an ungreased nonstick skillet over medium heat for about 2 to 3 minutes on each side.

4. Pour the undrained rice mixture into a shallow 11 x 7-inch baking dish. Place the steaks on top of the rice mixture.

5. Bake the casserole, uncovered, in the preheated hot oven (400°) for 20 to 25 minutes, or until the steaks are cooked through. Let the casserole stand for 5 minutes before serving it.

Salmon & Rice Salad

LOW-CHOLESTEROL

Makes 4 servings.

Nutrient Value Per Serving: 405 calories, 26 g protein, 17 g fat, 36 g carbohydrate, 799 mg sodium, 46 mg cholesterol.

1½ **cups packaged precooked rice**	2 **tablespoons chopped fresh dill**
¼ **teaspoon salt**	2 **teaspoons Dijon-style mustard**
1½ **cups boiling water**	1 **teaspoon honey**
1 **can (16 ounces) salmon**	1 **teaspoon lemon juice**
¼ **cup yogurt**	¼ **teaspoon freshly ground pepper**
¼ **cup mayonnaise**	1 **cup frozen peas, thawed**
2 **tablespoons chopped green onion**	

1. Combine the rice with the salt in a medium-size bowl. Pour in the boiling water, and stir to mix the ingredients. Cover the bowl, and let the rice stand for 5 minutes, or until the water is absorbed.

2. Place the salmon in a strainer, and rinse it under cold water. Carefully remove all the skin and bones, and flake the salmon coarsely.

3. Stir together the yogurt, mayonnaise, green onion, dill, mustard, honey, lemon juice and pepper in a small bowl. Stir the dressing into the rice along with the peas. Fold in the salmon, and toss gently to mix the ingredients.

Flounder Meunière

Makes 4 servings.

Nutrient Value Per Serving: 325 calories, 34 g protein, 16 g fat, 10 g carbohydrate, 430 mg sodium, 102 mg cholesterol.

1½ **pounds flounder fillets**	2 **tablespoons lemon juice**
½ **cup milk**	2 **tablespoons unsalted butter or margarine, in 4 pieces**
⅓ **cup all-purpose flour**	¼ **cup chopped parsley**
2 **tablespoons vegetable oil**	**Lemon slices, for garnish**
½ **teaspoon salt**	
¼ **teaspoon freshly ground pepper**	

1. Cut the flounder fillets into 8 pieces, and place them in a bowl. Pour the milk over the flounder, and let stand for 10 minutes. Drain the flounder.

2. Place the flour on a piece of wax paper. Coat the flounder pieces on both sides with the flour, shaking off the excess flour.

3. Heat 1 tablespoon of the oil in a large, nonstick skillet over medium-high heat. Add half the flounder pieces, and sauté for 1½ to 2 minutes, or until the pieces are browned on the bottom. Turn over the pieces, and brown the other side. Remove the flounder pieces from the skillet as soon as they are cooked, and sprinkle them with ¼ teaspoon of the salt and ⅛ teaspoon of the pepper. Keep the cooked flounder warm. Repeat with the remaining oil, flounder, salt and pepper.

4. Wipe the skillet clean. Pour in the lemon juice. Add the butter or margarine. Cook, stirring constantly, until the butter melts. Stir in the parsley. Pour the sauce over the flounder, and garnish with lemon slices.

SALAD FROM THE SEA

Salmon & Rice Salad

Pickled Beets & Apples
(recipe, page 149)

Crisp Wafers

Banana and Cherry Compote

o ❖ o

FISH IN A FLASH

Flounder Meunière

Zucchini Sauté
(recipe, page 153)

Tossed Green Salad

Chocolate Pudding

o ❖ o

Elegant Flounder Meunière with Zucchini Sauté (recipe, page 153) is delicious enough for company, and easy enough to make any night of the week.

43

Vegetables, Legumes & Pasta

A selection of mouth watering recipes using fresh vegetables, rice, beans or pasta. Not all these recipes are vegetarian!

Vegetable Curry with Pistachio Rice

To have the rice and curry ready at the same time, cut up the vegetables, start the rice cooking, then simmer the curry.

LOW-CHOLESTEROL · LOW-FAT
Makes 4 servings.
Nutrient Value Per Serving: 490 calories, 15 g protein, 12 g fat, 84 g carbohydrate, 560 mg sodium, 8 mg cholesterol.

1	tablespoon vegetable oil	1¼	cups water
1	tablespoon unsalted butter	4	ripe plum tomatoes (12 ounces), cut into eighths, and seeded
1	tablespoon curry powder		
½	teaspoon ground cumin	1	cup fresh peas
⅛	teaspoon ground hot red pepper	1	can (10½ ounces) chick peas, drained and rinsed
2	cloves garlic, halved and thinly sliced	1	teaspoon fresh thyme, chopped
1	large onion, halved, and each half cut into 8 wedges	½	teaspoon salt
1	small head cauliflower (1¾ pounds), cut into small flowerets (4 cups)	¼	teaspoon freshly ground pepper
			Pistachio Rice (recipe follows)

1. Heat the oil and the butter in a very large skillet over medium heat. Add the curry powder, cumin, ground hot red pepper and garlic, and sauté for 1 minute. Add the onion, and sauté for 3 minutes. Add the cauliflower and the water. Bring the mixture to boiling. Reduce the heat and simmer, covered, for 5 minutes, or just until the cauliflower is tender.

2. Stir in the tomatoes, peas, chick peas, thyme, salt and pepper. Cook, stirring occasionally, until the tomatoes wilt, for about 10 minutes. Serve the curry over the Pistachio Rice.

Pistachio Rice:

Combine 1 cup of long-grain white rice with ⅓ cup of golden raisins, the grated zest of 1 lemon (yellow part of the rind only), and ½ teaspoon of salt in a medium-size saucepan. Stir in 1¾ cups of water. Bring the rice mixture to full boiling over medium-high heat. Reduce the heat to very low, cover the saucepan, and cook for 20 minutes. Remove the saucepan from the heat. Let the rice mixture sit, covered, for 10 minutes. Just before serving, stir in ¼ cup of toasted and chopped shelled pistachio nuts.

MIDDLE EASTERN SENSATION

Vegetable Curry with Pistachio Rice

Endive and Watercress Salad

Fresh Nectarines and Bananas

◦ ❖ ◦

"Progress in civilization has been accompanied by progress in cookery."
—*Fannie Farmer*

UPSIDE DOWN DINNER PIE

Eggplant, Rice & Sausage Pie
Grated Carrot Salad
Breadsticks
Melon with Orange Mint Sauce
(recipe, page 202)

o ❖ o

PINE NUTS

Pine nuts are ivory-colored, sweet-tasting kernels. They actually are the edible seeds of the cones of a variety of pine tree that grows in the mountainous Southwest states. Pine nuts also are called Indian nuts, pignons or piñons. In Italy and France, pine nuts are known as *pinoleas* or *pignolias*. American-grown pine nuts are smaller than the European variety.
• Pine nuts can be found shelled or unshelled, but always are sold unroasted.
• One ounce of pine nuts has 158 calories and 8 grams of protein.

Eggplant, Rice & Sausage Pie

LOW-CHOLESTEROL

Broil eggplant for 5 minutes; bake pie at 350° for 30 minutes.
Makes 6 servings.
Nutrient Value Per Serving: 408 calories, 15 g protein, 23 g fat, 35 g carbohydrate, 843 mg sodium, 71 mg cholesterol.

¼	cup plus 1½ teaspoons olive oil
3	tablespoons packaged bread crumbs
1	eggplant (1 pound), cut into ¼-inch slices
1	cup long-grain white rice
½	pound sweet Italian sausage, casings removed
1	small onion, chopped (¼ cup)
2	cloves garlic, finely chopped
1	egg, slightly beaten
3	tablespoons tomato paste
1	teaspoon dried oregano, crumbled
1	teaspoon salt
½	teaspoon freshly ground pepper
2	ounces Provolone cheese, shredded (½ cup)
2	ounces mozzarella cheese, shredded (½ cup)
¼	cup pine nuts (optional)
	Cherry tomatoes, for garnish (optional)
	Parsley sprigs, for garnish (optional)

1. Preheat the broiler. Grease the bottom and sides of a 10-inch pie plate with 1½ teaspoons of the oil. Dust the plate with the bread crumbs, and set aside the plate.

2. Place the eggplant slices on a baking sheet, and brush both sides of the slices with the remaining ¼ cup of oil.

3. Broil the eggplant slices 4 inches from the heat source, turning the slices once, for 5 minutes, or until the slices are lightly browned on both sides.

4. Reduce the oven temperature to moderate (350°).

5. Cook the rice following the package directions, adding salt if you wish. Drain any excess liquid from the rice, and set aside the rice.

6. Lay the eggplant slices over the bottom and up the sides of the prepared pie plate; overlap the slices, if necessary.

7. Crumble the sausage into a large skillet, and lightly brown the sausage over medium heat. Carefully pour off the excess fat. Add the onion and the garlic to the skillet, and cook, stirring, for 3 minutes. Stir in the rice, egg, tomato paste, oregano, salt, pepper, Provolone cheese, mozzarella cheese and, if you wish, the pine nuts. Spoon the sausage mixture over the eggplant, packing down the mixture well. Cover the pie plate with aluminum foil.

8. Bake the pie in the preheated moderate oven (350°) for 30 minutes. Remove the pie from the oven. Place a serving plate over the pie plate, carefully invert both plates, and remove the pie plate. Let the pie stand for 10 minutes before slicing it. Garnish the pie with cherry tomatoes and parsley sprigs, if you wish.

Baked Eggplant Sandwiches

Bake eggplant at 450° for 10 minutes; bake sandwiches at 375° for 15 minutes.
Makes 4 servings.

Nutrient Value Per Serving: 514 calories, 25 g protein, 32 g fat,
32 g carbohydrate, 1,037 mg sodium, 80 mg cholesterol.

1 **eggplant (about 1 pound)**	2 **tablespoons chopped parsley**
½ **teaspoon salt**	2½ **cups sauce from Moroccan**
⅛ **teaspoon freshly**	**Pasta (recipe, page 53)**
ground pepper	**OR: prepared spaghetti**
2 **tablespoons olive oil**	**sauce, with or without meat**
1 **can (10 ounces) chick peas**	1 **tablespoon packaged**
¾ **cup shredded Fontina cheese**	**bread crumbs**
(3 ounces)	

1. Preheat the oven to very hot (450°).

2. Cut the eggplant crosswise into 16 equal slices. Sprinkle the slices with
the salt and the pepper. Brush both sides of the slices lightly with the oil.
Place the slices on a large baking sheet.

3. Bake the eggplant slices in the preheated very hot oven (450°) for
10 minutes, turning the slices once. Remove the slices from the oven.
Lower the oven temperature to moderate (375°).

4. Drain and rinse the chick peas. Mash the chick peas with a fork in a small
bowl. Stir in ½ cup of the Fontina cheese along with the parsley. Spread the
chick pea mixture, divided evenly, on 8 eggplant slices. Top with the
remaining slices. Spread ½ cup of the Moroccan Pasta sauce or prepared
spaghetti sauce in an 11 x 8-inch baking dish. Place the eggplant sandwiches
in a single layer in the dish. Spoon the remaining 2 cups of sauce over the
sandwiches. Combine the bread crumbs with the remaining ¼ cup of
Fontina cheese in a bowl, and sprinkle the mixture over the sandwiches.

5. Bake the eggplant sandwiches in the preheated moderate oven (375°)
for 15 minutes, or until the sandwiches are hot.

Individual Eggplant Lasagnas

Eggplant replaces the usual pasta in this new version of an old favorite.

LOW-CHOLESTEROL

Bake eggplant at 425° for 15 minutes; bake lasagnas at 425° for 20 to
25 minutes.
Makes 4 servings.

Nutrient Value Per Serving: 410 calories, 23 g protein, 28 g fat,
18 g carbohydrate, 486 mg sodium, 65 mg cholesterol.

Nonstick vegetable	1 **cup part-skim ricotta cheese**
cooking spray	⅛ **teaspoon freshly**
1 **eggplant (1 pound)**	**ground pepper**
3 **tablespoons olive oil**	½ **cup shredded part-skim**
2 **cups Bolognese Sauce**	**mozzarella cheese**
(recipe, page 52) OR:	**(2 ounces)**
prepared spaghetti sauce	2 **tablespoons grated**
	Parmesan cheese

EGGPLANT ITALIAN-STYLE

Baked Eggplant Sandwiches

Italian Bread

Tossed Green Salad

**Sliced Oranges with
Honey Orange Sauce**
(recipe, page 202)

◦ ❖ ◦

LOTSA LASAGNA!

Individual Eggplant Lasagnas
Italian Green Bean Toss
(recipe, page 153)
Fresh Strawberries

◦ ❖ ◦

1. Preheat the oven to hot (425°).

2. Coat a large baking sheet with nonstick vegetable cooking spray. Cut the eggplant crosswise into eight ⅜-inch-thick slices, and place the slices on the baking sheet. Brush the tops of the slices with the oil.

3. Bake the eggplant slices in the preheated hot oven (425°) for 15 minutes. Remove the eggplant slices from the oven. Leave the oven on.

4. Coat the inside of four 1½- to 2-cup individual casserole dishes with nonstick vegetable cooking spray.* Divide ½ cup of the Bolognese Sauce or spaghetti sauce evenly among the dishes. Top with half the eggplant slices. Combine the ricotta cheese with the pepper, and spread the ricotta mixture over the eggplant in the dishes. Sprinkle with 6 tablespoons of the mozzarella cheese, divided evenly. Add 1 cup of the sauce, divided evenly. Top each casserole with one of the remaining eggplant slices. Cover with the remaining ½ cup of sauce, divided evenly. Sprinkle with the remaining mozzarella cheese, then with the Parmesan cheese.

5. Bake the lasagnas in the preheated hot oven (425°) for 20 to 25 minutes, or until their tops are lightly browned and the eggplant is cooked through.

***Note:** The lasagna can be assembled and baked in an 8-inch square baking dish. Increase the baking time to 30 minutes.*

Enjoy the flavors of Italy with Individual Eggplant Lasagnas and Italian Green Bean Toss (recipe, page 153).

Tofu & Vegetable Stir-Fry

LOW-CALORIE · LOW-CHOLESTEROL

Makes 4 servings.

Nutrient Value Per Serving: 238 calories, 19 g protein, 13 g fat, 15 g carbohydrate, 313 mg sodium, 0 mg cholesterol.

3 **tablespoons reduced-sodium soy sauce**	1 **tablespoon vegetable oil**
1 **tablespoon honey**	½ **pound green beans, trimmed, and cut into 1½-inch lengths**
1 **pound extra firm tofu, cut into 1-inch chunks**	½ **zucchini, thinly sliced (½ cup)**
¼ **cup sliced green onion**	½ **sweet red pepper, cut into thin strips (¾ cup)**
1 **clove garlic, finely chopped**	**Cooked brown rice with cashews**
1 **teaspoon peeled, grated fresh ginger**	

1. Combine the soy sauce with the honey in a medium-size bowl. Add the tofu, and toss gently to coat it.

2. Sauté the green onion, garlic and ginger in the oil in a large skillet for 3 minutes, or until the vegetables are slightly softened. Add the green beans, zucchini and red pepper, and sauté for 5 minutes more. Fold in the tofu mixture, and heat it through. Serve the stir-fry with the brown rice.

FAR EAST FEAST

Hot & Sour Soup
Tofu & Vegetable Stir-Fry
Lemon Sherbet and Strawberries

∘ ❖ ∘

BROWN RICE

The seed of a cereal grass, rice has a long and fascinating history. Rice was one of the first cultivated foods, providing important nourishment to half the world's population. Rice did not originate in China, as many people believe, but in ancient Babylonia. Its popularity spread fast and far. It is said that Buddha himself once lived on a single grain of rice a day. In fact, the Buddhists were responsible for making rice a diet staple throughout the Orient. In 1694, a ship from Madagascar stopped at Charleston, South Carolina during a storm for repairs. The ship's captain gave the governor of the colony some rice seeds, and the governor had the grains planted. The plants flourished, and rice became one of the principal crops of the southeastern colonies.

● Brown rice is whole grain rice with only the outer hull removed. It has a savory, nutlike flavor. The cooking time for brown rice is longer than for regular white rice.

● One cup of cooked brown rice has 232 calories, 5 grams of protein, 50 grams of carbohydrates, and no cholesterol.

A fast treat from the Far East: Tofu & Vegetable Stir-Fry.

o ❖ o

TO EACH HIS OWN CASSEROLE

To make individual Spinach Cheese Casseroles, divide the bulgur-cheese mixture equally among 6 greased 6-ounce custard cups or baking dishes. Bake the casseroles in the preheated moderate oven (350°) for 30 minutes. Remove the casseroles to a wire rack, and let them stand for 10 minutes. Meanwhile, warm the tomato sauce in a small saucepan over medium-low heat. Run a thin metal spatula around the edge of each casserole to loosen it. Spoon some of the warm tomato sauce onto each of 6 individual dinner plates. Unmold a casserole into the center of each pool of sauce. Pour the remaining tomato sauce into a gravy boat and serve the sauce on the side.

Spinach Cheese Casserole

Cracked wheat, sharp Cheddar cheese, spinach and plum tomatoes combine to make a delicious vegetarian one-dish meal.

LOW-CALORIE

Bake at 350° for 30 minutes.

Makes 6 servings.

Nutrient Value Per Serving: 295 calories, 16 g protein, 14 g fat, 30 g carbohydrate, 952 mg sodium, 101 mg cholesterol.

2 cups water	**2** eggs
¾ teaspoon salt	**½** cup lowfat milk
1 cup bulgur (cracked wheat)	**6** ounces sharp Cheddar cheese, shredded (1¾ cups)
1 tablespoon vegetable oil	**1** package (10 ounces) frozen chopped spinach, thawed and well drained
1 large onion, finely chopped (1 cup)	
2 cloves garlic, finely chopped	**1** can (15 ounces) tomato sauce
3 large plum tomatoes, seeded and finely chopped	

1. Preheat the oven to moderate (350°). Lightly grease a 1½-quart casserole dish, and set aside the dish.

2. Bring the water and the salt to boiling in a medium-size saucepan. Add the bulgur. Lower the heat and simmer, uncovered, for 10 minutes, or until the liquid is absorbed. Set aside the saucepan.

3. Heat the oil in a medium-size skillet over medium heat. Add the onion and the garlic, and sauté for 5 minutes, or until the onion is softened. Stir in the tomatoes, and sauté for 5 minutes. Stir the tomato mixture into the bulgur mixture.

4. Beat together the eggs and the milk in a large bowl. Stir in the Cheddar cheese, spinach and bulgur-tomato mixture until they are well mixed. Turn the bulgur-cheese mixture into the prepared dish.

5. Bake the casserole in the preheated moderate oven (350°) for 30 minutes. Remove the casserole to a wire rack, and let it stand for 15 minutes. Meanwhile, warm the tomato sauce in a small saucepan, over medium-low heat. Pour the warm tomato sauce into a gravy boat and serve with the casserole.

Hearty Black Bean Soup

Serve the soup with warm tortillas for dipping. Instant rice makes the soup especially quick to prepare.

LOW-CHOLESTEROL · LOW-FAT

Makes 4 servings.

Nutrient Value Per Serving: 438 calories, 24 g protein, 7 g fat, 72 g carbohydrate, 1,205 mg sodium, 14 mg cholesterol.

1	tablespoon olive oil	2	cans (16 ounces each) black beans, drained and rinsed
1	large onion, finely chopped (1 cup)	1½	cups one-third-less-salt chicken broth
1	clove garlic, finely chopped	1	cup frozen corn kernels, thawed
1	large carrot, peeled and coarsely chopped	1	cup water
1	teaspoon ground cumin	1	lemon
4	ounces Canadian-style bacon, coarsely chopped (½ cup)	½	cup uncooked instant converted rice

1. Heat the oil in a medium-size saucepan over medium heat. Add the onion, garlic, carrot and cumin, and sauté, stirring, for 3 minutes. Add the bacon, and sauté for 1 minute. Remove the saucepan from the heat.

2. Place half the black beans and ½ cup of the broth in the container of a food processor or electric blender. Whirl until the mixture is puréed. Add the bean purée to the saucepan along with the remaining cup of broth, the remaining black beans, the corn and water. Bring the bacon-bean mixture to boiling. Reduce the heat to medium-low and simmer for 5 minutes, or until the carrot is tender.

3. Cut 4 slices from the lemon, and reserve them for garnish. Juice the remaining lemon.

4. Stir the lemon juice and the rice into the saucepan, and boil the soup for 1 minute. Cover the saucepan, and remove it from the heat. Let the soup stand for 7 minutes, or until the rice is tender. Ladle the soup into 4 bowls. Garnish each serving with a reserved lemon slice.

Fusilli with Turkey Tomato Sauce

LOW-FAT

Makes 4 servings.

Nutrient Value Per Serving: 606 calories, 34 g protein, 17 g fat, 78 g carbohydrate, 1,069 mg sodium, 83 mg cholesterol.

1	pound ground turkey	1	teaspoon salt
2	tablespoons olive oil	½	teaspoon dried basil, crumbled
1	large onion, chopped (1 cup)	1	bay leaf
3	cloves garlic, finely chopped	¼	teaspoon freshly ground pepper
1	can (35 ounces) tomatoes, undrained and broken up	12	ounces fusilli
1	teaspoon dried oregano, crumbled		

SOUP OF THE EVENING

Hearty Black Bean Soup

Warm Flour Tortillas

Salsa with Crisp Vegetables

Blueberry Crunch
(recipe, page 193)

○ ❖ ○

"No restaurants. The means of consoling oneself: reading cookbooks."
—Baudelaire

GREAT PASTA-BILITIES

Fusilli with Turkey Tomato Sauce

Garlic Bread

Mixed Green Salad

Jam-Filled Pastries
(recipe, page 190)

○ ❖ ○

1. Cook the turkey in the oil in a large skillet over medium heat for about 5 minutes. Add the onion and the garlic, and cook for about 5 minutes, or until the turkey no longer is pink. Stir in the tomatoes with their liquid, the oregano, salt, basil, bay leaf and pepper. Simmer, uncovered, for 30 minutes, or until the sauce has reached the desired consistency. Discard the bay leaf.

2. Cook the fusilli following the package directions until the fusilli is al dente, tender but firm to the bite. Drain the fusilli, and place it in a serving bowl. Add the sauce, and toss to coat the fusilli.

Linguine with Bacon & Peas

LOW-CALORIE · LOW-CHOLESTEROL · LOW-FAT

Makes 4 servings.

Nutrient Value Per Serving: 349 calories, 18 g protein, 8 g fat, 50 g carbohydrate, 758 mg sodium, 18 mg cholesterol.

8 ounces linguine	1¼ cups one-third-less-salt chicken broth
1 tablespoon olive oil	1 cup frozen peas
4 ounces Canadian-style bacon, cut into 2 x ¼-inch strips	1 tablespoon red wine vinegar
1 tablespoon all-purpose flour	¼ cup grated Parmesan cheese

1. Cook the linguine in a large pot of lightly salted boiling water following the package directions until the linguine is al dente, tender but firm to the bite. Drain the linguine well in a colander.

2. Meanwhile, heat the oil in a large skillet over medium heat. Add the bacon and cook, stirring, for 1 minute. Sprinkle the flour into the skillet. Cook the bacon mixture, stirring constantly, for 1 minute. Add the broth, and stir to dissolve the flour. Add the peas, and bring the bacon-peas mixture to boiling over medium-high heat. Reduce the heat to medium-low and simmer for 10 minutes, or until the bacon-peas mixture is slightly thickened. Remove the skillet from the heat. Stir in the vinegar and the Parmesan cheese.

3. Return the linguine to the large pot. Add the sauce, and toss to coat the linguine. Serve the linguine at once.

LONG LIVE LINGUINE!

Linguine with Bacon & Peas
Cherry Tomato Salad
Apple Berry Whirl
(recipe, page 204)

○ ❖ ○

BACON, CANADIAN-STYLE

This flavorful bacon is made from boneless pork loin that is cured and smoked. Canadian bacon tastes more like ham. It is sold sliced or by the piece.

● Store bacon in its original wrapper in the refrigerator. Freezing bacon for a long period of time is not recommended because the salt in the bacon draws out the moisture and affects the flavor.

● Bacon slices tear easily when they are cold, so take bacon out of the refrigerator 10 minutes before cooking it. If you forget, place a rubber spatula under one end of a slice, and run the spatula slowly between the slices to separate them.

Spaghetti with Bolognese Sauce

This recipe makes about 9 cups of sauce — enough for three meals. The leftover sauce can be stored in the refrigerator, tightly covered, for up to 1 week. Adding ground turkey makes the sauce a little leaner than usual.

LOW-CHOLESTEROL · LOW-FAT

Makes 4 servings, plus leftover sauce.

Nutrient Value Per Serving: 552 calories, 26 g protein, 16 g fat, 74 g carbohydrate, 440 mg sodium, 54 mg cholesterol.

3	tablespoons olive oil	1	teaspoon dried basil, crumbled
1	pound lean ground beef	½	teaspoon dried thyme, crumbled
1	pound ground turkey	¼	teaspoon salt
1	large onion, chopped (1 cup)	¼	teaspoon freshly ground pepper
1	carrot, shredded	⅓	cup chopped parsley
2	large cloves garlic, finely chopped	12	ounces spaghetti
2	cans (28 ounces each) tomatoes in tomato purée		Grated Parmesan cheese (optional)
1	can (13¾ ounces) beef broth		

1. Heat 1 tablespoon of the oil in a large, nonstick pot over medium-high heat. Crumble in the beef, and brown it well. Remove the beef to a medium-size bowl. Add another tablespoon of oil to the pot, and heat it. Crumble in the turkey, and brown it. Remove the turkey to the bowl with the beef. Add the remaining tablespoon of oil to the pot. Add the onion, carrot and garlic, and sauté, stirring often, until the vegetables are tender.

2. Place the tomatoes with their purée in the container of a food processor or electric blender. Whirl until the tomatoes are puréed. Add the purée to the vegetables in the pot along with the broth, meat, basil, thyme, salt and pepper. Bring the sauce to boiling. Lower the heat and simmer the sauce, partially covered and stirring occasionally, for 60 minutes, or until the sauce is thickened. Stir in the parsley.

3. Cook the spaghetti following the package directions until the spaghetti is al dente, tender but firm to the bite. Drain the spaghetti, and place it in a serving bowl. Add 3 cups of the sauce, and toss to coat the spaghetti. Refrigerate the remaining 6 cups of sauce for other meals. If you wish, sprinkle the spaghetti with grated Parmesan cheese.

SPAGHETTI TIME

Spaghetti with Bolognese Sauce

Tossed Green Salad

Parsley Cheese Bread
(recipe, page 161)

Vanilla Pudding with Sliced Bananas

∘ ❖ ∘

THE SAUCE SOLUTION

Plain pasta is virtually fat-free, but the traditional cream sauces for pasta are anything but! To make a creamy, health-smart sauce, start with a base of lowfat cottage cheese or part-skim ricotta. Grate in a little Parmesan or Romano cheese to add flavor. Then experiment by adding various herbs, garlic, spices, and vegetables to taste.

o ◦❖◦ o

LAMB

Lamb is tender, lean meat with a delicate but distinctive flavor. The meat comes from sheep that are less than 1 year old, most often 6-month-old lambs. Mutton is meat from mature sheep.

The domestic use of sheep and sheep products goes back some 8,000 years. In the Middle East and southern Europe, the sheep was valued as an animal that matured quickly and could exist in almost any kind of climate or terrain.

● Lamb is available fresh or frozen. Fresh lamb is pink to light red in color with firm, fine-textured flesh. Some cuts of lamb have a thin, papery skin called fell, that surrounds the fat. If the fell has not been removed, pull it off steaks and chops before cooking them; leave the fell intact on roasts to help them hold their shape during cooking.

● Some cuts of lamb, such as rib or loin chops, have given lamb a reputation for being expensive, but there are many other cuts that are both economical and excellent to use in everyday meals. Look for cuts from the shoulder, such as a shoulder arm roast or shoulder steaks, for example.

Moroccan Pasta

The distinctive taste of lamb adds an exotic touch to this sauce. As a bonus, the recipe makes enough sauce for Baked Eggplant Sandwiches (recipe, page 46) or another pasta supper.

LOW-CHOLESTEROL ▪ LOW-FAT

Makes 4 servings, plus leftover sauce.

Nutrient Value Per Serving: 617 calories, 29 g protein, 11 g fat, 72 g carbohydrate, 388 mg sodium, 66 mg cholesterol.

1	tablespoon olive oil
1	large onion, chopped (1 cup)
12	ounces ground round
12	ounces ground lamb
1	large clove garlic, finely chopped
¾	teaspoon ground cumin
½	teaspoon salt
⅛	teaspoon ground cinnamon
⅛	teaspoon ground hot red pepper
1	can (28 ounces) crushed tomatoes
12	ounces spaghetti
⅓	cup pitted black olives, sliced
2	tablespoons raisins
2	tablespoons chopped fresh cilantro OR: parsley

1. Heat the oil in a large pot. Add the onion, and sauté over medium heat for 3 minutes. Raise the heat to high. Crumble the beef and the lamb into the pot, and add the garlic. Brown the meat, breaking up the large clumps with a wooden spoon. Mix in the cumin, salt, cinnamon and ground hot red pepper. Add the tomatoes. Bring the mixture to boiling. Lower the heat and simmer, covered, for 15 minutes.

2. While the tomato mixture is simmering, cook the spaghetti following the package directions until the spaghetti is al dente, tender but firm to the bite. Drain the spaghetti, reserving 1 cup of the cooking water.

3. Add the olives and the raisins to the tomato mixture and simmer, covered, for 15 minutes. Stir in the cilantro or parsley. If the sauce is too thick, stir in some of the reserved spaghetti cooking water.

4. Place the spaghetti in a serving bowl. Add 3 cups of the sauce, and toss to mix. Refrigerate the remaining 2½ cups of sauce to use in Baked Eggplant Sandwiches, or another pasta supper.

Creamy Pasta Primavera

To save time midweek, make the creamy sauce several days in advance and refrigerate it.

LOW-CHOLESTEROL · LOW-FAT
Makes 6 servings.
Nutrient Value Per Serving: 398 calories, 22 g protein, 8 g fat, 60 g carbohydrate, 443 mg sodium, 6 mg cholesterol.

12 ounces wagon wheel pasta	2 cups broccoli flowerets
1 container (16 ounces) lowfat cottage cheese	½ sweet red pepper, cut into thin strips
¼ cup grated Parmesan cheese	1 carrot, peeled, and cut into thin strips
¼ teaspoon dried mint, crumbled	¼ teaspoon dried basil, crumbled
2 tablespoons olive oil	¼ pound mushrooms, sliced
1 medium-size onion, chopped (½ cup)	1 cup canned chick peas, drained and rinsed
1 clove garlic, finely chopped	

CHECK OUT CHICK PEAS

Widely used in the Mediterranean countries, chick peas are nutritious, ivory-hued legumes. In Spain and Mexico, the beans are known as *garbanzos*; Italians call them *ceci*; people throughout the Middle East know them as *hommos* or *hummus*.

● Chick peas are the seeds of a bushy plant that grows in dry regions. Although three varieties of chick peas are grown, only one is widely used in cooking. Dried chick peas are available in 1-pound packages, or are sold in bulk by the pound. Chick peas also are cooked and canned in 16- or 20-ounce-size cans.

● Use chick peas in soups, stews and salads, and mashed as a dip for snacks and appetizers.

● One cup of cooked chick peas has 269 calories, 15 grams of protein and 45 grams of carbohydrates. And chick peas contain no cholesterol!

Creamy Pasta Primavera uses lowfat cottage cheese rather than heavy cream in its tasty sauce.

1. Cook the pasta following the package directions until the pasta is al dente, tender but firm to the bite.

2. Meanwhile, combine the cottage cheese, Parmesan cheese and mint in the container of a food processor or electric blender. Whirl until the cheese mixture is puréed.

3. Heat the oil in a large, nonstick skillet. Add the onion and the garlic, and cook for 3 minutes, or until the vegetables are softened. Add the broccoli, red pepper, carrot and basil, and cook for 3 minutes; if necessary, sprinkle the mixture with water to prevent it from sticking. Add the mushrooms, and cook for 2 minutes more. Stir in the chick peas, and cook until they are heated through.

4. Drain the pasta, and transfer it to a serving bowl. Fold in the cheese mixture. Add the vegetable mixture, and toss to coat all the ingredients.

Western Macaroni & Cheese

Wagon wheel pasta makes this dish both fun to look at and good to eat.

Bake at 450° for 20 minutes.
Makes 4 servings.
Nutrient Value Per Serving: 655 calories, 32 g protein, 29 g fat, 65 g carbohydrate, 950 mg sodium, 92 mg cholesterol.

8 ounces wagon wheel pasta	**⅔** cup corn kernels, fresh OR: thawed frozen
3 tablespoons unsalted butter	
3 tablespoons all-purpose flour	**½** cup chopped sweet red pepper
3 cups lowfat milk	
¼ teaspoon salt	**¼** cup chopped green onion
6 ounces shredded Monterey Jack cheese	**2** tablespoons chopped canned mild green chili peppers
4 ounces thinly sliced baked ham, cut into strips	**3** tablespoons fine dry bread crumbs

1. Cook the pasta in a large pot of boiling salted water following the package directions until the pasta is al dente, tender but firm to the bite. Drain the pasta, rinse it, and drain it again.

2. Preheat the oven to hot (450°).

3. Melt the butter in a medium-size saucepan over medium-low heat. Whisk in the flour until it is smooth and cook, whisking constantly, for about 3 minutes. Whisk in the milk and the salt. Increase the heat to medium and simmer, whisking constantly, until the milk mixture is lightly thickened, for about 5 minutes. Stir in the Monterey Jack cheese, whisking until it is melted. Transfer the cheese mixture to a large mixing bowl.

4. Stir the ham, corn, red pepper, green onion, chili peppers and pasta into the cheese mixture. Spoon the pasta-cheese mixture into an 11 x 7-inch baking pan, and sprinkle the bread crumbs over the top.

5. Bake in the preheated hot oven (450°) for 20 minutes, or until bubbly and lightly browned on top.

WAGONS, HO!

Western Macaroni & Cheese

Cucumber & Romaine Salad with Cilantro Dressing
(recipe, page 148)

Cantaloupe and Honeydew Wedges

◦ ❖ ◦

"*A wonderful bird is the pelican, His bill will hold more than his belican. He can take in his beak Food enough for a week, But I'm damned if I see how the helican.*"

—*Dixon Lanier Merrit*

Pasta Niçoise

Use the leftover hard-cooked egg whites to make a low-cholesterol egg salad.

Makes 4 servings.

Nutrient Value Per Serving: 538 calories, 34 g protein, 23 g fat, 47 g carbohydrate, 495 mg sodium, 141 mg cholesterol.

2	hard-cooked egg yolks
1	anchovy (optional)
1	small clove garlic, crushed or pressed
1	teaspoon Dijon-style mustard
2½	tablespoons lemon juice
½	teaspoon dried marjoram, crumbled
¼	teaspoon freshly ground pepper
⅓	cup olive oil
8	ounces large bow tie OR: rotelle OR: raddiatore pasta
4	ounces green beans, trimmed, and cut into 2-inch lengths
¼	cup cured ripe olives, halved and pitted
1	cup cherry tomatoes, quartered
2	cans (6½ ounces each) light tuna packed in water, drained and flaked
¼	cup chopped parsley

1. Mash together the egg yolks, anchovy if you wish, garlic and mustard with a fork in a large bowl. Add the lemon juice, marjoram and pepper, and mash the mixture until it is almost smooth. Gradually whisk in the oil until it is blended. Set aside the dressing.

2. Cook the pasta following the package directions until the pasta is al dente, tender but firm to the bite. Add the green beans to the pasta for the last 5 minutes of cooking time. Drain the pasta and beans well. Add the pasta and beans to the dressing in the bowl, and toss to coat the pasta and beans. Add the olives, cherry tomatoes, tuna and parsley, and toss gently. Serve the pasta warm.

Shells, Salmon & Broccoli with Dill Sauce

LOW-CHOLESTEROL · LOW-FAT

Makes 4 servings.

Nutrient Value Per Serving: 426 calories, 33 g protein, 11 g fat, 54 g carbohydrate, 660 mg sodium, 45 mg cholesterol.

1	tablespoon olive oil
1	tablespoon all-purpose flour
1	cup lowfat milk
1	tablespoon tomato paste (optional)
¼	teaspoon salt
⅛	teaspoon freshly ground pepper
½	cup chopped fresh dill
2	tablespoons lemon juice (1 lemon)
8	ounces shell pasta
1	small head broccoli (about 1 pound), divided into flowerets
1	can (16 ounces) red salmon, bones and skin removed

TUNA SALAD, FRENCH-STYLE

Pasta Niçoise

Mixed Green Salad

Breadsticks

Frozen Strawberry Banana Cream
(recipe, page 212)

BEACHCOMBER'S DELIGHT

Shells, Salmon & Broccoli with Dill Sauce

Soft Breadsticks

Chocolate Pudding with Strawberries

1. Heat the oil in a small saucepan over medium-low heat. Whisk in the flour until it is smooth, and cook for 2 minutes. Slowly stir in the milk and cook, stirring, until the mixture is smooth and lightly thickened, for about 2 minutes. Stir in the tomato paste if you wish, the salt, pepper, dill and lemon juice, and cook for 1 minute. Keep the sauce warm.

2. Meanwhile, cook the pasta in a large pot of boiling salted water following the package directions until the pasta is al dente, tender but firm to the bite. Add the broccoli to the pasta for the last 5 minutes of cooking time. Drain the pasta and broccoli.

3. Combine the sauce with the pasta and broccoli in a serving bowl. Gently fold in the salmon, and serve.

An oh-so-easy meal for a summer's night: Shells, Salmon & Broccoli with Dill Sauce.

Weekday Breakfasts

Monday breakfast leaves you in a whirl? Not to mention Tuesday, Wednesday, and so on? End the morning madness with these healthy, delicious meals, and get your family off to a great start every day.

Mexican Eggs in Tortilla Cups

The tortilla cups bake in the time it takes to scramble the eggs. A fun way to serve an old favorite.

LOW-CALORIE

Bake tortilla cups at 450° for 7 to 8 minutes.

Makes 4 servings.

Nutrient Value Per Serving: 315 calories, 15 g protein, 17 g fat, 28 g carbohydrate, 776 mg sodium, 182 mg cholesterol.

	Nonstick vegetable cooking spray	3	**eggs**
4	**flour OR: corn tortillas (6-inch)**	3	**egg whites**
1	**tablespoon butter**	¼	**teaspoon salt**
1	**tablespoon vegetable oil**	½	**cup shredded Cheddar cheese**
1	**can (12 ounces) Mexican corn, drained and 2 tablespoons liquid reserved**		**Catsup OR: salsa (optional)**

1. Preheat the oven to very hot (450°). Spray 4 individual custard cups, or the 4 corner cups of a muffin pan, with nonstick vegetable cooking spray. Place the tortillas in a stack. Make four equally spaced 2-inch-long cuts, spoke fashion, from the outside of the stack toward the center.

2. Heat together the butter and the oil in a medium-size, nonstick skillet. Brush both sides of each tortilla lightly with the butter mixture. Fit each tortilla into a custard cup. Place the cups on a baking sheet.

3. Bake the tortilla cups in the preheated very hot oven (450°) for 5 minutes. Remove the cups from the oven. Leave the oven on.

4. Meanwhile, beat the reserved corn liquid with the eggs, egg whites and salt in a medium-size bowl until the ingredients are blended. Add the corn.

5. Heat the remaining butter mixture in the skillet over medium heat. Add the egg mixture and cook, stirring, for 6 minutes, or until the egg mixture is set. Divide the egg mixture equally among the tortilla cups. Sprinkle the Cheddar cheese on top.

6. Bake the tortilla cups in the very hot oven (450°) for 2 to 3 minutes more, or until the Cheddar cheese is melted. Run a knife around the edge of each tortilla cup, and gently remove the cup. Serve the tortilla cups with catsup or salsa, if you wish.

BREAKFAST FIESTA

Mexican Eggs in Tortilla Cups

Cherry Tomato Halves

Fruit Juice Fizz
(recipe, page 59)

Coffee, Tea or Milk

◦ ✤ ◦

EGG SMARTS

● Store eggs away from strong-smelling foods — the porous eggshells may absorb the odors.

● Hard-cook eggs perfectly every time. Place the eggs in a saucepan, cover them with water, and bring the water to a simmer. Remove the saucepan from the heat, cover the saucepan, and let the eggs stand for 12 minutes.

● To make peeling hard-cooked eggs easier, use week-old eggs; their shells come off more readily. Plunge the eggs in cold water immediately after cooking, and peel them under cold running water.

● For a new twist on a breakfast favorite, bake eggs in hollowed-out baked potatoes or tomatoes.

● Poach eggs the easy way — in the microwave. Place ¼ cup of water, broth or tomato juice in an individual custard cup. Break an egg into the cup, and gently pierce the yolk so it doesn't burst or spurt. Microwave at full power for 45 to 60 seconds.

Fruit Juice Fizz

Makes 4 servings.
Nutrient Value Per Serving: 65 calories, 0 g protein, .03 g fat,
16 g carbohydrate, 1 mg sodium, 0 mg cholesterol.

	Ice cubes	**Fresh fruit, for garnish (optional)**
2	**cups fruit juice**	
2	**cups seltzer water**	

Place ice cubes in each of 4 water glasses. Add ½ cup of the fruit juice and
½ cup of the seltzer water to each glass, and stir to blend. Garnish the
fizzes with fresh fruit, if you wish.

Overnight French Toast

*The easiest French toast yet! Prepared the night before, the bread is baked in
the same pan in which it is soaked.*

Bake at 425° for 10 minutes.
Makes 4 servings.
Nutrient Value Per Serving: 354 calories, 11 g protein, 12 g fat,
54 g carbohydrate, 407 mg sodium, 180 mg cholesterol.

2	**tablespoons butter**	½	**teaspoon vanilla**
8	**slices whole wheat OR: white bread**	2	**teaspoons sugar**
3	**eggs**		**Pinch salt**
¾	**cup lowfat milk**		**Pineapple Maple Syrup (recipe follows)**

1. Spread the butter evenly on the bottom of a jelly-roll pan. Cut out the
centers of the bread slices with 2-inch cookie cutters. Arrange the bread
slices and cutouts in a single layer in the prepared pan.

2. Whisk together the eggs, milk, vanilla, sugar and salt in a bowl. Pour the
egg mixture over the bread, tilting the pan to spread the egg mixture in an
even layer. Cover the pan, and refrigerate the French toast overnight.

3. To cook the French toast, preheat the oven to hot (425°). Uncover the
jelly-roll pan.

4. Bake the French toast in the preheated hot oven (425°) for 10 minutes.
Remove the pan from the oven, and flip over the French toast. Serve
2 slices and 2 cutouts per serving, topped with the Pineapple Maple Syrup.

Pineapple Maple Syrup:
Combine 1 cup of drained pineapple tidbits with ⅓ cup of maple syrup in a
small bowl. If you wish, heat the mixture in a small saucepan.

OVERNIGHT SENSATION

Overnight French Toast
Fresh Strawberries
Milk

∘ ❖ ∘

**SNAPPY SOLUTIONS
AND SUBSTITUTIONS**

● Use packaged shredded potatoes
(sold in the dairy section of the
supermarket) to whip up extra-fast
hash browns or potato pancakes.
● For a taste treat, stir jam, jelly
or maple syrup rather than sugar
into hot cereal.
● Peanut butter isn't just for
lunch — kids will love it on toasted
frozen waffles or English muffins.

Quicky Sticky Buns

These buns are made the night before with packaged bread dough. Just pop them in the oven right from the refrigerator.

Bake at 350° for 35 to 40 minutes.
Makes 8 buns.

Nutrient Value Per Bun: 294 calories, 5 g protein, 11 g fat, 46 g carbohydrate, 346 mg sodium, 8 mg cholesterol.

Sticky Buns:

1 **pound frozen packaged bread dough**
2 **tablespoons unsalted butter**
¼ **cup firmly packed dark brown sugar**
3 **tablespoons dark corn syrup**
¾ **teaspoon ground cinnamon**

¾ **cup pecan halves**

Cinnamon Sugar:

¼ **cup granulated sugar**
½ **teaspoon ground cinnamon**
    Pinch ground nutmeg

GOOD MORNING SHAKE & BAKE

Peanut Butter & Banana Shake
(recipe, page 61)
Quicky Sticky Buns

> "*A simple enough pleasure, surely, to have breakfast alone with one's husband, but how seldom married people in the midst of life achieve it.*"
>
> —*Anne Morrow Lindbergh*

A breakfast bonanza of good taste: Quicky Sticky Buns with a Peanut Butter & Banana Shake (recipe, page 61).

**QUICK & EASY
BREAKFAST TIPS**

● Use an ice cream scoop to ladle just the right amount of batter for a pancake or waffle.

● Test a heated pan or griddle by sprinkling it with a few drops of water. When the water starts to bounce and dance around, the pan is ready for cooking.

● Try baking your bacon. Place bacon strips on a wire cake rack set in a jelly-roll pan, and bake them at 350° until they are crisp. Drain the bacon on paper toweling. To reheat bacon strips, wrap them in aluminum foil.

1. Prepare the Sticky Buns: Defrost the bread dough following the package directions.

2. Place the butter in a 9-inch square or round metal cake pan. Place the pan over low heat until the butter is melted. Remove the pan from the heat. Stir the brown sugar, 2 tablespoons of the corn syrup and the cinnamon into the butter in the pan until the ingredients are combined. Sprinkle the pecan halves in an even layer over the bottom of the pan.

3. Prepare the Cinnamon Sugar: Combine the granulated sugar, cinnamon and nutmeg in a small bowl.

4. Roll out the dough on a floured surface to a 12 x 9-inch rectangle; if the dough is too cold or resistant to roll, let it rest for 15 minutes. Drizzle the remaining tablespoon of corn syrup over the dough, and spread the syrup on the dough with the back of a spoon. Sprinkle the Cinnamon Sugar evenly over the dough.

5. Roll up the dough from a long side, jelly-roll style. Cut the roll crosswise into 8 equal pieces. Arrange the pieces, cut side down, in the prepared pan. Cover the pan with plastic wrap. Let the buns rise in a warm place, away from drafts, for 1 to 1¼ hours. Or refrigerate the buns overnight.

6. Preheat the oven to moderate (350°). Uncover the pan.

7. Bake the buns in the preheated moderate oven (350°) for 35 to 40 minutes. If the buns brown too quickly, tent them with aluminum foil during the last 10 minutes of baking. Invert the buns onto a serving plate; be careful of any dripping hot caramel. Serve the buns hot or warm.

Peanut Butter & Banana Shake

This shake provides a fast and healthy start to the day. If you wish, substitute your favorite fruits for the banana.

LOW-CALORIE ▪ LOW-CHOLESTEROL
Makes 2 servings.
Nutrient Value Per Serving: 280 calories, 11 g protein, 10 g fat, 42 g carbohydrate, 165 mg sodium, 5 mg cholesterol.

1	banana, peeled and sliced	2	tablespoons smooth peanut butter OR: 3 tablespoons apple butter
½	cup plain lowfat yogurt		
2	tablespoons honey	¾	cup skim milk

Combine the banana, yogurt, honey, peanut butter or apple butter and the milk in the container of an electric blender or food processor. Whirl until the mixture is smooth. Refrigerate the shake until serving time. To serve, pour the shake into 2 tall glasses.

Ricotta Cheese Blintzes

To save time in the morning, make the crêpes for the blintzes a day or two ahead of time. Filled blintzes freeze well, and are good to have on hand for easy Sunday suppers.

LOW-CALORIE

Makes 8 blintzes.

Nutrient Value Per Blintz: 232 calories, 10 g protein, 10 g fat, 25 g carbohydrate, 176 mg sodium, 112 mg cholesterol.

1 **container (15 ounces) part-skim ricotta cheese**	1 **tablespoon chopped walnuts (optional)**
1 **egg**	½ **cup blueberry pourable fruit jelly**
2 **tablespoons sugar**	
1 **teaspoon grated lemon zest (yellow part of rind only)**	½ **teaspoon vegetable oil**
8 **crêpes (recipe follows)**	1½ **teaspoons butter**

1. Beat together the ricotta cheese, egg, sugar and lemon zest in a medium-size bowl. Spoon about ¼ cup of the ricotta mixture into the center of one of the crêpes. Fold the crêpe as you would an envelope, and roll it up to close it. Place the blintz, seam side down, on a baking sheet. Repeat with the remaining filling and crêpes. (The blintzes can be prepared up to 1 day in advance, and refrigerated.)

2. If you wish, stir 1 tablespoon of chopped walnuts into the pourable fruit. Heat the fruit topping in a small saucepan, if you wish.

3. Heat together the oil and the butter in a medium-size, nonstick skillet over medium heat. Add the blintzes and cook for 5 minutes, or until the blintzes are golden, turning over the blintzes halfway through the cooking time. Serve the blintzes with the fruit topping.

Crêpes:

Combine 1 cup of all-purpose flour, 2 tablespoons of sugar, ¼ teaspoon of salt, 1 cup of lowfat or skim milk, 4 eggs and 2 tablespoons of melted butter in the container of an electric blender or food processor. Whirl until the mixture is smooth, scraping down the sides of the container as necessary. Spray a 10-inch skillet with nonstick vegetable cooking spray. Heat the skillet over medium heat. Ladle 2 tablespoons of the batter into the skillet, tilting the pan to coat the bottom evenly. Cook for 1 to 2 minutes, or until the bottom of the crêpe is lightly browned. Turn over the crêpe, and cook for about 1 minute more, or until the second side is lightly spotted. Repeat with the remaining batter to make a total of 14 crêpes, stacking them on a piece of wax paper. The crêpes can be prepared in advance, and refrigerated for up to 1 week or frozen for up to 2 months. Thaw frozen crêpes, in their wrapping, in the refrigerator.
Makes 14 crêpes.

BREAKFAST BLINTZES

Ricotta Cheese Blintzes

Grapes

Orange Slices

∘ ⋇ ∘

TASTY TREATS

● For new takes on breakfast, use packaged crêpes (sold in the produce or dairy section of the supermarket). For a morning quickie, fill the crêpes with ricotta cheese and jelly.

● For a spicy start to the day, stew mixed dried fruits with fresh pears or apples in apple cider flavored with a cinnamon stick, a few cloves and some honey. Serve with plain yogurt, or lowfat cottage cheese.

● Treat the kids to a non-traditional breakfast once in a while. Rice pudding, homemade English muffin pizzas, or peanut butter and jelly or grilled cheese sandwiches all are nourishing and fast.

A continental-style treat for breakfast, Ricotta Cheese Blintzes also are great for supper.

Banana Bran Muffins

The batter for these breakfast goodies can be stored in the refrigerator for up to 1 week.

LOW-FAT
Bake at 400° for 20 minutes.
Makes 2½ dozen muffins.
Nutrient Value Per Muffin: 137 calories, 4 g protein, 3 g fat,
27 g carbohydrate, 206 mg sodium, 28 mg cholesterol.

3	eggs	1	tablespoon ground cinnamon
2⅓	cups buttermilk	1½	teaspoons vanilla
1	cup unsweetened apple juice	3	cups bran cereal
½	cup sugar	½	cup raisins
½	cup honey	2½	cups all-purpose flour
¼	cup safflower OR: corn oil	1	tablespoon baking soda
1	medium-size ripe banana, peeled and sliced		

1. Preheat the oven to hot (400°).

2. Combine the eggs with 1 cup of the buttermilk, the apple juice, sugar, honey, safflower or corn oil, banana slices, cinnamon and vanilla in the container of a food processor or electric blender. Whirl until most of the banana is puréed.

3. Place the bran cereal in a large bowl. Add the egg mixture, the remaining 1⅓ cups of buttermilk and the raisins. Let the bran mixture stand for 15 minutes.

4. Sift together the flour and the baking soda into the bran mixture. Stir until the flour mixture is absorbed; do not overmix the batter. Use the batter at once, or store it in the refrigerator for up to 1 week.

5. Place paper liners in muffin-pan cups. Spoon the batter into the prepared muffin-pan cups, filling each cup about three-quarters full.

6. Bake the muffins in the preheated hot oven (400°) for 20 minutes, or until the tops spring back when lightly touched with your fingertip. Serve the muffins warm. Or cool the muffins and freeze them for up to 1 month.

A FESTIVAL OF FRUIT

Banana Bran Muffins
Ricotta Fruit Parfaits
(recipe, page 65)

∘ ❖ ∘

MUFFIN MAGIC

To make light, even-textured muffins every time:
• Combine the beaten liquid ingredients with the dry ingredients with a few quick stirring strokes just to moisten the dry ingredients.
• The batter should be lumpy; if it pours smoothly from the spoon, you have overbeaten it. Overbeating causes coarse texture and tunneling throughout the muffins.
• Fill greased muffin-pan cups only two-thirds to three-quarters full.

Ricotta Fruit Parfaits

Made ahead easily, these wholesome parfaits fit into the active family's life style. If you wish, double the ricotta mixture, and refrigerate half to use another morning. Top with fruit or crunchy cereal before serving.

LOW-CHOLESTEROL · LOW-FAT
Makes 4 servings.
Nutrient Value Per Serving: 390 calories, 17 g protein, 12 g fat, 57 g carbohydrate, 169 mg sodium, 38 mg cholesterol.

1 bag (12 ounces) frozen dry-pack cherries **OR:** 1½ cups drained canned cherries	**1** container (15 ounces) part-skim ricotta cheese
⅓ cup apricot **OR:** peach jam	**2** tablespoons dark brown sugar
½ cantaloupe, peeled, seeded and cubed (2 cups)	**¼** cup granola-type cereal

1. If using frozen cherries, rinse them in a colander under hot running water, and dry them on paper toweling.

2. Melt 3 tablespoons of the apricot or peach jam in a small saucepan. Toss in the cherries and the cantaloupe. Set aside the fruit mixture.

3. Combine the ricotta cheese with the remaining jam and the brown sugar in the container of an electric blender or food processor. Whirl until the ricotta mixture is smooth.

4. Pour the following, in layers, into each of 4 parfait glasses: ¼ cup of the ricotta mixture, ½ cup of the fruit mixture, ¼ cup of the ricotta mixture, and ¼ cup of the fruit mixture. (The parfaits can be prepared the night before, covered, and refrigerated.) To serve, sprinkle the granola over the tops of the parfaits.

A creamy breakfast treat that can be made ahead, Ricotta Fruit Parfaits are sure to become a family favorite.

Weekday Lunches

Try a change of taste for midday meals with the following luscious lunchables.

Picadillo Pockets

LOW-CHOLESTEROL · LOW-FAT
Bake at 375° for 15 to 18 minutes.
Makes 4 pockets.
Nutrient Value Per Pocket: 418 calories, 21 g protein, 12 g fat,
57 g carbohydrate, 1,039 mg sodium, 41 mg cholesterol.

	Nonstick vegetable cooking spray	1	can (8 ounces) tomato sauce
1	tablespoon vegetable OR: olive oil	2	tablespoons raisins (optional)
1	medium-size onion, chopped (½ cup)	¼	cup sliced green OR: black olives (optional)
1	clove garlic, chopped	2	tablespoons blanched, slivered almonds
½	pound ground turkey	1	pound frozen bread dough, thawed according to package directions
2	teaspoons chili powder		
¼	teaspoon dried oregano, crumbled		All-purpose flour

1. Spray a baking sheet with nonstick vegetable cooking spray.

2. Heat the vegetable or olive oil in a skillet over medium-high heat. Add the onion and the garlic, and cook for 4 minutes. Add the turkey, chili powder and oregano, and cook for 6 minutes, breaking up the turkey with a wooden spoon.

3. Add the tomato sauce, raisins if you wish, green or black olives if you wish, and the almonds, and cook for 4 minutes, or until the turkey-tomato mixture is thickened. Cool the turkey-tomato mixture.

4. Meanwhile, divide the dough into 4 equal pieces. Working on a floured surface, pat or roll one piece of dough into a 7 x 5-inch oval. Spoon about ½ cup of the turkey-tomato mixture lengthwise down the center of the oval, leaving a 1-inch border at each end. Fold the oval in half lengthwise over the filling, gently pressing out the air with your fingertips. Press the dough edges together to seal the pocket. Place the pocket on the prepared baking sheet. Repeat with the remaining dough and turkey-tomato mixture. Sprinkle the top of each pocket lightly with flour. Let the pockets rise in a warm place, away from drafts, for 20 minutes.

5. Preheat the oven to moderate (375°).

6. Bake the pockets in the preheated moderate oven (375°) for 15 to 18 minutes, or until the pockets are golden brown. Cool the pockets completely on a wire rack, wrap them in aluminum foil, and refrigerate them. To serve the pockets, bring them to room temperature, or reheat them in the toaster oven or microwave oven. If you wish, serve the pockets sliced in half crosswise.

POCKET LUNCH

Picadillo Pockets
Cheese Cubes
Apple

○ ❖ ○

BROWN BAG BASICS

● Use food storage bags that have write-on labels, or use masking tape strips as labels. On each label, write the person's name and any directions for assembling the lunch.

● In the morning, make sandwiches with frozen bread slices; the bread will keep perishable fillings cold, and will defrost by lunchtime.

● Single-serving cartons of frozen juice, milk or applesauce make great cold packs.

Pasta Salad with Turkey Ham Cubes

LOW-CALORIE · LOW-CHOLESTEROL · LOW-FAT

Makes 4 servings.

Nutrient Value Per Serving: 244 calories, 15 g protein, 8 g fat,
30 g carbohydrate, 719 mg sodium, 2 mg cholesterol.

8 **ounces alphabet OR: other fun-shaped pasta**	½ **cup bottled low-calorie Italian OR: vinaigrette dressing**
2 **cups broccoli flowerets, cut small**	¼ **teaspoon salt**
1 **cup shredded carrots**	1 **tablespoon lemon juice**
½ **cup frozen corn kernels (optional)**	1½ **cups (about 10 ounces) cubed turkey ham OR: boiled ham**
½ **cup part-skim ricotta cheese**	

1. Cook the pasta in a large pot of boiling salted water following the package directions until the pasta is al dente, tender but firm to the bite. Stir in the broccoli for the last 4 minutes of cooking time. When the broccoli is crisply tender, stir in the carrot and, if you wish, ½ cup of frozen corn kernels, and cook until the vegetables are warmed through. Drain the pasta mixture, and rinse it under cold running water.

2. Combine the ricotta cheese, Italian or vinaigrette dressing, salt and lemon juice in the container of a food processor or electric blender. Whirl until the ricotta mixture is blended and smooth. Mix the ricotta mixture with the pasta mixture in a medium-size bowl. Toss in the ham cubes to mix them. Cover the bowl, and refrigerate the salad for 1 to 12 hours. If the salad is too dry, add more dressing.

3. Pack the salad in a chilled thermos just before brown-bagging.

Date Nut Bread Sandwiches with Ricotta & Jam

LOW-CHOLESTEROL · LOW-FAT

Makes 4 sandwiches.

Nutrient Value Per Sandwich: 380 calories, 10 g protein, 10 g fat,
65 g carbohydrate, 401 mg sodium, 26 mg cholesterol.

½ **cup part-skim ricotta cheese**

8 **slices date nut bread, homemade or purchased**

2 **tablespoons jam OR: jelly**

1. Line a sieve with a coffee filter. Drain the ricotta cheese in the sieve for 8 hours, or overnight.

2. Spread 4 of the bread slices with the drained ricotta cheese. Spread the remaining 4 bread slices with the jam or jelly. Place a jam-coated slice on each ricotta-coated slice, coated sides facing. Wrap the sandwiches in plastic wrap. (The sandwiches can be prepared up to 12 hours in advance, and refrigerated.)

Ham Salad Roll-Ups

LOW-CALORIE • LOW-CHOLESTEROL • LOW-FAT

Makes 3 servings.

Nutrient Value Per Serving: 338 calories, 20 g protein, 8 g fat, 40 g carbohydrate, 1,226 mg sodium, 6 mg cholesterol.

- **1 green onion, cut into 1-inch pieces**
- **½ pound turkey ham OR: boiled ham, cut into 1-inch cubes**
- **3 tablespoons reduced-calorie mayonnaise**
- **1 tablespoon prepared honey mustard***
- **1 teaspoon red wine vinegar**
- **4 drops liquid red pepper seasoning**
- **¼ teaspoon ground allspice**
- **3 medium-size pita breads**

1. Place the green onion and the ham in the container of a food processor or electric blender. Whirl until the ham mixture is medium-chopped. Add the mayonnaise, mustard, vinegar, liquid red pepper seasoning and allspice. Pulse just until the ingredients are combined.

2. Split the pita breads in half. Spread ¼ cup of the ham-mayonnaise mixture on each pita half, and roll the pita half into a log. Secure the roll-ups with wooden picks, or cut the roll-ups into 1-inch pieces and secure the pieces with wooden picks. Remove the picks before eating.

***Note:** *You can make your own honey mustard by blending together equal parts of honey and prepared mustard.*

Pizza Muffin Sandwiches

LOW-CALORIE • LOW-CHOLESTEROL • LOW-FAT

Makes 2 sandwiches.

Nutrient Value Per Sandwich: 189 calories, 8 g protein, 3 g fat, 32 g carbohydrate, 604 mg sodium, 1 mg cholesterol.

- **2 English muffins, split and lightly toasted**
- **4 tablespoons bottled tomato pasta sauce**
- **2 tablespoons grated carrot**
- **1 teaspoon grated Parmesan cheese**
- **Chopped parsley (optional)**
- **2 slices turkey ham, cut into quarters**

1. Spread each muffin half with 1 tablespoon of the pasta sauce. Sprinkle the carrot, Parmesan cheese and, if you wish, chopped parsley, divided evenly, on 2 of the muffin halves. Top with the ham quarters, divided evenly, and the remaining 2 muffin halves.

2. Wrap the muffin sandwiches in aluminum foil or plastic wrap, and refrigerate them overnight. To serve the sandwiches, bring them to room temperature, or unwrap them and reheat them in the toaster oven or microwave oven.

MUNCHABLE LUNCHABLE

Ham Salad Roll-Ups
Mini Skewers with Pickles and Vegetables
Cantaloupe

"When ordering lunch the big executives are just as indecisive as the rest of us."

— William Feather

FUN FARE

Pizza Muffin Sandwiches
String Cheese
Banana Raisin Squares
(recipe, page 69)

Banana Raisin Squares

LOW-CALORIE

Bake at 350° for 20 minutes.

Makes 16 squares.

Nutrient Value Per Square: 147 calories, 3 g protein, 6 g fat, 22 g carbohydrate, 62 mg sodium, 27 mg cholesterol.

Nonstick vegetable cooking spray

Crust:

1	cup whole wheat flour
3	tablespoons firmly packed brown sugar
¼	teaspoon salt
2	tablespoons margarine, chilled
¼	cup vegetable oil
1	cup old-fashioned oats

Filling:

⅔	cup golden raisins
1	large banana (8 ounces), quartered
¼	cup firmly packed brown sugar
½	teaspoon ground ginger
1	teaspoon grated orange zest (orange part of rind only)
2	eggs

1. Preheat the oven to moderate (350°). Spray a 9-inch square baking pan evenly with nonstick vegetable cooking spray.

2. Prepare the Crust: Combine the flour, brown sugar, salt, margarine and oil in the container of a food processor or electric blender. Whirl until the mixture is the texture of coarse cornmeal. Add the oats. Pulse just until the oats are combined. Remove and reserve 1 cup of the crust mixture.

3. Scrape the remaining crust mixture into the prepared pan. Spread the crust mixture so it is level, pressing it down evenly in the pan.

4. Prepare the Filling: Combine the raisins, banana, brown sugar, ginger and orange zest in the unwashed container of the food processor. Whirl for 1 minute, or until the mixture is smooth. Add the eggs, and whirl until they are blended. Pour the filling into the pan. Sprinkle the reserved crust mixture, crumbled, over the filling in the pan.

5. Bake the cake in the preheated moderate oven (350°) for 20 minutes, or until a knife inserted in the center comes out clean. Cool the cake in the pan on a wire rack. Cut the cake into 16 squares. Wrap the squares individually in plastic wrap for easy packing. The wrapped squares can be stored in the refrigerator for up to 5 days.

CHAPTER 2

Holiday Meals & Menus and Special Gatherings

From spectacular feasts to intimate dinners, this chapter is full of delightful menus to suit every "special occasion" in your life. Whether you're a novice cook, gourmet chef or, like most of us, somewhere in between, you'll enjoy creating these marvelous meals when the time permits and the occasion inspires.

When you want to entertain friends and family, we offer menus to help make the event deliciously fun. Chase away the winter blues with "A Taste of the Tropics," a sampling of sunny recipes from Hawaii and Jamaica. Take a ride on the "Orient Express" and see how easy stir-fry can be. Or plan a weekend get-away, and treat everyone to the delicacies of the "Brunch Basket."

Holidays provide a natural inspiration to culinary greatness. We offer a Thanksgiving feast overflowing with nature's bounty, a selection of Christmas cookies to please young and old, and a lavish — and unique — spread for Christmas Eve. There's even a "new fashioned" clam bake for the Fourth of July.

Entertaining is an art unto itself. This chapter will help you to create your own mealtime masterpieces time and again.

From lower left, clockwise: Maple-Glazed Carrots (recipe, page 111), Peanut Pumpkin Soup (recipe, page 107), Roast Turkey with Chestnut Bread Stuffing (recipe, page 106), Candied Sweet Potatoes with Pineapple (recipe, page 110) and Cranberry Orange Sauce (recipe, page 111).

Saturday Night with Friends

The antidote to a wild work week: settling down in your home for a relaxing evening of feasting and friendship.

Roast Pork with Onion Thyme Gravy

Ask the butcher to cut through the chine or backbone for easy carving.

LOW-CALORIE · LOW-CHOLESTEROL
Roast at 325° for about 1½ hours.
Makes about 12 servings.
Nutrient Value Per Serving: 293 calories, 20 g protein, 22 g fat, 2 g carbohydrate, 342 mg sodium, 67 mg cholesterol.

¾ teaspoon dried thyme, crumbled	1 large onion, finely chopped (1 cup)
1 teaspoon salt	1½ cups chicken broth
¼ teaspoon freshly ground pepper	1 tablespoon cornstarch
1 large clove garlic, crushed	Additional salt and freshly ground pepper, to taste
1 center cut pork rib roast (about 4 pounds), cut through backbone	

MENU

Layered Vegetable Pâté
(recipe, page 154)

**Roast Pork with
Onion Thyme Gravy**
(recipe, at left)

**Steamed Carrots, Brussels Sprouts
& New Potatoes**

Honey Pear Spice Cake
(recipe, page 189)

◦ ❖ ◦

4 STEPS TO A PERFECT ROAST:

1. Season the roast following the recipe, sprinkling or rubbing the herbs onto all the meat surfaces. Place the roast on a rack in a roasting pan, insert a regular meat thermometer, if you're using one, and set the pan in a preheated oven. (Or use an instant-read thermometer to check the temperature.) Use the charts on pages 76 to 79 to determine the total cooking time. (The photos show the preparation of a pork roast, but the basic principles are the same for all roasts.)

A feast for your friends and family — Roast Pork with Onion Thyme Gravy surrounded by steamed carrots, Brussels sprouts and new potatoes.

1. Preheat the oven to slow (325°).

2. Combine ½ teaspoon of the thyme with the 1 teaspoon of salt, the ¼ teaspoon of pepper and the garlic in a small bowl. Rub the thyme mixture over the outside of the pork roast. If you wish, insert a regular meat thermometer in the thickest part of the roast without touching the bone. Place the roast in a roasting pan, fat side up and elevated on the rib bones.

3. Roast the pork in the preheated slow oven (325°) for about 1½ hours; the meat thermometer should register 160° for medium or 170° for well done. About 45 minutes before the roast is done, stir the onion into the roasting pan. Check the onion once or twice; if it is browning too fast, add a little water to the pan.

4. Remove the pan from the oven. Place the pork roast on a cutting board or serving platter, and cover the roast loosely with aluminum foil. Carefully pour the pan drippings into a 2-cup measure. Let the drippings stand for a few minutes to let the fat rise to the top. If necessary, spoon off all but 3 tablespoons of the fat. Stir 1 cup of the broth into the roasting pan, and place the pan over medium heat. Using a wooden spoon, scrape the browned bits from the bottom of the pan. Pour the pan drippings into the pan, and add the remaining ¼ teaspoon of thyme. Whisk the cornstarch into the remaining ½ cup of broth in a small bowl until the mixture is smooth. Pour the cornstarch mixture into the pan. Cook the gravy over medium heat, stirring constantly, for 2 to 3 minutes, or until the gravy thickens and boils. Season the gravy with the additional salt and pepper.

5. To carve the roast, cut away and discard the backbone. Cut along each side of the rib bones, skipping every other cut along the left sides; alternate slices will contain a bone. Serve the pork roast with the gravy.

2. About 45 minutes before the roast is done, add any onions or other vegetables to the roasting pan, distributing them evenly. Continue roasting to the desired doneness.

3. Remove the roast from the pan. To make gravy, pour the pan drippings into a measuring cup, and spoon off the fat. Place seasoned liquid, such as broth or wine, and the degreased drippings into the pan. Bring the liquid to a boil, and thicken it following the recipe.

4. To carve Roast Pork, cut away the backbone, and slice the meat along each side of the rib bones, skipping every other cut along the left sides; alternate slices will contain a bone.

Sunday Suppers

Two taste-tempting dinners to share with friends, or for special family meals.

Roast Pork Tenderloins with Peppers & Onions

LOW-CALORIE · LOW-CHOLESTEROL

Bake vegetables at 425° for 15 minutes; roast pork with vegetables at 425° for 20 to 25 minutes.
Makes 8 servings.

Nutrient Value Per Serving: 206 calories, 24 g protein, 9 g fat, 9 g carbohydrate, 156 mg sodium, 67 mg cholesterol.

2	pork tenderloins (13 ounces to 1 pound each), trimmed	¼	teaspoon salt
4	medium-size onions, halved	¼	teaspoon freshly ground pepper
5	large cloves garlic, crushed	1	can (14½ ounces) reduced-sodium chicken broth
3	tablespoons olive oil		
½	teaspoon dried thyme, crumbled	2	teaspoons Worcestershire sauce
2	large sweet red peppers, cored, seeded, and cut lengthwise into 6 pieces	1	teaspoon coarse-grained mustard
2	large sweet green peppers, cored, seeded, and cut lengthwise into 6 pieces	1	tablespoon cornstarch
			Additional salt, freshly ground pepper, and coarse-grained mustard (optional)

1. Combine the pork, onion, garlic, oil and thyme in a large bowl, and toss to mix the ingredients. Add the red and green peppers, and toss to mix them. Cover the bowl, and refrigerate the pork mixture for 2 to 3 hours, stirring occasionally. Remove the bowl from the refrigerator, and let the pork mixture stand at room temperature for 30 minutes.

2. Preheat the oven to hot (425°).

3. Sprinkle the pork with the ¼ teaspoon of salt and the ¼ teaspoon of pepper. Transfer only the vegetables and garlic to 1 large roasting pan, or two 13 x 9 x 2-inch roasting pans, dividing the vegetables and garlic evenly.

4. Bake the vegetables and garlic in the preheated hot oven (425°) for 15 minutes. Push the vegetables and garlic to one side of the pan. Add the pork; if using 2 pans, place 1 tenderloin in each pan. Roast the pork with the vegetables for 20 to 25 minutes, or just until the pork juices run clear and the pork is cooked through; do not overcook the pork.

5. Transfer the pork and vegetables to a serving platter, and keep them warm; discard the garlic. Measure out ¼ cup of the broth, and reserve it. If there are any browned bits in the roasting pan, place the pan over high heat. Add some of the remaining broth, and scrape the browned bits with a spoon from the bottom of the pan. Place the broth mixture in a saucepan. Add the remaining broth, the Worcestershire sauce and the 1 teaspoon of mustard. Boil the mustard mixture for 2 minutes.

MENU

Roast Pork Tenderloins with Peppers & Onions
(recipe, at left)

Confetti Corn Salad
(see Tip, below)

Green Salad with Assorted Cheeses

Walnut Pear Torte
(recipe, page 197)

∘ ❖ ∘

CONFETTI CORN SALAD

In a large bowl, combine 4 cups of fresh, cooked corn kernels, 2 cups of cooked rice, ½ cup of sliced green onion, 1 large Red Delicious apple, cored and cut into ¼-inch dice (about 1¼ cups), and 1 tablespoon of chopped fresh dill. Add ¼ cup of apple juice, 2 tablespoons of apple cider vinegar, 1 tablespoon of olive oil, ¾ teaspoon of salt, and ½ teaspoon of freshly ground pepper. Toss to combine the ingredients thoroughly. Cover the bowl, and refrigerate the salad, tossing it occasionally, for about 2 hours, or until the salad is chilled. Serve the salad chilled.
Makes 8 servings.

6. Whisk the cornstarch into the reserved ¼ cup of broth in a small bowl until the mixture is smooth. Slowly whisk the cornstarch mixture into the mustard mixture in the saucepan. Boil the gravy, whisking constantly, for 1 minute, or until the gravy is thickened. Strain the gravy through a sieve into a bowl; you should have about 3 cups of gravy. If you wish, season the gravy with additional salt, ground pepper and coarse-grained mustard.

7. To serve, slice the pork diagonally into thin medallions. Spoon the gravy over the pork, and serve the pork with the vegetables.

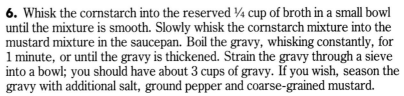

Beef & Rice Strata

LOW-CALORIE · LOW-CHOLESTEROL
Bake at 350° for 50 minutes.
Makes 12 servings.
Nutrient Value Per Serving: 338 calories, 20 g protein, 14 g fat, 33 g carbohydrate, 676 mg sodium, 54 mg cholesterol.

1½	cups long-grain white rice	1	egg
	Nonstick vegetable cooking spray	1	container (16 ounces) lowfat cottage cheese
1	pound ground beef	1	package (8 ounces) part-skim mozzarella cheese, shredded
1	medium-size onion, chopped (½ cup)		
¼	cup chopped sweet green pepper	¼	cup grated Parmesan cheese
1	jar (32 ounces) prepared spaghetti sauce		

1. Cook the rice following the package directions, adding salt if you wish.

2. Preheat the oven to moderate (350°). Coat a 13 x 9 x 2-inch baking dish with nonstick vegetable cooking spray.

3. Brown the beef in a large skillet over medium-high heat, breaking up the large clumps with a wooden spoon. Carefully pour off the excess fat from the skillet. Add the onion and the green pepper to the skillet, and cook, stirring, for 2 minutes. Add the spaghetti sauce.

4. Beat the egg slightly in a medium-size bowl. Stir in the cottage cheese and the mozzarella cheese.

5. Spread half the meat sauce over the bottom of the prepared dish. Spoon half the rice evenly over the sauce, and top with half the cheese mixture. Repeat. Sprinkle the top with the Parmesan cheese.

6. Bake the strata in the preheated moderate oven (350°) for 50 minutes, or until the strata is hot and bubbly. Let the strata stand for 10 minutes before serving it.

MENU

Beef & Rice Strata
(recipe, at right)
Sesame Breadsticks
Tossed Green Salad
Country Apple Bars
(recipe, page 196)

○ ❈ ○

"All human history attests That happiness for man —the hungry sinner!— Since Eve ate apples, much depends on dinner."

—George Gordon, Lord Byron

Beef Roasting Time Chart

Cut & Weight	RARE 140°	MEDIUM 160°	WELL DONE 170°	OVEN TEMP
Rib, Bone in				
4 to 6 pounds	1¾ to 2½ hours	2¼ to 3½ hours	2¾ to 4 hours	325°
6 to 8 pounds	2¼ to 3 hours	2¾ to 3¾ hours	3¼ to 4¼ hours	325°
Rib Eye, Bone in				
4 to 6 pounds	1¼ to 1¾ hours	1½ to 2 hours	1¾ to 2¼ hours	350°
Sirloin Tip, Boneless				
3½ to 4 pounds	2¼ hours	2½ hours	2¾ hours	325°
6 to 8 pounds	3 to 4 hours	3 to 4¼ hours	3¼ to 4½ hours	325°
Tenderloin,				
Whole 4 to 6 pounds		45 to 60 minutes		425°
Half 2 to 3 pounds		40 to 50 minutes		425°

ROASTED TO PERFECTION

Roasting is a simple, time-honored method of slow-cooking meat with dry heat. Once the meat is in the oven, it requires little attention. The result? Tender cuts that are crusty on the outside, succulent on the inside, with tasty gravy.

● Remove the roast from the oven when it's a few degrees below the desired doneness — the meat will continue to cook a little while standing — you will never overcook a roast again!

○ ❖ ○

HERBS TO USE WITH BEEF

● Basil and oregano
● Thyme and marjoram
● Bay leaf and parsley
● Chili powder and cumin

Pork Roasting Time Chart

CARVING COMMENTS

- Let a cooked roast stand for about 10 minutes before carving it. This lets the hot juices settle into the meat, and makes carving easier.
- Carve only enough slices from the roast to serve everyone once; carve seconds upon request.

∘ ❖ ∘

HERBS TO USE WITH PORK

- Garlic and caraway seeds — or paprika
- Ground hot red pepper and ginger
- Sage and thyme

Cut & Weight	RARE 140°	MEDIUM 160°	WELL DONE 170°	OVEN TEMP
Center Loin, Bone in 3 to 5 pounds		1¼ to 2 hours	1½ to 2½ hours	325°
Center Loin, Boneless 2 to 4 pounds		¾ to 1½ hours	1¼ to 2 hours	325°
Whole Leg, Bone in 12 to 16 pounds			4¾ to 6 hours	325°
Half Leg, Boneless 3½ pounds			2¼ to 2½ hours	325°
Tenderloin ½ to 1 pound		20 to 25 minutes	25 to 30 minutes	425°

Lamb Roasting Time Chart

Cut & Weight	RARE 140°	MEDIUM 160°	WELL DONE 170°	OVEN TEMP
Whole Leg, Bone in				
5 to 7 pounds	1¾ to 2¾ hours	2 to 3¼ hours	2½ to 4 hours	325°
7 to 9 pounds	2¼ to 3 hours	3 to 3¾ hours	3½ to 4½ hours	325°
Half Leg, Bone in Shank				
3 to 4 pounds	1½ to 1¾ hours	1½ to 2 hours	1¾ to 2¼ hours	325°
Sirloin				
3 to 4 pounds	1¼ to 1¾ hours	1¾ to 2½ hours	2¼ to 3 hours	325°
Leg, Boneless				
3 to 5 pounds	1¼ to 2¼ hours	1½ to 2½ hours	1¾ to 3 hours	325°
5 to 7 pounds	2 to 3 hours	2½ to 3½ hours	3¼ to 4¼ hours	325°
Rib (rack)				
1½ to 2 pounds	¾ hour	1 hour	1¼ hours	375°
2 to 3 pounds	1 hour	1¼ hours	1½ hours	375°

THE HEAT OF THE MEAT

There are two kinds of meat thermometers, and either is fine for gauging the internal heat of most roasts. A regular meat thermometer is inserted in the meat before roasting, and stays in during the entire cooking time. An instant-read meat thermometer is inserted in the meat for 10 seconds after cooking just to register the degrees, then the thermometer is removed.

o ❖ o

HERBS TO USE WITH LAMB

- Rosemary and thyme
- Dill and lemon
- Curry powder and turmeric
- Mustard and chives

Veal Roasting Time Chart

ROASTING PAN POINTERS

- Always use an open roasting pan.
- Place the roast on a rack in the pan to raise the meat above the pan drippings and allow the heat to circulate. If the roast has rib bones, a rack is unnecessary.
- Place the roast on the rack fat side up so the meat will baste itself as it cooks.

o ❖ o

HERBS TO USE WITH VEAL

- Rosemary and tarragon — or sage
- Marjoram and parsley — or thyme

Cut & Weight	RARE 140°	MEDIUM 160°	WELL DONE 170°	OVEN TEMP
Rump or Round, Boneless 2 to 3 pounds		¾ to 1 hour	55 to 75 minutes	325°
Loin, Bone in 3 to 4 pounds		1¾ to 2¼ hours	2 to 2½ hours	325°
Shoulder, Boneless 2½ to 3 pounds		1¼ to 1¾ hours	1½ to 2 hours	325°

*T*he Brunch Basket

All things baked and beautiful!

Carrot Cornbread Rolls

LOW-CHOLESTEROL · LOW-FAT
Bake rolls at 375° for 20 minutes; or bake loaf at 375° for 30 minutes.
Makes 24 rolls, or 1 large loaf (24 slices).
Nutrient Value Per Roll: 138 calories, 3 g protein, 2 g fat,
26 g carbohydrate, 298 mg sodium, 14 mg cholesterol.

⅔ **cup milk**	1 **egg**
3 **tablespoons butter,**	2 **packages active dry yeast**
cut into pieces	¼ **cup warm water**
1½ **cups cornmeal**	½ **teaspoon sugar**
1 **tablespoon salt**	3½ **to 4 cups all-purpose flour**
⅓ **cup molasses**	
1 **cup finely shredded carrot**	
(3 medium-size carrots)	

1. Combine the milk with the butter in a saucepan. Heat the milk mixture over low heat just until bubbles form around the edge of the pan. Combine the cornmeal with the salt in a large bowl. Stir in the milk mixture until it is blended. Stir in the molasses, carrot and egg until they are blended.

2. Sprinkle the yeast over the water and the sugar in a small cup, and stir to dissolve the yeast. Set aside the yeast mixture for 5 minutes, or until the mixture is foamy. Stir the yeast mixture into the cornmeal mixture.

3. Stir 3 cups of the flour into the cornmeal-yeast mixture to form a stiff dough. Turn out the dough onto a floured surface. Knead the dough for 8 to 10 minutes, or until the dough is smooth and elastic, kneading in as much of the remaining flour as needed to prevent the dough from sticking. Place the dough in a greased bowl, and turn the greased side up. Cover the bowl, and let the dough rise in a warm place, away from drafts, until the dough is doubled in size, for about 1 hour.

4. Punch down the dough. To make rolls, divide the dough into 24 equal pieces. Knead each piece into a smooth ball. Place the dough balls in a greased 13 x 9 x 2-inch baking pan, with the sides of the balls touching. Cover the balls, and let them rise in a warm place, away from drafts, until they are doubled in size, for about 45 minutes. To make a loaf, sprinkle a baking sheet with cornmeal. Shape the dough into an 8-inch round loaf, and place the loaf on the prepared baking sheet. Cover the loaf, and let it rise in a warm place, away from drafts, until it is doubled in size, for about 1 hour.

5. Preheat the oven to moderate (375°). Using a sharp small knife, cut a shallow X in the top of each roll or the loaf.

6. Bake the rolls in the preheated moderate oven (375°) for 20 minutes, or until the rolls are well browned. Or bake the loaf in the preheated moderate oven (375°) for 30 minutes, or until the loaf sounds hollow when tapped with your fingertips. Remove the rolls or loaf from the pan to a wire rack to cool.

MENU

Carrot Cornbread Rolls
(recipe, at left)

Cranberry Oatmeal Muffins
(recipe, page 83)

Multi-Grain Buttermilk Rolls
(recipe, page 82)

Assorted Jams & Jellies

Cream Cheese

Butter or Margarine

Assorted Fruit Juices

Coffee, Tea & Hot Chocolate

○ ✢ ○

" *L*ife, within doors, has few pleasanter prospects than a neatly arranged and well-provisioned breakfast-table. "

—*Nathaniel Hawthorne*

From left: Carrot Cornbread Rolls, Cranberry Oatmeal Muffins (recipe, page 83) and Multi-Grain Buttermilk Rolls (recipe, page 82).

Multi-Grain Buttermilk Rolls

This dark, seeded dough can be shaped into rolls or jumbo loaves.

LOW-FAT

Bake rolls at 375° for 25 to 30 minutes; or bake loaves at 375° for 40 to 45 minutes.

Makes 32 rolls, or 2 large loaves (16 slices each).

Nutrient Value Per Roll: 198 calories, 7 g protein, 6 g fat, 30 g carbohydrate, 265 mg sodium, 22 mg cholesterol.

2	cups buttermilk	1	tablespoon salt
1	cup plus 1 tablespoon water	1	tablespoon unsweetened cocoa powder
½	cup (1 stick) butter or margarine, cut into pieces	½	teaspoon baking soda
¼	cup molasses	1	cup sunflower seeds
3½	cups all-purpose flour	½	cup old-fashioned oats
3	cups whole wheat flour	2	eggs, slightly beaten
2	cups rye flour	1	egg white
½	cup wheat germ		Additional sunflower seeds
½	cup oat bran		OR: sesame seeds
2	packages active dry yeast		OR: caraway seeds

1. Combine the buttermilk with 1 cup of the water and the butter or margarine in a medium-size saucepan. Heat the buttermilk mixture over low heat just until bubbles form around the edge of the pan. Pour the buttermilk mixture into a very large bowl. Stir in the molasses.

2. Meanwhile, whisk 2 cups of the all-purpose flour with the whole wheat flour, rye flour, wheat germ, oat bran, yeast, salt, cocoa powder and baking soda in a large bowl until the ingredients are blended. Stir in the 1 cup of sunflower seeds and the oats.

3. Using a wooden spoon, gradually stir the flour mixture and the beaten whole eggs into the molasses-buttermilk mixture to form a soft dough. Knead the remaining 1½ cups of all-purpose flour into the dough in the bowl. Turn out the dough onto a floured surface. Knead the dough for 10 minutes, or until it is smooth and elastic. Place the dough in a greased bowl, and turn the greased side up. Cover the bowl, and let the dough rise in a warm place, away from drafts, until it is is doubled in size, for about 1½ hours.

4. Punch down the dough. Shape the dough into 32 rolls or twists, or two 9 x 4-inch oval loaves, or 1 loaf and 16 rolls. Place the rolls or loaves on greased baking sheets. Cover the baking sheets, and let the rolls or loaves rise in a warm place, away from drafts, until they are doubled in size, for about 1 hour.

5. Preheat the oven to moderate (375°). Using a sharp small knife, make shallow cuts across the tops of the rolls or loaves. Mix the egg white with the remaining tablespoon of water. Brush the tops of the rolls or loaves with the glaze. Sprinkle the tops with the additional sunflower seeds, or sesame or caraway seeds.

6. Bake the rolls in the preheated moderate oven (375°) for 25 to 30 minutes, or the loaves for 40 to 45 minutes, or until the rolls or loaves are well browned and sound hollow when tapped with your fingertips. Remove the rolls or loaves from the baking sheets to wire racks to cool.

GREAT GRAINS!

Whole grains are superior to refined grains. Refined grains have had their most nutritious parts—the bran and germ—removed. One cup of cooked whole grains offers 3 to 8 grams of fiber, while 1 cup of refined grains offers 1 gram or less.

● **Oats:** All versions (steel-cut, old-fashioned, quick, instant, and oat bran) are high in cholesterol-cutting soluble fiber; none are refined.

● **Barley:** Although most commonly found pearled (without the hull and germ), this is a good source of soluble fiber.

● **Cornmeal:** Corn kernels— yellow, white or blue—that are ground to use in baking; a good fiber source.

● **Wheat:** Comes in many forms: whole as berries, cracked (bran and germ intact), bulgur (bran removed), wheat germ (vitamin-packed center), or semolina (usually refined).

● **Rye:** The darker the rye flour, the more bran and nutrients it has.

● **Buckwheat:** Actually not a grain, but the seeds of a plant. Available crushed as groats, roasted as "kasha," and ground as flour. Rich in trace minerals.

o ❖ o

"Oats.
A grain, which in
England is generally
given to horses,
but in Scotland
supports the people. "
—*Samuel Johnson*

Cranberry Oatmeal Muffins

Bake muffins at 350° for 20 minutes; or bake loaf at 350° for 50 minutes.
Makes 16 muffins, or 1 loaf (12 slices).
Nutrient Value Per Muffin: 165 calories, 3 g protein, 6 g fat,
26 g carbohydrate, 219 mg sodium, 21 mg cholesterol.

1½ **cups all-purpose flour**	¾ **cup old-fashioned oats**
1 **tablespoon baking powder**	3 **tablespoons butter, softened**
¾ **teaspoon salt**	¾ **cup firmly packed light**
½ **cup walnuts, finely chopped**	**brown sugar**
½ **cup dried cranberries**	¾ **cup milk**
OR: dried pitted cherries	1 **egg**
OR: raisins	

1. Preheat the oven to moderate (350°). Grease 16 muffin-pan cups, or an 8½ x 4½-inch loaf pan.

2. Whisk together the flour, baking powder and salt in a large bowl. Toss the chopped walnuts and the cranberries, cherries or raisins with 1 teaspoon of the flour mixture in a small bowl to coat the walnuts and cranberries. Set aside the walnut mixture. Stir the oats into the remaining flour mixture.

3. Beat together the butter, brown sugar, milk and egg in a small bowl until they are blended. Add the milk mixture to the flour mixture, stirring just until the dry ingredients are evenly moistened; do not overmix. Fold the walnut mixture into the flour-milk mixture. Turn the batter into the prepared muffin-pan cups or loaf pan.

4. Bake the muffins in the preheated moderate oven (350°) for 20 minutes, or the loaf for 50 minutes, or until a wooden pick inserted in the centers comes out clean. Cool the muffins in the pan on a wire rack for 5 minutes; cool the loaf for 10 minutes. Loosen the sides of the muffins or loaf with a small metal spatula, and invert the muffins or loaf onto the rack. Serve the muffins warm, or at room temperature. Cool the loaf completely before serving it.

Three Cheers for Chicken!

Try Chicken Fajitas with Tomato Salsa, or California-style Chicken Roulades with Sun-Dried Tomato Sauce.

Chicken Roulades with Sun-Dried Tomato Sauce

Use sun-dried tomatoes wrapped in cellophane, not those packed in oil.

Bake at 375° for 30 to 35 minutes.
Makes 4 servings.
Nutrient Value Per Serving: 370 calories, 41 g protein, 14 g fat, 20 g carbohydrate, 871 mg sodium, 144 mg cholesterol.

Butter OR: nonstick vegetable cooking spray

Chicken Roulades:
- 1 tablespoon olive oil
- 2 tablespoons chopped shallots OR: green onion
- ½ cup cooked fresh OR: frozen spinach, squeezed dry and chopped
- ⅓ cup part-skim ricotta cheese
- 2 tablespoons grated Parmesan cheese
- ¼ teaspoon freshly ground pepper
- ¼ teaspoon fennel seeds, crushed
- ⅛ teaspoon salt
- 4 boned, skinless chicken breast halves (about 5 ounces each), pounded to ¼-inch thickness

- 1 egg, slightly beaten
- ½ cup bread crumbs

Sun-Dried Tomato Sauce:
- 1 ounce (about 4 pieces) sun-dried tomatoes (not oil-packed), chopped
- ½ teaspoon olive oil
- 1 medium-size onion, chopped (½ cup)
- 1 clove garlic, finely chopped
- 1 can (8 ounces) tomato sauce
- 1 teaspoon dried basil, crumbled
- ½ teaspoon sugar
- ⅛ teaspoon freshly ground pepper

1. Preheat the oven to moderate (375°). Grease a 15 x 10 x 1½-inch jelly-roll pan, or spray it with nonstick vegetable cooking spray.

2. Prepare the Chicken Roulades: Heat half the oil in a medium-size skillet over medium heat. Add the shallots or green onion, and cook for about 3 minutes, or until the shallots are soft. Add the spinach, and cook for 2 minutes. Let the spinach mixture cool. Combine the spinach mixture with the ricotta and Parmesan cheeses, the pepper, fennel and salt in a bowl.

3. Spread out the chicken pieces flat. Place ¼ cup of the filling in the center of each chicken piece. Roll up both sides of each chicken piece, and secure the roulade with a wooden pick.

MENU

Champagne & Chili Nuts

Chicken Roulades with Sun-Dried Tomato Sauce (recipe, at left)

Basmati Rice

Steamed Carrots & Snow Peas

Brownies & Ice Cream

❖

"*Oh, better no doubt is a dinner of herbs, when season'ed by love, which no rancor disturbs.*"
— *Owen Meredith*

4. Place the egg in a shallow dish or pie plate. Place the bread crumbs in a separate dish or pie plate. Dip the roulades in the egg, then in the bread crumbs, making sure to cover the entire surface of each roulade. Place the roulades in the prepared pan. Drizzle the roulades with the remaining oil.

5. Bake the roulades in the preheated moderate oven (375°) for 30 to 35 minutes, or until the roulades are cooked through. Remove the roulades from the oven, and let them stand for 10 minutes before slicing them. Cut the roulades crosswise into slices.

6. Meanwhile, prepare the Tomato Sauce: Place the sun-dried tomatoes in ¼ cup of hot water in a small bowl. Set aside the tomatoes to rehydrate.

7. Heat the oil in a small saucepan. Add the onion and the garlic, and cook for about 5 minutes, or until the vegetables are soft. Add the tomato sauce, sun-dried tomatoes with their water, the basil, sugar and pepper. Lower the heat, cover the saucepan, and simmer the sauce for 15 minutes. Spoon the sauce over the sliced roulades, or arrange the sliced roulades in a pool of the sauce. Serve the roulades immediately.

Chicken Fajitas with Tomato Salsa

LOW-FAT

Broil chicken for 8 minutes.

Makes 4 servings.

Nutrient Value Per Serving: 452 calories, 44 g protein, 4 g fat, 58 g carbohydrate, 972 mg sodium, 83 mg cholesterol.

1	container (8 ounces) nonfat yogurt
2	tablespoons lime juice
1	clove garlic, finely chopped
1	teaspoon ground cumin
¼	teaspoon salt
¼	teaspoon freshly ground pepper
4	boned, skinless chicken breast halves (about 5 ounces each)

Tomato Salsa:

3	medium-size ripe tomatoes, chopped
2	green onions, finely sliced
1	teaspoon balsamic vinegar
1	teaspoon olive oil
½	teaspoon salt
¼	teaspoon freshly ground pepper
¼	cup chopped fresh cilantro
8	warmed flour tortillas

1. Combine the yogurt, lime juice, garlic, cumin, the ¼ teaspoon of salt and the ¼ teaspoon of pepper in a pie plate or shallow dish. Add the chicken pieces, and turn to coat them. Marinate the chicken pieces in the refrigerator for 2 hours.

2. Prepare the Tomato Salsa: Mix together the tomatoes, green onion, vinegar, oil, salt, pepper and cilantro in a bowl. Set aside the salsa.

3. Preheat the broiler. Remove the chicken pieces from the marinade, reserving any remaining marinade. Line the broiler pan with aluminum foil. Arrange the chicken pieces, smooth side down, on the broiler-pan rack.

4. Broil the chicken pieces, with the bottom of the pan 6 inches from the heat source, for 4 minutes. Turn over the chicken pieces, and spoon the reserved marinade over them. Broil the chicken pieces for 4 minutes more, or until the pieces are lightly browned and cooked through.

5. Slice the chicken pieces diagonally into strips. Place the chicken strips, divided evenly, on the tortillas. Top with the Tomato Salsa, divided evenly. Fold the tortillas, and serve the fajitas immediately.

MENU

Margaritas

Bean Nachos
(see Tip, page 15)

Chicken Fajitas with Tomato Salsa
(recipe, at right)

Tossed Green Salad

Corn on the Cob

Strawberry Shortcake
(recipe, page 186)

o ❖ o

A SLIMMING SUBSTITUTE

Substituting nonfat yogurt for oil in the marinade for Chicken Fajitas with Tomato Salsa (recipe, at right) lowers the fat, and produces a delicious, moist piece of chicken. If you're cooking for a large crowd, this recipe can be doubled easily.

Meatless Feast

Mouth-watering lasagna filled with sweet red peppers, mushrooms and tomatoes is the perfect choice for a meal without meat.

Vegetarian Lasagna

LOW-CHOLESTEROL
Bake at 375° for 30 minutes.
Makes 9 servings.
Nutrient Value Per Serving: 405 calories, 22 g protein, 20 g fat, 35 g carbohydrate, 720 mg sodium, 44 mg cholesterol.

White Sauce:

2	tablespoons unsalted butter
2	tablespoons all-purpose flour
2¾	cups lowfat milk
½	teaspoon salt
⅛	teaspoon ground nutmeg

Vegetable Filling:

2	tablespoons olive oil
1	large onion, finely chopped (1 cup)
2	large cloves garlic, finely chopped
1	carrot, peeled and finely chopped
1	large sweet red pepper, cored, seeded and finely chopped
1	pound zucchini, coarsely chopped
1	cup sliced mushrooms (3 ounces)
1	can (28 ounces) tomatoes, drained and chopped
¼	cup cured black olives, pitted and finely chopped
¼	teaspoon salt
⅛	teaspoon freshly ground pepper
1	cup packed fresh basil, finely chopped
9	lasagna noodles
8	ounces part-skim mozzarella cheese, shredded
8	ounces Provolone cheese, shredded
½	cup grated Parmesan cheese

1. Prepare the White Sauce: Melt the butter in a saucepan over medium-low heat. Whisk in the flour until it is blended. Cook the flour mixture, stirring, for 3 minutes. Gradually whisk in the milk. Add the salt. Bring the milk mixture to boiling over medium heat. Reduce the heat to low. Simmer, whisking often, for 30 minutes, or until the milk mixture is thickened. Stir in the nutmeg. Cover the saucepan, and set aside the white sauce.

2. Prepare the Vegetable Filling: Heat 2 teaspoons of the oil in a large skillet over medium heat. Add the onion, garlic and carrot, and sauté for 3 minutes. Remove the onion mixture to a bowl. Wipe out the skillet. Heat 2 more teaspoons of the oil in the same skillet over medium heat. Add the red pepper, and sauté for 3 minutes. Remove the red pepper to the bowl with the onion mixture. Wipe out the skillet. Heat the remaining 2 teaspoons of oil. Add the zucchini, and sauté for 5 minutes. Add the mushrooms, and sauté for 3 minutes. Return the onion-red pepper mixture to the skillet. Add the tomatoes, olives, salt and pepper. Bring the vegetable mixture to boiling. Cover the saucepan, lower the heat, and simmer for 15 minutes. Stir in the basil.

MENU

Vegetarian Lasagna
(recipe, at left)
Sesame Breadsticks
Shredded Romaine Salad
Strawberry Raspberry Tart
(recipe, page 191)

o ✦ o

VIVA LA VEGGIES!

Eating vegetarian meals doesn't mean depriving your taste buds. It means centering dishes around delicious foods you already enjoy: fruits, fresh vegetables, rice and other grains, potatoes, salads, soups, pastas, and breads.
● Try to cut down your use of animal products by preparing large, crunchy, main course salads, and adding only small amounts of meat, chicken, fish, or cheese.
● Enjoy traditional side dishes —potatoes, rice, soups, pasta, and hot breads—as satisfying main courses, accompanied by raw or steamed vegetables and salads.
● Try tofu. It can be substituted for cheese in lasagna, for chicken in tacos, for beef in spaghetti sauce, or for lamb in stuffed peppers. There are excellent tofu "burgers" and "dogs" available commercially.
● Keep in mind that changing the way you and your family eat takes time. Don't set rigid rules—just follow your new eating plan as well, and as often, as you can.

3. Preheat the oven to moderate (375°). Lightly grease a 13 x 9 x 2-inch baking dish.

4. Cook the noodles following the package directions. Drain the noodles. Combine the mozzarella and Provolone cheeses with ¼ cup of the Parmesan cheese in a medium-size bowl.

5. Spread ½ cup of the vegetables over the bottom of the prepared dish. Lay 3 noodles over the vegetables. Spread half the remaining vegetables over the noodles. Spread one third of the white sauce over the vegetables. Sprinkle with half the cheese mixture. Top with 3 noodles. Spread the remaining vegetables over the top. Top with half the remaining white sauce. Sprinkle with the remaining cheese mixture. Top with the remaining 3 noodles. Spread the remaining white sauce over all. Sprinkle with the remaining ¼ cup of Parmesan cheese.

6. Bake the lasagna in the preheated moderate oven (375°) for 30 minutes, or until the top is golden brown. Let the lasagna stand for at least 10 minutes before cutting it.

Vegetarian Lasagna combines carrots, sweet red peppers, zucchini and a trio of cheeses in one delicious dish.

Catch the Orient Express

Enjoy almost effortless entertaining when you stir-fry a feast of marinated flank steak and colorful vegetables.

Confetti Stir-Fry

LOW-CALORIE • LOW-CHOLESTEROL
Makes 4 servings.
Nutrient Value Per Serving: 299 calories, 20 g protein, 20 g fat, 12 g carbohydrate, 666 mg sodium, 44 mg cholesterol.

¼ **cup reduced sodium soy sauce**
2 **tablespoons dry sherry**
2 **teaspoons cornstarch**
½ **teaspoon sugar**
⅛ **teaspoon red pepper flakes**
1 **flank steak (12 ounces)**
1 **inch piece of fresh ginger**

2 **cloves garlic, finely chopped**
2 **zucchini (1 pound)**
1 **large sweet red pepper, cored and seeded**
3 **tablespoons vegetable oil**
⅓ **cup canned baby corn (half 14-ounce can)**

1. Stir together the soy sauce, sherry, cornstarch, sugar and red pepper flakes in a small bowl until the marinade is smooth.

MENU

Confetti Stir-Fry
(recipe, at left)
Hot Cooked Rice
Steamed Snow Peas
Raspberry Sherbet
(recipe, page 208)

○ ✤ ○

STIR-FRY MADE SIMPLE

The prize-winning formula for this super-speedy cooking technique? A little preparation, a hot wok, a splash of oil, and some sleight of hand work. The results? Juicier meats, and crisply tender vegetables that are bright in color and full of vitamins. Check out the basics on page 89, then whip up spicy Confetti Stir-Fry (recipe, at left).

SUPER STEAK SLICING

Slicing raw flank steak evenly can be a bit tricky. For easier slicing, roll up the flank steak lengthwise, then cut it into ¼-inch-thick slices. Or lay the steak flat in the freezer for 45 minutes, or until the meat is firm enough to slice easily.

2. Slice the steak across the grain into ¼-inch-thick slices. Place the slices in the marinade, and stir to coat them.

3. Peel the ginger, and cut it lengthwise into thin slices. Cut the slices into fine matchstick pieces. Place the ginger in a bowl along with the garlic.

4. Cut the zucchini lengthwise into ¼-inch-thick slices. Cut the slices into ¼-inch-thick sticks. Cut the sticks into 3-inch lengths. Cut the red pepper into ¼-inch-thick strips, and halve the strips.

5. Heat a wok or large skillet until it is hot. Add 1 tablespoon of the oil, pouring it down the side of the wok to coat the entire surface. Add the ginger mixture to the wok and stir-fry for 30 seconds, or until the ginger mixture is lightly browned. Remove the ginger mixture, and set it aside.

6. Drain the steak slices, reserving the marinade. Reheat the wok, and add 1 more tablespoon of the oil. Stir-fry the steak slices for about 2 minutes, or until they are browned. Remove the steak slices from the wok to a plate.

7. Reheat the wok, and add the remaining tablespoon of oil. Add the zucchini and the red pepper, and stir-fry until the vegetables are crisply tender, for about 3 minutes. Add the ginger mixture, steak slices and corn. Stir the reserved marinade, and pour it into the wok. Cook, stirring constantly, just until the mixture is bubbly. Serve immediately.

FLASH-IN-THE-PAN: QUICK & EASY STIR-FRYING

1. If food needs to be marinated, mix the marinade, add the food, and stir to coat the food with the marinade. Refrigerate as directed to let the food absorb the flavors.

2. Prepare all the ingredients before beginning to stir-fry; once you start cooking, you should not have to stop. Cut meat into strips, slivers or chunks. Cut vegetables into the same shape and size as the meat. Finely chop seasonings such as garlic or ginger. Measure out the liquids. Working with small amounts of food (less than a pound of meat) that are cut into small pieces is what makes stir-frying a quick cooking technique.

3. Place all the ingredients within easy reach of the wok. Heat the wok until it is very hot. Test the wok heat by sprinkling with a few drops of water — when the drops sizzle and jump around, the wok is ready for cooking. Pour peanut or vegetable oil in a thin stream down the side of the wok, turning the wok to coat it.

4. Add small amounts of each ingredient, one after the other, following the sequence in the recipe. Keep the wok very hot so the ingredients fry rather than simmer. Constantly stir the ingredients. When the ingredients are almost cooked, use a Chinese shovel or a pancake turner to move them from the center up the sides of the wok, or to remove them from the wok. When all the food is fully cooked, add the seasonings or reserved marinade, and stir-fry just until they are hot. Serve the stir-fry immediately.

Fun-in-the-Sun Summer Suppers

Beat the heat with a poolside pizza party, or a backyard barbecue.

Focaccia with Cheese & Grilled Vegetables

LOW-CHOLESTEROL
Broil vegetables for 4 to 5 minutes; bake focaccia at 425° for 9 to 13 minutes.
Makes 4 servings.
Nutrient Value Per Serving: 421 calories, 21 g protein, 20 g fat,
37 g carbohydrate, 626 mg sodium, 33 mg cholesterol.

Basil Dressing:

1	clove garlic, peeled
¼	cup firmly packed fresh basil
2	teaspoons fresh thyme OR: ½ teaspoon dried thyme, crumbled
⅔	cup olive oil
⅓	cup balsamic OR: red wine vinegar
⅛	teaspoon salt
⅛	teaspoon freshly ground pepper

½	zucchini, thinly sliced (½ cup)
½	sweet red pepper, cored, seeded, and cut into thin strips (¾ cup)
1	cup cherry tomatoes, halved
1	package (10 ounces) ready-made pizza dough
1	package (8 ounces) shredded part-skim mozzarella cheese

1. Prepare the Basil Dressing: Place the garlic, basil and thyme in the container of a food processor or electric blender. Whirl until the ingredients are chopped. Blend in the oil, balsamic or red wine vinegar, salt and pepper. Pour the dressing into a measuring cup; you should have 1 cup.

2. Preheat the broiler.

3. Toss the zucchini, red pepper and cherry tomatoes with ¼ cup of the dressing in a medium-size bowl. Refrigerate the remaining dressing to use with salads. Line the broiler pan with aluminum foil. Arrange the vegetables on the broiler pan.

4. Broil the vegetables 6 inches from the heat source for 4 to 5 minutes. Reduce the oven temperature to hot (425°). Lightly grease a 12-inch pizza pan. Roll out the pizza dough to a 14-inch circle following the package directions. Press the dough into the prepared pan.

5. Bake the dough in the preheated hot oven (425°) for 5 to 8 minutes, or just until the crust begins to brown. Sprinkle the mozzarella cheese over the crust. Top with the vegetables. Bake for 4 to 5 minutes more, or until the mozzarella cheese melts. Serve the focaccia immediately.

MENU

Focaccia with Cheese & Grilled Vegetables
(recipe, at left)

Tossed Green Salad

Tri-Colored Sherbet Mold
(recipe, page 206)

o ❖ o

" Summer afternoon —summer afternoon; to me those have always been the two most beautiful words in the English language. "
—Henry James

∘ ❖ ∘

GAME HENS

Known both as Rock Cornish game hens, or simply Cornish hens, these birds were developed by crossing a Cornish game cock with a white Rock hen. The Cornish game hen is a very small bird that is marketed at 4 to 6 weeks of age, and weighs 1½ pounds or less.

• Both fresh and frozen Cornish game hens are widely available.

Barbecued Cornish Game Hens

Bake at 375° for 35 minutes, then broil for 10 minutes.
Makes 4 servings.
Nutrient Value Per Serving: 357 calories, 35 g protein, 17 g fat, 14 g carbohydrate, 170 mg sodium, 110 mg cholesterol.

2	**Cornish hens, split, and backbone removed**
¼	**teaspoon salt**
¼	**teaspoon freshly ground pepper**
½	**cup prepared chili sauce**
¼	**cup finely chopped onion (1 small onion)**
1	**clove garlic, finely chopped**
1	**tablespoon honey**
1	**tablespoon red wine vinegar**
1	**teaspoon Worcestershire sauce**

1. Preheat the oven to moderate (375°). Line the bottom of the broiler pan with aluminum foil.

2. Sprinkle the Cornish hens with the salt and the pepper. Arrange the hens, cut side down, on the broiler-pan rack.

3. Bake the hens in the preheated moderate oven (375°), basting them once or twice with the pan drippings, for 20 minutes.

4. Meanwhile, combine the chili sauce, onion, garlic, honey, vinegar and Worcestershire sauce in a small bowl.

5. Remove the hens from the oven, and turn them over. Cover the hens with half the chili sauce mixture. Bake the hens for 15 minutes more. Remove the hens from the oven, and increase the oven temperature to broil. Turn over the hens again, and cover them with the remaining chili sauce mixture.

6. Broil the hens for 10 minutes, or until the hens are cooked through and no longer pink near the bone. Serve the hens immediately.

A piquant barbecue sauce gives these Barbecued Cornish Game Hens a fantastic flavor boost.

A *Taste of the Tropics*

A scrumptious combination of tropical tastes from Jamaica to Hawaii, this is a perfect party menu to brighten the dog days of summer.

Jamaican Jerk Chicken

This highly seasoned dish uses a fair amount of allspice, a favorite Jamaican flavoring. Since individual tastes vary, we've included a range on the hot seasonings, so you can make this dish as hot or mild as you wish.

Bake at 400° for 35 minutes, then broil for 4 to 5 minutes.
Makes 6 servings.

Nutrient Value Per Serving: 416 calories, 32 g protein, 28 g fat, 8 g carbohydrate, 282 mg sodium, 103 mg cholesterol.

4 teaspoons allspice berries, crushed in mortar with pestle OR: 1 teaspoon ground allspice	¼ to ½ teaspoon freshly ground pepper
6 cloves garlic, crushed and peeled	½ teaspoon salt
2 tablespoons peeled, chopped fresh ginger	⅓ cup olive oil
2 tablespoons dark brown sugar	⅓ cup sliced green onion
1 teaspoon ground cinnamon	¼ cup red wine vinegar
½ to 1 teaspoon seeded, chopped, jalapeño pepper	2 tablespoons lime juice
¼ to ½ teaspoon ground hot red pepper	1 chicken (3½ pounds), cut into 12 pieces (2 legs, 2 thighs, breasts cut into 4 pieces, wing tips removed and wings halved)

1. Combine the allspice, garlic, ginger, brown sugar, cinnamon, jalapeño pepper, ground hot red pepper, black pepper, salt, oil, green onion, vinegar and lime juice in the container of a food processor or electric blender. Whirl until the marinade is smooth.

2. Place the chicken pieces in a large, nonreactive pan, and rub them with the marinade. Gently lift up the skin of each piece, rub the marinade over the meat under the skin, and pull the skin back in place. Cover the chicken pieces with plastic wrap, and refrigerate them for 2 hours.

3. Preheat the oven to hot (400°).

4. Place the chicken pieces in a broiler-proof baking pan that will hold the pieces in a single layer. Bake the chicken pieces in the preheated hot oven (400°) for 35 minutes. Raise the oven temperature to broil. Broil the chicken pieces 4 inches from the heat source for 4 to 5 minutes, or until the pieces are lightly crisped.

MENU

Jamaican Jerk Chicken
(recipe, at left)

Fried Bananas
(recipe, page 94)

Empanadas
(recipe, page 94)

Marinated Beef & Apricot Kebabs
(recipe, page 96)

Papaya Salad
(recipe, page 96)

Macadamia Coconut Cookies
(recipe, page 98)

Ginger Pineapple Punch
(recipe, page 97)

o ⚬ o

COOKIN' CHICKEN

● To oven bake chicken pieces, dip them in egg, egg white or honey mustard, and roll the pieces in bread crumbs to coat them.

● To broil chicken, rub the pieces with oil or butter. If you wish, sprinkle them with herbs and spices.

● To poach chicken, place the pieces in a saucepan with enough water to cover them. Season the water with carrot, thyme, celery and a bay leaf. Simmer the chicken pieces in the water until they are cooked through.

● To braise chicken, first brown the pieces in fat, then cook them, covered, in a small amount of liquid. Add vegetables such as mushrooms, onions, sweet peppers or carrots, and/or herbs such as tarragon, marjoram or garlic.

● To sauté or stir-fry chicken, add the pieces to a hot pan with a small amount of oil, and fry quickly.

Jamaican Jerk Chicken is marinated in a spicy mixture of allspice, lime and ginger. Fried Bananas (recipe, page 94), with a crunchy cornmeal coating, are a perfect partner.

Fried Bananas

For the best flavor, use firm, ripe bananas.

LOW-CHOLESTEROL · LOW-SODIUM
Makes 8 servings.
Nutrient Value Per Serving: 162 calories, 1 g protein, 9 g fat,
21 g carbohydrate, 35 mg sodium, 0 mg cholesterol.

¼ **cup cornmeal**
⅛ **teaspoon salt**
2 **pounds firm, ripe bananas
(5 to 6 bananas), peeled,
and diagonally sliced
½ inch thick**

⅓ **cup olive OR: vegetable oil**

1. Combine the cornmeal with the salt on a piece of wax paper. Dip the banana slices in the cornmeal mixture to coat the slices evenly.

2. Heat the olive or vegetable oil in a large, nonstick skillet over medium heat. Add the banana slices, and cook until they are golden brown and crisp, for about 1 minute on each side. Serve the fried bananas immediately.

Empanadas

These are perfect for entertaining. The dough can be made in advance and frozen, or the empanadas can be baked in advance, and reheated at serving time. Use fresh or frozen cod, or any firm-fleshed white fish—just make sure there are no bones.

LOW-CALORIE
Bake at 400° for 12 minutes.
Makes 5 dozen empanadas.
Nutrient Value Per Empanada: 74 calories, 3 g protein, 5 g fat,
6 g carbohydrate, 75 mg sodium, 13 mg cholesterol.

Dough:
2½ **cups all-purpose flour**
½ **cup yellow cornmeal**
1 **tablespoon sugar**
¾ **teaspoon salt**
¾ **teaspoon ground coriander**
½ **teaspoon ground cumin**
½ **teaspoon ground hot
red pepper**
1 **cup (2 sticks) unsalted butter
or margarine, cut into pieces**
1 **container (8 ounces) plain
lowfat yogurt**

Filling:
4 **tablespoons olive oil**
1¼ **pounds cod fillets, fresh
OR: thawed frozen**
6 **cloves garlic, finely chopped**
4 **green onions, trimmed and
thinly sliced**
½ **cup oil-cured black olives,
pitted and coarsely chopped**
¼ **cup chopped fresh cilantro
OR: parsley**
2 **tablespoons lime juice**

1. Prepare the Dough: Combine the flour, cornmeal, sugar, salt, coriander, cumin and ground hot red pepper in a large bowl. Using a pastry blender or 2 forks, cut in the butter or margarine until the mixture resembles coarse meal. Stir in the yogurt just until it is combined. Divide the dough in half, and flatten each half into a disk. Wrap the disks individually in plastic wrap, and refrigerate them for 2 hours, or overnight.

ODE TO OLIVES

Olives have been a dietary staple in Mediterranean countries for at least 4,000 years. Cultivation of the gnarled, evergreen olive tree, with its small leaves, began in the ideal climate of the Middle East. Franciscan monks brought the tree to California in the 1700's. No one knows how humans discovered that the olive tree's bitter fruit could be eaten. Freshly picked olives are unappetizing because they contain an acrid-tasting natural substance called glucoside. Credit for discovering the olive's appeal is given to shepherds who observed their flocks nibbling on the fruit of an olive branch that had fallen into a stream; the leaching in water had removed the acrid substance from the olives. Today, olive leaching is done with salt water, or salt alone.

> "*My life,
> my joy,
> my food,
> my all the world.*"
> —*William Shakespeare*

2. Prepare the Filling: Heat 2 tablespoons of the oil in a large skillet over medium heat. Add the cod fillets and cook, breaking up the fillets with a fork, until they are cooked through, for about 5 minutes; the timing will vary depending on the thickness of the fillets. Transfer the cod to a strainer, and drain off all the liquid.

3. Heat the remaining 2 tablespoons of oil in the skillet. Add the garlic and the green onion, and sauté over low heat until the garlic mixture is tender, for about 2 minutes. Combine the cod with the garlic mixture, olives, cilantro or parsley and the lime juice in a small bowl.

4. Preheat the oven to hot (400°).

5. Roll out each dough disk on a lightly floured surface to a ⅛-inch thickness. Using a 3-inch round, straight or scalloped biscuit cutter, cut out rounds as close to each other as possible. Spoon a rounded measuring teaspoon of the filling in the center of each round. Moisten the bottom half of each round with a little water, fold over the top half, and press the edges together to seal them. Place the empanadas on ungreased baking sheets.

6. Bake the empanadas in the preheated hot oven (400°) for 12 minutes, or until the empanadas are golden and crisp. Serve the empanadas immediately. Or cool the empanadas to room temperature, and refrigerate them. Reheat the empanadas in a preheated moderate oven (350°) until they are heated through.

Spicy Empanadas, crusty codfish turnovers laced with cilantro and olives, are sharply accented with Papaya Salad (recipe, page 96).

Marinated Beef & Apricot Kebabs

In Argentina, beef is the meat of choice, and often it is paired with fruit. Our version of the combination is seasoned with oregano and garlic.

LOW-CALORIE · LOW-CHOLESTEROL

Broil for 8 to 10 minutes.

Makes 8 skewers.

Nutrient Value Per Skewer: 153 calories, 12 g protein, 7 g fat, 10 g carbohydrate, 211 mg sodium, 31 mg cholesterol.

1½	teaspoons dried oregano, crumbled	1	pound eye round OR: sirloin, cut ¾ inch thick
1	teaspoon coarse (kosher) salt	1	medium-size onion, cut into 1-inch chunks
⅛	teaspoon freshly ground pepper	½	teaspoon sugar
5	cloves garlic, finely chopped (1 tablespoon)	1	tablespoon olive oil
		32	dried apricots (about ¾ cup)

1. Combine the oregano, salt, pepper and garlic in a small bowl. Place the beef in a small, shallow pan, and rub the oregano mixture into the beef. Cover the pan, and refrigerate the beef for 2 hours.

2. Combine the onion, sugar and oil in a small bowl. Let the onion mixture stand at room temperature.

3. Place the apricots in a small bowl, and cover them with warm water. Let the apricots stand for 30 minutes to soften. Drain the apricots.

4. Preheat the broiler.

5. Cut the beef into thirty-two ¾-inch cubes. On each of 8 metal skewers, alternate 4 beef cubes, 4 apricots, and 4 onion chunks. Place the skewers on the broiler-pan rack.

6. Broil the skewers 4 inches from the heat source, turning the skewers once, for 8 to 10 minutes, or until the beef is browned and medium-rare. Serve the kebabs immediately.

Papaya Salad

This cool and refreshing salad is a nice foil for spicy chicken.

LOW-CHOLESTEROL · LOW-SODIUM

Makes 8 servings.

Nutrient Value Per Serving: 104 calories, 1 g protein, 5 g fat, 15 g carbohydrate, 80 mg sodium, 0 mg cholesterol.

1	small red onion, halved and thinly sliced	2	tablespoons lime juice
	Ice water	1¼	teaspoons ginger juice*
2	navel oranges	½	teaspoon Dijon-style mustard
2	grapefruits, preferably pink	¼	teaspoon salt
1	ripe papaya (about 1 pound)	3	tablespoons olive oil
1	sweet red pepper, cored, seeded, and cut into thin strips		Boston OR: leaf lettuce (optional)
1	sweet yellow pepper, cored, seeded, and cut into thin strips		

PAPAYA

A greenish-yellow, oval fruit with soft golden-pink flesh, papaya grows on a subtropical tree. An average papaya fruit is about 6 inches long and 3 inches wide. With some varieties, the fruit weighs up to 20 pounds. Most papayas are grown in Hawaii, Puerto Rico, Florida and southern California. Papaya also is called pawpaw. Fully ripe papaya is eaten alone as a dessert, made into sherbet or ice cream, and used in salads and pies. Unripe, or green, papaya can be cooked as a vegetable, and tastes somewhat like squash. Half-ripe papaya is a source of papain, an enzyme used in meat tenderizers. Ripe papaya has little or no papain present.

● A 3½-ounce serving of papaya has 39 calories, and is an excellent source of vitamins A and C.

● The numerous tiny black seeds inside a papaya are edible, and are considered an aid to digestion. Place the seeds in the container of a food processor or electric blender, and whirl until the seeds are finely ground. Add the ground seeds to the dressing for a fruit salad.

● Papaya is available year-round, with the best supplies in late winter and early spring. The fruit is picked firm, and will ripen in 3 to 5 days at room temperature. Select firm, mostly yellow fruit with no bruises or soft spots. Store ripe papaya in the refrigerator.

1. Place the onion in a small bowl, and cover the onion with the ice water. Let the onion stand at room temperature for 30 minutes. Drain the onion, and dry it on paper toweling.

2. Section the oranges, removing the peel and reserving 2 tablespoons of the juice. Section the grapefruits the same way, but do not reserve any juice. Peel the papaya, then halve, seed and thickly slice it.

3. Drain the orange and grapefruit sections well. Combine the citrus sections with the onion, papaya and red and yellow peppers in a large salad bowl.

4. Whisk the lime juice together with the reserved orange juice, the ginger juice, mustard and salt in a small bowl. Whisk in the oil until it is well blended. Pour the dressing over the salad, and toss to mix well. If you wish, serve the salad on a bed of Boston or leaf lettuce.

Note: *To make ginger juice, peel and grate a 2-inch-long piece of fresh ginger. Squeeze the grated ginger through a strainer to extract the juice.*

Ginger Pineapple Punch

LOW-CHOLESTEROL · LOW-SODIUM · LOW-FAT

Makes 8 servings.

Nutrient Value Per Serving: 163 calories, 0 g protein, .27 g fat, 41 g carbohydrate, 5 mg sodium, 0 mg cholesterol.

1 cup sugar	3 cups fresh pineapple chunks
2½ cups water	1 cup pineapple juice
1½ tablespoons chopped crystallized ginger	¼ cup lemon juice
1 vanilla bean, split lengthwise	2 tablespoons grenadine
4 strips (3 x ½ inch) lemon zest (yellow part of rind only)	Ice cubes

1. Stir together the sugar, water, ginger, vanilla bean and lemon zest in a small saucepan until the sugar is dissolved. Bring the sugar syrup to boiling, and boil for 1 minute. Remove the saucepan from the heat. Cover the saucepan, and let the sugar syrup stand for 30 minutes.

2. Combine the pineapple chunks, pineapple juice, lemon juice and grenadine in the container of an electric blender or food processor. Whirl until the pineapple mixture is smooth.

3. Strain the sugar syrup, and discard the solids. Add the sugar syrup to the pineapple mixture in the blender. Whirl until the mixture is well combined. Pour the punch into a pitcher. If the blender container gets too full, work in batches, and stir the batches together in the pitcher. Cover the pitcher, and refrigerate the punch until it is chilled. Serve the punch in tall glasses over ice cubes.

PINEAPPLE

A tropical fruit, pineapple is so named because it resembles a pine cone. A 4-pound pineapple takes almost 2 years to grow. The pineapple plant is grown from slips or crowns, not seeds. Smooth Cayenne is the leading variety of pineapple grown in Hawaii, Honduras, Mexico, the Dominican Republic, the Philippines, Thailand, and Costa Rica.

● Pineapple is used in desserts and salads, and as an accompaniment to pork and ham. It is a good source of vitamin C, with only 52 calories per 3½-ounce serving.

● Fresh pineapples are marketed year-round, with peak supplies between April and June. A pineapple does not ripen after it is harvested. Select a pineapple that is firm, with fresh looking, green crown leaves. The larger the fruit, the greater the proportion of edible flesh. Larger fruits also are a better buy, because pineapple usually is sold by the piece rather than by weight. A very slight separation of the eyes, and the presence of a fresh "pineapple" fragrance are signs of ripeness.

● Store pineapple at room temperature, away from heat or sun, and use it within 3 days. Before serving pineapple, refrigerate it just until it is cold.

Macadamia Coconut Cookies

These cookies are rich, mouthwatering, and easy to prepare.

Toast coconut at 325° for 7 minutes; bake cookies at 325° for 15 to 17 minutes.
Makes 2 dozen cookies.

Nutrient Value Per Cookie: 103 calories, 1 g protein, 7 g fat,
9 g carbohydrate, 28 mg sodium, 10 mg cholesterol.

½ **cup flaked coconut (about 1½ ounces)**	1 **teaspoon vanilla**
1 **cup sifted all-purpose flour**	½ **cup macadamia nuts, finely chopped**
¼ **teaspoon salt**	2 **tablespoons strained apricot jam**
½ **cup (1 stick) unsalted butter, at room temperature**	12 **macadamia nuts, halved**
⅓ **cup firmly packed light brown sugar**	

1. Preheat the oven to slow (325°). Place the coconut in a small baking pan or pie pan.

2. Bake the coconut in the preheated slow oven (325°), shaking the pan occasionally, for about 7 minutes, or until the coconut is toasted and golden. Leave the oven on.

3. Sift together the flour and the salt onto wax paper.

4. Beat the butter in a small bowl until it is creamy. Add the brown sugar, and beat until the mixture is light colored. Beat in the vanilla. Gradually beat in the flour mixture until it is combined. Stir in the coconut.

5. Roll the dough into 24 walnut-size balls. Roll each ball in the chopped macadamia nuts, and place the balls 2 inches apart on ungreased baking sheets. Make a thumbprint in the center of each ball. Spoon ¼ teaspoon of the apricot jam into each thumbprint, and place a macadamia half on top.

6. Bake the cookies in the preheated slow oven (325°) for 15 to 17 minutes, or just until the cookies are set and the macadamia nuts are lightly browned. Cool the cookies on the baking sheets on wire racks for 1 minute. Remove the cookies to the wire racks to cool completely.

MACADAMIA MANIA

Macadamia nuts are the edible seeds of silk oak trees, which are native to Australia but now are grown in Hawaii and California. The flavor of the macadamia nut is similar to that of the Brazil nut. Macadamia nuts are white, crisp, sweet, and high in oil content.

● Macadamia nuts have shiny, round, brown shells that are about an inch in diameter. The nuts seldom are sold in their shells, however, because these are very thick and difficult to crack. Most macadamia nuts are sold in cans shelled, roasted, and salted.

A tropical delight, Macadamia Coconut Cookies feature the world's two most delicious nuts.

Fall Foliage Dinner

Celebrate the advent of autumn with a fragrant roast chicken and brown rice.

Garlic & Rosemary Roast Chicken with Brown Rice Stuffing

Roast at 425° for 15 minutes, then at 325° for 2¼ hours.
Makes 8 servings.
Nutrient Value Per Serving: 472 calories, 39 g protein, 26 g fat, 18 g carbohydrate, 324 mg sodium, 117 mg cholesterol.

Brown Rice Stuffing:

1	medium-size onion, chopped (½ cup)
1	tablespoon olive oil
½	cup brown rice
1¼	cups low-sodium chicken broth
¼	teaspoon dried thyme, crumbled
¼	teaspoon dried rosemary, crumbled
¼	teaspoon freshly ground pepper
3	ounces prosciutto, chopped
⅓	cup golden raisins
2	tablespoons pignoli nuts

Roast Chicken:

1	roasting chicken (about 5 pounds)
1	tablespoon olive oil
1	teaspoon dried rosemary, crumbled
2	cloves garlic, finely chopped
¼	teaspoon salt

Herb Gravy:

2	tablespoons all-purpose flour
¼	cup white wine
1	teaspoon dried rosemary, chopped
1	cup low-sodium chicken broth
1	teaspoon lemon juice
¼	teaspoon freshly ground pepper

1. Prepare the Brown Rice Stuffing: Sauté the onion in the oil in a saucepan over medium heat for 5 minutes, or until the onion is lightly golden. Add the brown rice and sauté for 5 minutes, or until the rice is lightly golden. Add the broth, thyme and rosemary. Bring the rice mixture to boiling. Lower the heat, cover the saucepan, and simmer the rice mixture for 40 minutes, or until the liquid is absorbed and the rice is tender. Stir in the pepper, prosciutto, raisins and pignoli nuts. Set aside the stuffing.

2. Preheat the oven to hot (425°).

3. Prepare the Roast Chicken: Remove the neck and giblets from the chicken. Rinse the chicken well inside and out with cold water. Pat the chicken dry inside and out with paper toweling. Starting from the edge of the cavity, gently loosen and lift the skin covering the breasts and legs, being careful not to tear the skin. Combine the oil, rosemary and garlic in a small bowl. Rub the oil mixture over the meat under the skin. Carefully press the skin back in place.

4. Spoon the stuffing loosely into the cavity. Tie the legs to the tail with string, and skewer the neck skin to the back. Place the chicken on a rack in a roasting pan. Sprinkle the chicken with the salt.

MENU

Split Pea Soup

Garlic & Rosemary Roast Chicken with Brown Rice Stuffing
(recipe, at left)

Oven-Roasted Red Potatoes

Green Beans with Sweet Red Pepper

Cherry Tomato & Chicory Salad

Individual Apple Pies
(recipe, page 194)

o ❖ o

CHICKEN: SAFE & SENSIBLE

● **Shopping:** Carefully examine the chicken in the package. Check the skin for blemishes or discoloration — normal color varies from yellow to white. The flesh should be pink, not gray. Make sure the package is intact. As soon as you get home, open the package and smell the chicken. If the chicken has an "off" odor, return it.

● **Thawing:** Thaw raw chicken in the refrigerator or microwave. Never leave raw chicken to thaw at room temperature, because bacteria may grow on it. For peak flavor, cook chicken shortly after thawing it.

MORE SAFE & SENSIBLE CHICKEN

● **Handling:** To prevent any bacteria present in raw chicken from being transferred to other foods, scrub your hands, utensils and work surfaces with soap and water right after handling raw chicken. Scour the cutting board, rinse it, and dry it. Use a different cutting board to prepare any vegetables that will be eaten raw.

● **Storing:** Uncooked chicken will keep in the refrigerator for up to 2 days; the chicken can be left in the store package. When storing uncooked chicken in the freezer, wrap the chicken with aluminum foil or more plastic wrap for double protection. Use frozen chicken within 2 months for best quality. Never leave raw or cooked chicken at room temperature for more than 2 hours.

● **Cooking:** To insure the destruction of salmonella bacteria, which cause food poisoning, be sure to cook chicken thoroughly; salmonella bacteria are killed by heat. There are several ways to test chicken for doneness. Insert a meat thermometer in the thickest part of the chicken, without touching a bone. A whole chicken is well done when the thermometer registers 180°; chicken parts are well done when the thermometer registers 160°. Pierce the chicken; the juices should run clear. Check the color of the flesh; well done chicken is opaque white, not translucent pink.

5. Roast the chicken, uncovered, in the preheated hot oven (425°) for 15 minutes. Reduce the oven temperature to slow (325°). Roast the chicken, basting it frequently with the pan drippings, for 2¼ hours more, or until an instant-read thermometer inserted in the thickest part of the thigh without touching the bone registers 180°. If the chicken browns too quickly, cover it with aluminum foil.

6. Remove the chicken to a warmed serving platter. Let the chicken stand for 20 minutes before carving it.

7. Prepare the Herb Gravy: Degrease the pan drippings. Pour off all but 1 tablespoon of the drippings from the pan. Set the pan over medium heat. Sprinkle the flour over the pan drippings, stirring to make a paste. Add the wine and the rosemary, stirring to loosen the browned bits from the bottom of the pan. Slowly add the broth, stirring constantly until the mixture is smooth. Bring the broth mixture to boiling. Lower the heat and simmer, stirring, for 3 to 5 minutes, or until the broth mixture is slightly thickened. Stir in the lemon juice and the pepper. Pour the gravy into a warmed gravy boat. Serve the chicken with the gravy.

CHICKEN COOKING TIME CHART

Chicken Type/ Part	Baking or Roasting 350° to 400°	Broiling 6 to 8 inches from heat	Poaching or Braising	Sautéing or Frying 350° to 375°
Breast quarter	40 to 60	15 to 20 per side		25
Leg/thigh combo	40 to 45	8 to 10 per side		15 to 20
Breast half, bone in	35 to 45	8 to 10 per side	20 to 25	20 to 25
Breast half, boned	25 to 30	5 per side	15 to 20	10 to 12
Breast half, flattened	15	2 to 3 per side		2 to 4
Fillet	15 to 20	2 to 3 per side		4 to 6
Drumstick	40 to 45	8 to 10 per side	25 to 30	15 to 20
Thigh	45 to 50	10 to 12 per side	30 to 35	20 to 25
Wing	25 to 35	5 to 8 per side	15 to 20	10 to 15
Whole fryer	1½ to 2¼ hours			
Whole roaster	2 to 3 hours			
Cornish game hen, 1 pound	60 to 70			

Cooking times are approximate, and given in minutes unless noted.

Savory Broth & Bread

A sure-fire winter warmer-upper — the perfect meal after skiing, sledding or just playing in the snow.

Caraway Rye Batter Bread

Yogurt adds tangy flavor and a tender crumb to this no-knead yeast loaf.

Bake loaves at 350° for 35 minutes; or bake rolls at 350° for 25 minutes.
Makes 2 loaves (12 slices each), or 2 dozen rolls.
Nutrient Value Per Slice: 130 calories, 4 g protein, 5 g fat,
18 g carbohydrate, 246 mg sodium, 29 mg cholesterol.

2	**packages active dry yeast**
½	**cup plus 1 tablespoon warm water (105° to 115°)***
½	**teaspoon sugar**
3	**cups all-purpose flour**
1½	**cups rye flour**
2	**teaspoons salt**
¼	**teaspoon baking soda**

2	**tablespoons caraway seeds**
1	**container (8 ounces) plain lowfat yogurt**
½	**cup (1 stick) butter or margarine, melted**
2	**eggs**
1	**egg white**
	Additional caraway seeds

MENU

Scotch Barley Broth
(recipe, page 103)
Caraway Rye Batter Bread
(recipe, at left)
Herbal Teas

> " *L*ittle Tom Tucker
> *Sings for his supper;*
> *What shall he eat?*
> *White bread*
> *and butter.*
> *How will he cut it*
> *Without e'er a knife?*
> *How will he*
> *be married*
> *Without e'er a wife?* "
>
> —Anonymous

Caraway Rye Batter Bread combines the earthy flavor of rye with the tanginess of yogurt.

1. Grease two 1-quart casserole or soufflé dishes, or 24 muffin-pan cups, or 1 casserole dish and 12 muffin-pan cups. Sprinkle the yeast over ½ cup of the warm water and the sugar in a large bowl. Stir to dissolve the yeast. Let the yeast mixture stand for 5 minutes, or until the mixture is foamy.

2. Stir 1½ cups of the all-purpose flour together with the rye flour, salt, baking soda and the 2 tablespoons of caraway seeds in a medium-size bowl.

3. Beat the yogurt, butter or margarine and the eggs into the yeast mixture until they are blended. Add the flour mixture. Beat the yeast-flour mixture with an electric mixer at medium-high speed for 1 minute. Add the remaining 1½ cups of all-purpose flour, and beat until they are well blended. Cover the bowl, and let the dough rise in a warm place, away from drafts, until it is doubled in size, for about 1 hour.

4. Punch down the dough. Divide the dough evenly among the prepared dishes or cups. Cover the dishes or cups, and let the dough rise in a warm place, away from drafts, until it is doubled in size, for about 45 minutes.

5. Preheat the oven to moderate (350°). Mix the egg white with the remaining tablespoon of warm water. Brush the tops of the loaves or rolls with the glaze. Sprinkle the tops with the additional caraway seeds.

6. Bake the loaves in the preheated moderate oven (350°) for 35 minutes, or the rolls for 25 minutes, or until the loaves or rolls are golden brown and sound hollow when tapped with your fingertips. Invert the loaves or rolls onto wire racks to cool.

__Note:__ Warm water should feel tepid when dropped on your wrist.

Scotch Barley Broth

LOW-FAT

Makes 6 servings.

Nutrient Value Per Serving: 214 calories, 10 g protein, 7 g fat, 29 g carbohydrate, 655 mg sodium, 20 mg cholesterol.

1 **pound lamb neck**	1 **all-purpose potato, peeled, and cut into ½-inch dice**
1 **can (14½ ounces) chicken broth**	1 **stalk celery, cut into ¼-inch-thick slices**
4 **cups water**	½ **teaspoon salt**
½ **cup pearl barley**	¼ **teaspoon freshly ground pepper**
2 **leeks, cut into ¼-inch-thick slices, and well rinsed**	1 **can (14½ ounces) tomatoes, undrained and chopped**
2 **carrots, peeled, and cut into ¼-inch-thick slices**	½ **cup frozen peas, thawed**
1 **medium-size turnip, peeled, and cut into ½-inch dice**	2 **tablespoons chopped parsley**

1. Combine the lamb, broth, water and barley in a large saucepan. Bring the mixture to boiling, skimming the foam from the surface.

2. Add the leek, carrot, turnip, potato, celery, salt and pepper to the saucepan. Cover the saucepan, and bring the mixture to boiling. Lower the heat and simmer the mixture for 1 hour, stirring occasionally.

3. Remove the lamb from the saucepan, and cut the meat from the bone. Return the lamb meat to the saucepan. Add the tomatoes with their liquid and the peas. Simmer the soup, covered, for 20 minutes, or until the soup is heated through. Remove the saucepan from the heat. Stir in the parsley, and serve the soup at once.

BARLEY

Like wheat, barley is a member of the grass family and was one of the first grains to be cultivated. At one time, barley was used extensively to make bread, but its low gluten content resulted in a heavy loaf. So barley gave way in bread-making to wheat flour, which is higher in protein as well as gluten. Today, most of the world's barley is used in the production of beer and scotch whiskey.

● Barley makes a tasty addition to hearty soups and stews. The barley sold in supermarkets is labeled pearl barley, which means the hull has been removed from the grain by a special polishing method. Store barley in an airtight container in the cupboard.

Culture Club

A delicious blending of cultures: Italian polenta and Spanish gazpacho.

Cheese Polenta & Chili

Polenta is easy to make with this soaking method, and the mild cornmeal mixture is a perfect complement to the spicy vegetable chili. The polenta can be made 1 or 2 days in advance; broil it just before serving.

LOW-CHOLESTEROL
Broil polenta for 3 minutes.
Makes 4 servings.
Nutrient Value Per Serving: 494 calories, 17 g protein, 21 g fat, 63 g carbohydrate, 1,201 mg sodium, 33 mg cholesterol.

Cheese Polenta:

1	cup yellow cornmeal
2½	cups water
½	teaspoon salt
1	cup shredded Fontina, Monterey Jack OR: Gruyère cheese (4 ounces)

Chili:

1	large onion, finely chopped (1 cup)
2	cloves garlic, finely chopped
1	medium-size sweet red pepper, cored, seeded and finely chopped
1	tablespoon chili powder
½	teaspoon ground cumin
1	small jalapeño pepper, seeded and finely chopped (optional)

1	tablespoon vegetable oil
8	ounces zucchini, chopped
8	ounces yellow squash, coarsely chopped
1	cup fresh corn kernels
1	can (28 ounces) tomatoes in juice, drained and ½ cup juice reserved
1	can (10½ ounces) red kidney beans, drained and rinsed
½	teaspoon salt
¼	teaspoon freshly ground pepper

Vegetable oil

1	cup shredded Fontina, Monterey Jack OR: Gruyère cheese (4 ounces) (optional)

1. Prepare the Cheese Polenta: Stir together the cornmeal, water and salt in a medium-size, nonstick saucepan. Let the cornmeal mixture stand for 20 minutes. Bring the cornmeal mixture to boiling over medium heat, whisking constantly. Lower the heat and simmer, stirring often, for 30 minutes; the cornmeal mixture will be very stiff. Stir in the Fontina, Monterey Jack or Gruyère cheese. Spread the polenta evenly in an 8-inch square baking pan.

2. Prepare the Chili: Sauté the onion, garlic, red pepper, chili powder, cumin and, if you wish, jalapeño pepper in the oil in a very large skillet over medium heat for 5 minutes, or until the onion is tender.

3. Stir in the zucchini, squash, corn, tomatoes, reserved tomato juice, kidney beans, salt and pepper, breaking up the tomatoes with a wooden spoon. Simmer the chili, covered, for 15 to 20 minutes, or until the vegetables are tender.

MENU

Cheese Polenta & Chili
(recipe, at left)

White Gazpacho
(recipe, page 105)

Tossed Green Salad

Piña Colada Sherbet
(recipe, page 209)

○ ❖ ○

"Never commit yourself to cheese without having first examined it."
— *T.S. Eliot*

4. Meanwhile, preheat the broiler. Cut the polenta into 4 squares, and cut each square diagonally into 2 triangles. Place the polenta triangles on a greased baking sheet. Brush the triangles with vegetable oil.

5. Broil the polenta 6 inches from the heat source for 3 minutes, or until the polenta is crisp and golden on top. Top the polenta with the chili and, if you wish, 1 cup of shredded Fontina, Monterey Jack or Gruyère cheese.

White Gazpacho

LOW-CHOLESTEROL • LOW-FAT

Makes 4 servings.

Nutrient Value Per Serving: 110 calories, 7 g protein, 2 g fat, 18 g carbohydrate, 622 mg sodium, 7 mg cholesterol.

3	**cups buttermilk**
2	**tablespoons cider vinegar**
1	**tablespoon sugar**
¾	**teaspoon salt**
4	**to 6 drops liquid red pepper seasoning**
2	**green onions, trimmed**
1	**small sweet red pepper, cored, seeded, and cut into small pieces**

1	**medium-size tomato, cored, seeded, and cut into small pieces**
1	**clove garlic**
1	**large cucumber, seeded, and cut into cubes**
1	**stalk celery, cut into cubes**
	Chives, for garnish (optional)

1. Combine the buttermilk, vinegar, sugar, salt and liquid red pepper seasoning in a medium-size bowl. Place the bowl inside a larger bowl of ice water to chill the buttermilk mixture.

2. Slice the green parts of the green onion, and add them to the buttermilk mixture. Add the red pepper and the tomato.

3. Place the garlic and the white parts of the green onion in the container of a food processor or electric blender. Whirl until the garlic and onion are finely chopped. Add the cucumber and the celery, and whirl until they are finely chopped.

4. Stir the chopped vegetables into the buttermilk-tomato mixture. Cover the bowl, and chill the gazpacho for 30 minutes. Serve the gazpacho well chilled. If you wish, garnish the gazpacho with chives.

GLORIOUS GAZPACHO

Born in the sunny south of Spain, gazpacho is a chilled soup that most often is made with a tomato base. The name is derived from the Moorish, and means "soaked bread." Gazpacho is a light and lively meal-opener or, paired with a sandwich, a cooling summer supper. The tomato base makes this soup particularly rich in vitamin C.

Giving Thanks

Gathering together with family and friends to celebrate the bounty of the earth—what could be more wonderful?

Roast Turkey with Chestnut Bread Stuffing

To keep the turkey from drying out, roast it in a slow oven from start to finish, and keep it tightly covered for the first 3½ hours. Be sure to make the Turkey Giblet Stock before starting the stuffing.

LOW-FAT

Roast turkey at 300° for 4½ to 5 hours; bake extra stuffing at 350° for 30 to 35 minutes.

Makes 12 servings, plus leftovers.

Nutrient Value Per Serving: 757 calories, 85 g protein, 22 g fat, 49 g carbohydrate, 860 mg sodium, 254 mg cholesterol.

Chestnut Bread Stuffing:

1	large onion, coarsely chopped (1 cup)
6	large stalks celery, coarsely chopped (2 cups)
¼	cup (½ stick) butter
4	teaspoons poultry seasoning
1½	teaspoons rubbed sage
1	teaspoon salt
½	teaspoon freshly ground pepper
⅓	cup chopped parsley
2	eggs, beaten
1¼	cups Turkey Giblet Stock (see Tip, at right)
1	large loaf (2 pounds) stale white bread, cut into ¾-inch cubes
1	can (1 pound) unsweetened whole chestnuts, drained and quartered
1	oven-ready turkey (14 pounds), with giblets and fat removed
2	tablespoons melted butter
	Turkey Giblet Gravy (recipe, page 109)

1. Preheat the oven to slow (300°).

2. Prepare the Chestnut Bread Stuffing: Cook the onion and the celery in the butter in a large, heavy Dutch oven for 10 minutes, or until the vegetables are softened. Remove the Dutch oven from the heat. Stir in the poultry seasoning, sage, salt, pepper, parsley, eggs and Turkey Giblet Stock. Stir in the bread cubes and the chestnuts.

3. Spoon the stuffing lightly into the turkey neck cavity, and skewer the neck skin to the back. Twist the wing tips until they rest flat against the skewered neck skin. Spoon the stuffing lightly into the body cavity. Lace the opening closed with poultry pins and string, and truss the legs close to the body. Place the extra stuffing in a buttered 3-quart casserole dish. Cover the dish, and refrigerate the extra stuffing.

4. Brush the turkey with the melted butter. Place the turkey, breast side up, on a rack in a roasting pan. Cover the turkey snugly with a lid, or tent it with aluminum foil.

○ ❖ ○

TURKEY GIBLET STOCK

Combine the turkey giblets and liver with 4 cups of water in a small, heavy saucepan. Simmer the stock for 10 minutes. Remove the liver, and refrigerate it. Cook the stock for 10 minutes more. Remove the giblets, and refrigerate them with the liver.

- Read through your holiday recipes and make a list of the special ingredients you'll need, such as whole vanilla beans or chocolate sprinkles. Stock up on these before the holiday crush.
- Freeze fresh, raw cranberries when they first come in season. Grind or chop them later to add to muffins or sauces.
- Buy extra freezer storage bags to have on hand for storing holiday baked goods and leftovers.
- Purchase canned pumpkin, evaporated or condensed milk, nutmeg, cinnamon, allspice, ground ginger, cookie decorations, and dried fruits well ahead of holiday baking time; stores often run out of these items during the holidays.

5. Roast the turkey in the preheated slow oven (300°) for 3½ hours. Uncover the turkey. Roast the turkey, basting it every 30 minutes with the pan drippings, for 1 to 1½ hours more, or until the turkey is richly browned and an instant-read thermometer inserted in the meatiest part of the thigh without touching the bone registers 175°.

6. Remove the turkey from the oven. Raise the oven temperature to 350°. Bake the extra stuffing for 30 to 35 minutes, or until it is heated through.

7. Meanwhile, remove the pins and string from the turkey. Cover the turkey with aluminum foil, and let the turkey stand for 25 minutes.

8. Prepare the Turkey Giblet Gravy.

9. Serve the turkey with the stuffing and the gravy.

Peanut Pumpkin Soup

Make this soup 1 or 2 days in advance, and refrigerate it until serving time. Bring the soup just to a simmer before serving it, or serve it cold.

Makes 10 servings.
Nutrient Value Per Serving: 343 calories, 13 g protein, 25 g fat, 21 g carbohydrate, 631 mg sodium, 25 mg cholesterol.

4	medium-size onions, chopped (about 2 cups)	1	can (13¾ ounces) beef broth
6	shallots, finely chopped (½ cup)	1	can (29 ounces) solid-pack pumpkin (not pumpkin pie filling)
4	cloves garlic, finely chopped (1½ tablespoons)	1	cup firmly packed creamy peanut butter
1	teaspoon dried marjoram, crumbled	2	cups milk
½	teaspoon dried thyme, crumbled	2	cups half-and-half
¼	teaspoon freshly grated nutmeg	1	teaspoon liquid red pepper seasoning
3	tablespoons peanut OR: vegetable oil	½	cup coarsely chopped dry-roasted peanuts, for garnish (optional)
1	can (13¾ ounces) chicken broth		

1. Sauté the onion, shallot, garlic, marjoram, thyme and nutmeg in the peanut or vegetable oil in a large saucepan or Dutch oven for 5 minutes, or until the vegetables are golden. Reduce the heat to low, cover the saucepan and cook for 25 minutes, or until the vegetables are limp.

2. Add the chicken broth and the beef broth to the saucepan. Simmer the broth mixture, covered, for 20 minutes. Cool the broth mixture for 15 minutes. Working in batches, purée the broth mixture in the container of a food processor or electric blender. Or force the broth mixture through a food mill.

3. Return the broth mixture to the saucepan. Stir in the pumpkin, peanut butter, milk, half-and-half and liquid red pepper seasoning. Bring the soup to a simmer over medium heat, and serve it immediately. Or refrigerate the soup, tightly covered, until shortly before serving it. Serve the soup chilled. Or reheat the soup over medium-low heat for about 10 minutes, or until the soup is simmering. If you wish, garnish the soup with ½ cup of coarsely chopped dry-roasted peanuts.

Creamed Onions

Freshly grated nutmeg adds an extra special flavor. Save the onion cooking water for the cream sauce and for Turkey Giblet Gravy (recipe, page 109).

Makes 10 servings.

Nutrient Value Per Serving: 183 calories, 3 g protein, 14 g fat, 14 g carbohydrate, 179 mg sodium, 45 mg cholesterol.

3	pounds small white onions	⅛	teaspoon freshly ground pepper
2	quarts boiling water	1	cup heavy cream
¼	cup (½ stick) butter or margarine	½	teaspoon salt
3	tablespoons all-purpose flour		Additional freshly grated nutmeg (optional)
¼	teaspoon freshly grated nutmeg		

1. Blanch the onions in boiling water in a large saucepan just until the outer skins wrinkle. Drain the onions. When the onions are cool, slip off the skins. Trim the root ends.

2. Cook the onions in the 2 quarts of boiling water in the same saucepan, covered, for 10 minutes, or until the onions are fork tender. Drain the onions, reserving the cooking liquid.

3. Melt the butter or margarine in the same saucepan. Stir in the flour, the ¼ teaspoon of nutmeg and the pepper. Add the cream and 1 cup of the onion cooking liquid; reserve the remaining onion cooking liquid for Turkey Giblet Gravy. Cook the cream sauce, stirring constantly, for 3 minutes, or until the sauce is thickened and smooth, and no raw flour taste remains. Stir in the salt.

4. Return the onions to the saucepan, and heat them in the cream sauce for 2 to 3 minutes. Pour the creamed onions into a serving dish. If you wish, sprinkle the creamed onions with additional freshly grated nutmeg.

THANKSGIVING TIMESAVING TIPS

- Include plenty of make-ahead dishes, such as Peanut Pumpkin Soup (recipe, page 107), Cranberry Orange Sauce (recipe, page 111), Pumpkin Cheesecake (recipe, page 114) and Apple Walnut Pie (recipe, page 112).

- Do as much food preparation as possible in advance. For example, mix the dry ingredients for the stuffing the day before and store them in the refrigerator. Add the remaining ingredients just before stuffing the turkey.

- Set the table well ahead of time. Have all the serving dishes and flatware out and ready.

- Encourage the kids to pitch in. They can peel and trim vegetables, make place cards, set the table, arrange baskets of fruit and flowers.

A tasty part of the holiday feast: Creamed Onions.

Turkey Giblet Gravy

LOW-CHOLESTEROL
Makes twenty-four ¼ cup servings.
Nutrient Value Per Serving: 65 calories, 1 g protein, 5 g fat,
5 g carbohydrate, 236 mg sodium, 4 mg cholesterol.

½ **cup fat skimmed from turkey pan drippings***	2 **to 3 teaspoons salt**
1 **cup quick-mixing flour**	½ **teaspoon freshly ground pepper**
3 **cups vegetable cooking liquids from Maple-Glazed Carrots, Creamed Onions, and Mashed Potatoes OR: canned reduced-sodium chicken broth**	**Cooked turkey giblets from Turkey Giblet Stock, finely chopped**
2½ **cups Turkey Giblet Stock (see Tip, page 106)**	**Cooked turkey liver from Turkey Giblet Stock, finely chopped (optional)**

Stir together the fat and the flour in a large, heavy saucepan until they are
blended. Stir in the vegetable cooking liquids or broth, the Turkey Giblet
Stock, salt and pepper. Simmer the mixture, stirring, for 5 minutes, or until
the mixture is thickened and no raw flour taste remains. Stir in the turkey
giblets and, if you wish, turkey liver, and cook for 2 minutes, or until the
gravy is heated through.

*Note: *If there is not enough fat from the turkey pan drippings, add melted
butter to equal ½ cup.*

Mashed Potatoes

*These mashed potatoes are unusually fluffy because they're put through a food
mill. Mill them in batches, adding some of the butter and milk to each batch.*

Makes 10 servings.
Nutrient Value Per Serving: 253 calories, 5 g protein, 11 g fat,
34 g carbohydrate, 564 mg sodium, 32 mg cholesterol.

8 **large baking potatoes (5 to 5½ pounds), peeled, and cut into 2-inch chunks**	2 **cups milk**
	2 **teaspoons salt**
½ **cup (1 stick) butter or margarine**	½ **teaspoon freshly ground pepper**

1. Place the potatoes in a large saucepan with enough cold water to cover
them. Gently boil the potatoes, covered, for 2 minutes, or until the
potatoes are fork tender. Drain the potatoes, reserving the cooking liquid
for Turkey Giblet Gravy *(recipe, above).*

2. Place one quarter of the potatoes in a food mill set over a large,
heatproof bowl. Add one quarter each of the butter or margarine and the
milk. Push the potatoes through the mill. Repeat 3 times. Beat in the salt
and the pepper. Taste the mashed potatoes, and adjust the seasonings if
necessary. Return the mashed potatoes to the saucepan, cover the
saucepan, and keep the mashed potatoes warm.

○ ❖ ○

FABULOUS FOOD GIFTS

• Bake and freeze extra cookies,
muffins, pies and breads for last
minute gifts and guests.
• Mix a variety of salad dressings,
such as tarragon, citrus and dill.
Pour the dressings into pretty
bottles, and attach "from the kitchen
of" labels. For a special gift, give a
bottle of dressing in a salad bowl
along with salad servers.
• Wrap food gifts in yellow, rust,
red and brown tissue paper, or a
combination of autumn colors. Or
wrap food items in pretty cloth
napkins or dish towels.
• Write your favorite recipes in a
pretty book with blank pages as a
great gift for a loves-to-cook friend.

Candied Sweet Potatoes with Pineapple

These candied sweet potatoes can be prepared in advance, and baked just before serving time.

LOW-CHOLESTEROL ▪ LOW-SODIUM ▪ LOW-FAT

Bake sweet potatoes at 400° for 1 hour; bake candied sweet potatoes at 350° for 35 minutes.

Makes 10 servings.

Nutrient Value Per Serving: 272 calories, 3 g protein, 5 g fat, 55 g carbohydrate, 73 mg sodium, 12 mg cholesterol.

5½ **pounds sweet potatoes**	½ **teaspoon ground allspice**
⅓ **cup firmly packed dark brown sugar**	¼ **teaspoon freshly grated nutmeg**
¼ **cup (½ stick) butter or margarine, at room temperature**	⅛ **teaspoon freshly ground pepper**
1 **can (8½ ounces) crushed pineapple, drained with 3 tablespoons liquid reserved**	

1. Preheat the oven to hot (400°).

2. Bake the sweet potatoes in the preheated hot oven (400°) for 1 hour, or until the sweet potatoes are fork tender. Cool the sweet potatoes to room temperature.

3. Slip the skins off the sweet potatoes. Place the sweet potatoes in a large bowl and mash them.

4. Beat in the brown sugar, butter or margarine, pineapple, reserved pineapple liquid, allspice, nutmeg and pepper. Spoon the candied sweet potatoes into a buttered 3-quart casserole dish. Cover the casserole dish with plastic wrap, and refrigerate the candied sweet potatoes until 1 hour before serving.

5. Remove the casserole dish from the refrigerator and let the candied sweet potatoes stand at room temperature, covered, for 25 minutes.

6. Preheat the oven to moderate (350°).

7. Bake the candied sweet potatoes, uncovered, in the preheated moderate oven (350°) for 35 minutes, or until the candied sweet potatoes are heated through.

PERFECT PLANNING

A perfect party requires advance planning to run smoothly. Here are some guidelines to get you through the holiday cooking crunch with your spirit intact.

● Write out the menu, including the time it takes to prepare and cook each dish. Note which dishes can be prepared in advance. Be sure you have enough top burners on your stove to accommodate the number of pots you'll need for cooking the day of the dinner.

2 Days Ahead:
● Buy the perishables.
● Trim the vegetables. Store them in plastic bags in the refrigerator.
● Make the cranberry sauce, and refrigerate it.

1 Day Ahead:
● Bake the pies.
● Wash and dry the salad ingredients, and store them separately in the refrigerator.
● Set the table.
● Assemble the serving dishes and utensils in the kitchen.
● Prepare the stuffing's dry and liquid ingredients separately. Store them separately in the refrigerator.

Early in the Morning:
● Finish making the stuffing, stuff the bird, and put the bird in the oven. Prepare and cook the breads, relishes, first courses, side dishes, vegetables, and salads.

Maple-Glazed Carrots

LOW-CHOLESTEROL · LOW-SODIUM · LOW-FAT

Makes 10 servings.

Nutrient Value Per Serving: 119 calories, 1 g protein, 3 g fat, 24 g carbohydrate, 66 mg sodium, 6 mg cholesterol.

2½ **pounds uniform-size carrots, cut into 3 x ½ x ½-inch strips**	2 **tablespoons firmly packed dark brown sugar**
6 **cups boiling water**	½ **cup maple syrup**
2 **tablespoons butter**	

1. Cook the carrots in the boiling water in a large saucepan, covered, for 20 minutes, or just until the carrots are tender. Drain the carrots, reserving the cooking liquid for Turkey Giblet Gravy (*recipe, page 109*).

2. Meanwhile, melt the butter in a large, heavy skillet. Add the brown sugar and the maple syrup. Simmer the glaze, uncovered, for 8 to 10 minutes, or until the glaze is thick and syrupy.

3. When the carrots are done, add them to the skillet and toss them until they are glossy. Keep the glazed carrots warm. Toss the carrots again just before serving them.

Cranberry Orange Sauce

LOW-CHOLESTEROL · LOW-SODIUM · LOW-FAT

Makes 5 cups.

Nutrient Value Per Tablespoon: 27 calories, 0 g protein, 0 g fat, 7 g carbohydrate, 2 mg sodium, 0 mg cholesterol.

1 **cinnamon stick, broken in half**	2 **packages (12 ounces each), fresh OR: frozen cranberries**
4 **whole cloves**	1 **box (1 pound) light brown sugar**
2 **whole allspice, crushed**	2 **tablespoons lemon juice**
1 **navel orange with rind, finely chopped**	

1. Wrap a small piece of cheesecloth around the cinnamon stick halves, cloves and allspice, and tie the spice bag closed. Place the spice bag in a large, non-reactive saucepan.

2. Place the orange in a 4-cup liquid measure. Add enough cold water to equal 2½ cups. Add the orange mixture to the saucepan along with the cranberries, brown sugar and lemon juice. Simmer the cranberry sauce, uncovered, for 12 to 15 minutes, or until the sauce is thickened and the cranberry skins have popped. Cool the cranberry sauce to room temperature. Remove and discard the spice bag. Store the cranberry sauce in the refrigerator for up to 1 week.

Apple Walnut Pie

Bake at 350° for 40 minutes.

Makes 8 servings.

Nutrient Value Per Serving: 584 calories, 5 g protein, 27 g fat, 87 g carbohydrate, 264 mg sodium, 31 mg cholesterol.

Filling:

2½ pounds Golden Delicious apples (about 5 to 6 medium-size apples), peeled, cored, and sliced ¼ inch thick (8 cups)

2 tablespoons lemon juice

1 cup granulated sugar

1¼ teaspoons ground cinnamon

½ teaspoon freshly grated nutmeg

½ teaspoon finely grated lemon zest (yellow part of rind only)

3 tablespoons arrowroot paste OR: 2 tablespoons cornstarch blended with ¼ cup cold water

Topping:

¾ cup firmly packed dark brown sugar

¾ cup all-purpose flour

¾ cup coarsely chopped walnuts

½ cup (1 stick) melted butter or margarine

Baked 9-inch pie shell with high fluted edge (if using frozen crust, use deep-dish kind, and crimp edge again to make higher)

1 cup heavy cream, whipped to stiff peaks (optional)

1. Preheat the oven to moderate (350°).

2. Prepare the Filling: Place the apples in a very large, heavy skillet. Sprinkle the apples with the lemon juice. Combine the granulated sugar, cinnamon, nutmeg and lemon zest in a small bowl. Sprinkle the sugar mixture over the apples. Bring the apple mixture to boiling over medium heat. Adjust the heat so the apple mixture bubbles gently, and boil the mixture, uncovered, stirring occasionally, for 10 to 12 minutes, or until the apples give up most of their juices.

3. Increase the heat to high and boil the apple mixture, uncovered, stirring occasionally, for 5 minutes, or until the mixture is reduced by half.

4. Reduce the heat to low. When the apple mixture stops bubbling furiously, quickly pour the arrowroot paste or cornstarch mixture over the top of the apple mixture, and mix it in. Cook the filling, stirring, for about 2 minutes, or just until the filling clears and turns very thick.

5. Prepare the Topping: Mix the brown sugar, flour and chopped walnuts in a small bowl. Add the butter or margarine, and toss the topping with a fork just until it is crumbly.

6. Spoon the filling into the pie shell, mounding the filling in the center. Crumble the topping thickly over the filling, mounding the topping in the center; do not pack down the topping.

7. Bake the pie in the preheated moderate oven (350°) for 40 minutes, or just until the filling bubbles and the topping is crisp. Cool the pie for several hours. If you wish, top each serving with a dollop of whipped cream.

ARROWROOT

A plant grown in the West Indies, the root of which yields a starch used to thicken sauces. Arrowroot is sold in powder form. Use it as an alternative to flour or cornstarch to thicken sauces, puddings, soups and gravies. Arrowroot also is used in making cookies.

○ ❖ ○

"*Driven from every other corner of the earth, freedom of thought and the right of private judgment in matters of conscience direct their course to this happy country as their last asylum.*"

—Samuel Adams

*Apple Walnut Pie and Pumpkin
Cheesecake (recipe, page 114)
are spectacular make-ahead
desserts for the holiday.*

Pumpkin Cheesecake

This cheesecake can be baked 1 or 2 days in advance.

Bake at 350° for 60 minutes, then at 450° for 10 minutes.
Makes 20 servings.

Nutrient Value Per Serving: 411 calories, 7 g protein, 27 g fat,
36 g carbohydrate, 254 mg sodium, 121 mg cholesterol.

Crust:

2	**cups graham cracker crumbs**
1	**cup pecans, finely chopped**
½	**cup granulated sugar**
½	**teaspoon ground cinnamon**
½	**teaspoon ground ginger**
¼	**teaspoon ground nutmeg**
½	**cup (1 stick) melted butter or margarine**

Filling:

3	**packages (8 ounces each) cream cheese, softened**
1¼	**cups firmly packed light brown sugar**
6	**eggs**

1	**can (1 pound) solid-pack pumpkin (not pumpkin pie filling)**
1	**teaspoon orange extract**
1	**teaspoon rum extract**
1	**teaspoon ground cinnamon**
1	**teaspoon ground ginger**
¼	**teaspoon ground nutmeg**

Topping:

1½	**cups dairy sour cream**
⅓	**cup firmly packed light brown sugar**
1	**teaspoon rum extract**
⅛	**teaspoon ground nutmeg**
⅓	**cup coarsely chopped pecans**

1. Preheat the oven to moderate (350°).

2. Prepare the Crust: Combine the graham cracker crumbs, chopped pecans, granulated sugar, cinnamon, ginger, nutmeg and butter or margarine in a large bowl. Spoon the crust into a 10-inch springform pan. Pat the crust firmly across the bottom and halfway up the sides of the pan. Place the pan on a baking sheet.

3. Prepare the Filling: Beat together the cream cheese and the brown sugar in a large bowl until the mixture is smooth. Beat in the eggs, pumpkin, orange and rum extracts, cinnamon, ginger and nutmeg until the filling is smooth. Scrape the filling into the prepared pan.

4. Bake the cheesecake in the preheated moderate oven (350°) for 60 minutes, or until the filling is set in the center. Cool the cheesecake on a wire rack for 20 minutes. Increase the oven temperature to 450°.

5. Meanwhile, prepare the Topping: Stir together the sour cream, brown sugar, rum extract and nutmeg in a small bowl until they are blended. Spread the mixture evenly on the cooled cheesecake. Sprinkle the chopped pecans over the top.

6. Bake the cheesecake in the preheated very hot oven (450°) for 10 minutes. Cool the cheesecake on the wire rack to room temperature. Refrigerate the cheesecake for at least 8 hours, or overnight. Serve the cheesecake chilled.

SEASONAL SCENT-SATIONS

Fill your home with the scents of the holiday season.

● Make a spicy simmering potpourri by combining ½ cup of carnation petals, ¼ cup of dried sweet woodruff leaves, 3 tablespoons of unpeeled dried apple, one 3-inch-long cinnamon stick, 1½ teaspoons of grated nutmeg (1 whole nutmeg), 1 tablespoon of whole cloves, 3 drops of cinnamon- or vanilla-scented oil, and several long strands of lemon, lime and orange peel. Place 1 tablespoon of the potpourri in a pot of water, bring the water to boiling, and simmer the potpourri over low heat until the entire house is scented.

● For a fragrant fire, try adding one of the following: Tiny pieces of orange peel, to give your home a wonderful citrus smell; bits of pine cones, to bring the scent of the woods indoors; cinnamon sticks, to fill the house with a rich, spicy fragrance.

Christmas Cookie Bake

Get out the aprons, bowls and baking sheets! Here's a spectacular selection of festive holiday cookies.

Apricot Diamonds

If you wish, make these diamonds sparkle with an apricot glaze.

Bake crust at 350° for 15 minutes; bake diamonds at 350° for 25 minutes.
Makes about 7 dozen diamonds.
Nutrient Value Per Diamond: 51 calories, 1 g protein, 2 g fat,
7 g carbohydrate, 13 mg sodium, 12 mg cholesterol.

Crust:
¾ **cup (1½ sticks) unsalted butter, cut into pieces**
1½ **cups all-purpose flour**
⅓ **cup 10X (confectioners' powdered) sugar**
⅛ **teaspoon salt**

Topping:
6 **ounces dried apricots**
1½ **cups granulated sugar**

½ **cup pecans**
3 **eggs**
3 **tablespoons lemon juice**
2 **tablespoons all-purpose flour**
¾ **teaspoon baking powder**
⅛ **teaspoon salt**

½ **cup apricot preserves, for glaze (optional)**
2 **tablespoons shelled pistachio nuts, chopped (optional)**

1. Preheat the oven to moderate (350°).

2. Prepare the Crust: Combine the butter, flour, 10X (confectioners' powdered) sugar and salt in the container of a food processor or electric blender. Whirl until the ingredients are combined. Press the crust into an even layer across the bottom of a 15 x 10-inch jelly-roll pan.

3. Bake the crust in the preheated moderate oven (350°) for 15 minutes. Leave the oven on.

4. Prepare the Topping: Cover the apricots with boiling water in a small bowl. Let the apricots stand for 5 minutes to soften. Drain the apricots well, and pat them dry with paper toweling. Combine the apricots with the granulated sugar and the pecans in the processor container. Whirl until the apricots are chopped. Remove the apricot mixture. Place the eggs in the processor container. Whirl until the eggs are light colored. Add the lemon juice, flour, baking powder, salt and apricot mixture. Whirl just until the ingredients are mixed. Pour the topping over the crust.

5. Bake the cake in the preheated moderate oven (350°) for 25 minutes, or until the topping is set. Cool the cake in the pan on a wire rack. If you wish, glaze the cake by melting ½ cup of apricot preserves in a small saucepan. Brush the glaze over the top of the cake. If you wish, sprinkle the cake with 2 tablespoons of chopped shelled pistachio nuts. Cut the cake into 1¼-inch diamonds or squares.

Swedish Ginger Cutouts

Bake at 375° for 6 to 8 minutes.
Makes 2 dozen stockings OR: 3⅓ dozen candy canes.
Nutrient Value Per Stocking: 97 calories, 1 g protein, 4 g fat,
14 g carbohydrate, 38 mg sodium, 19 mg cholesterol.

1¾ **cups all-purpose flour**	1 **tablespoon grated orange zest (orange part of rind only)**
1 **teaspoon baking soda**	
1 **teaspoon ground cinnamon**	
½ **teaspoon ground ginger**	1 **tablespoon light corn syrup**
¼ **teaspoon ground cloves**	**Nonstick vegetable cooking spray**
½ **cup (1 stick) unsalted butter, softened**	1 **cup Decorator Icing (recipe, page 119)**
¾ **cup sugar**	
1 **egg**	

1. Stir together the flour, baking soda, cinnamon, ginger and cloves on wax paper until the ingredients are well mixed. Set aside the flour mixture.

2. Beat together the butter, sugar, egg, orange zest and corn syrup in a medium-size bowl until the butter mixture is light colored and fluffy. Stir in the flour mixture until it is well blended. Divide the dough into quarters, and flatten each quarter into a disk. Wrap the disks individually in plastic wrap, and chill them thoroughly.

3. When ready to bake the cutouts, preheat the oven to moderate (375°). Spray several baking sheets with nonstick vegetable cooking spray.

4. Roll out each dough disk on a lightly floured surface to a ⅛-inch thickness. Cut out the dough with floured 4-inch stocking-shaped cookie cutters, or 3½-inch candy cane-shaped cookie cutters. Place the cutouts 2 inches apart on the prepared baking sheets. Reroll and cut out the scraps as necessary.

5. Bake the cutouts in the preheated moderate oven (375°) for 6 to 8 minutes, or until the cutouts are lightly browned. Cool the cutouts on the baking sheets on wire racks for 5 minutes. Remove the cutouts to the wire racks to cool completely. Frost the cutouts with the Decorator Icing.

Mincemeat Squares

A spicy treat that's perfect for the holiday season, or any time of year.

Bake at 350° for 35 minutes.
Makes 9 squares.
Nutrient Value Per Square: 348 calories, 5 g protein, 16 g fat,
47 g carbohydrate, 376 mg sodium, 51 mg cholesterol.

1¾ **cups all-purpose flour**	½ **cup sugar**
1 **teaspoon baking soda**	1 **egg**
½ **teaspoon baking powder**	1 **teaspoon vanilla**
¼ **teaspoon salt**	1 **cup prepared mincemeat**
½ **cup (1 stick) butter or margarine, softened**	½ **cup chopped walnuts**

MINCEMEAT

Mincemeat is a finely chopped mixture of fruit and spices, such as apples, currants, candied citrus peel, cinnamon, nutmeg, mace and cloves. It can be prepared with or without meat; meatless versions of mincemeat have become increasingly popular. Brandy often is added to cooked mincemeat.

● Commercially prepared mincemeat is available in jars. Dried, condensed mincemeat is sold in packages, and can be reconstituted with water. Mincemeat is used to make breads, sauces, pies, and other desserts.

1. Preheat the oven to moderate (350°). Grease a 9 x 9 x 2-inch square baking pan.

2. Combine the flour, baking soda, baking powder and salt in a small bowl. Beat the butter or margarine with the sugar in a large bowl until the butter mixture is creamy. Add the egg and the vanilla, and beat well.

3. Gradually beat the flour mixture into the butter mixture. Stir in the mincemeat and the chopped walnuts until they are well mixed. Spread the batter in the prepared pan.

4. Bake the cake in the preheated moderate oven (350°) for 35 minutes, or until a wooden pick inserted in the center comes out clean. Cool the cake in the pan on a wire rack. Cut the cake into 9 squares.

Pinwheel Cookies

Because of their swirled design, these also are called "dreidel" cookies, after the spinning top game played during the celebration of Hanukkah.

Bake at 350° for 15 to 20 minutes.
Makes about 5 dozen pinwheels.
Nutrient Value Per Pinwheel: 86 calories, 1 g protein, 7 g fat, 6 g carbohydrate, 63 mg sodium, 16 mg cholesterol.

Pastry:
1	cup (2 sticks) butter, softened
1	package (8 ounces) cream cheese, softened
¼	cup dairy sour cream
2¼	cups sifted all-purpose flour
½	teaspoon salt

Filling:
2	cups finely ground walnuts
½	cup sugar
1	teaspoon ground cinnamon
1	egg
1	teaspoon grated orange zest (orange part of rind only)

1. Prepare the Pastry: Beat together the butter and the cream cheese in a large bowl with an electric mixer until the mixture is creamy. Beat in the sour cream. Stir in the flour and the salt until a firm dough forms; add more flour, if necessary. Divide the dough in half, and flatten each half into a 4-inch square. Wrap the squares individually in plastic wrap, and refrigerate them overnight.

2. When the dough is ready, prepare the Filling: Combine the ground walnuts with the sugar, cinnamon, egg and orange zest in a small bowl.

3. Roll out one dough square on a floured surface to a ¼-inch-thick 9-inch square. Spread ¾ cup of the filling evenly over the square, and roll up the square jelly-roll style. Wrap the roll in aluminum foil. Repeat with the remaining dough square and filling. Refrigerate the rolls for at least 3 hours.

4. When ready to bake the cookies, preheat the oven to moderate (350°). Lightly grease 2 large baking sheets. Using a serrated knife, slice the rolls ¼ inch thick. Place the slices ½ inch apart on the prepared baking sheets; reshape the slices into rounds, if necessary.

5. Bake the cookies in the preheated moderate oven (350°) for 15 to 20 minutes, or until the cookies are firm and golden brown. Cool the cookies on the baking sheets on wire racks for 10 minutes. Remove the cookies to the wire racks to cool completely.

BAKING THE BEST COOKIES

● Carefully measure the amounts called for in a recipe, and follow the recipe directions exactly.

● When working with a soft dough, try to avoid extremes in kitchen temperatures. If the room is too cool, the dough will become too stiff to work with; if the room is too hot, the dough will become too soft.

● If a recipe calls for firm, chilled dough, keep the bowl of dough in the refrigerator and remove only the amount needed to roll or cut out.

● Don't use baking sheets that touch the sides of the oven. This prevents the circulation of heat necessary for even baking.

● Use nonstick vegetable cooking spray, or a very thin layer of vegetable shortening, to grease baking sheets.

● Leave plenty of room between the cookies on the baking sheets so the cookies won't spread out and merge while baking.

● Invest in an oven thermometer. An oven's actual temperature may vary widely from the temperature indicated on its dial; a good oven thermometer is the most accurate way to gauge oven temperature.

● Position the oven rack in the center of the oven to insure evenly baked cookies.

● Check the cookies for doneness at the minimum baking time. The maximum baking time may be too long, and the cookies may burn.

Orange Stars

Bake largest stars at 350° for 8 to 10 minutes; bake smaller stars at 350° for 5 to 7 minutes.

Makes about 3¼ dozen star stacks.

Nutrient Value Per Star Stack: 107 calories, 1 g protein, 6 g fat, 13 g carbohydrate, 58 mg sodium, 25 mg cholesterol.

1 **cup plus 2 tablespoons (2¼ sticks) unsalted butter, softened**	1 **teaspoon vanilla**
⅔ **cup sugar**	2 **egg yolks**
1 **teaspoon salt**	3½ **cups all-purpose flour**
2 **tablespoons dark rum**	**Nonstick vegetable cooking spray**
1 **tablespoon grated orange zest (orange part of rind only)**	2 **tablespoons orange marmalade**
	1 **cup Decorator Icing (recipe, page 119)**

1. Beat together the butter, sugar, salt, rum, orange zest, vanilla and egg yolks in a large bowl until the mixture is light colored and fluffy. Stir in the flour until it is well blended.

2. Divide the dough into quarters, and flatten each quarter into a disk. Wrap each disk individually in plastic wrap. Refrigerate the disks for at least 2 hours, or overnight.

3. When ready to bake, preheat the oven to moderate (350°). Spray several baking sheets with nonstick vegetable cooking spray.

4. Roll out each dough disk on a piece of lightly floured wax paper to a ⅛-inch thickness. Using 3-inch, 2-inch and 1-inch star-shaped cookie cutters, cut out an equal number of each size star. Place the largest stars 1 inch apart on one baking sheet, and the smaller stars on another baking sheet. Reroll and cut out the scraps as necessary.

5. Bake the largest stars in the preheated moderate oven (350°) for 8 to 10 minutes, and the smaller stars for 5 to 7 minutes, or until the stars are very lightly colored. Cool the stars on the baking sheets on wire racks for 1 minute. Remove the stars to the wire racks to cool completely.

6. To assemble the star stacks, spread the bottoms of a medium-size and small star with some of the orange marmalade. Press the medium-size star onto a large star, and the small star onto the medium-size star to make a graduated stack. Repeat with the remaining stars and marmalade.

7. Frost the stars with the Decorator Icing.

THE GREAT CHRISTMAS COOKIE SWAP

A cookie swap is a wonderful way to make the most of your Christmas baking, and have a good time with friends, too! Here are some simple guidelines to make this year's cookie swap the best ever.

● Limit the number of guests to 10 or fewer; more than 10 people at a swap can be overwhelming.

● Schedule the swap for the 2nd week in December. This is far enough ahead of Christmas that the swap won't overlap last-minute shopping time, but close enough to Christmas that the cookies won't become stale before holiday entertaining begins.

● Ask each guest to bring 3 or 4 dozen cookies; the guests should take home the same number of cookies they bring to the swap.

● Remind guests to bring empty containers for their swap cookies. Have a few sturdy paper plates on hand for those who forget.

● Ask the guests to include their favorite cookie recipes, on 3 x 5-inch file cards, with their swap cookies; most people enjoy exchanging the recipes as well as the cookies.

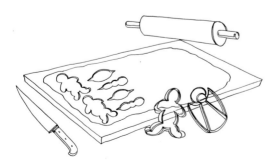

Linzer Jewels

Bake at 350° for 30 minutes.

Makes about 5 dozen cookies.

Nutrient Value Per Cookie: 113 calories, 1 g protein, 5 g fat, 17 g carbohydrate, 40 mg sodium, 17 mg cholesterol.

1¼ **cups (2½ sticks) unsalted butter, softened**	1 **egg yolk**
¾ **cup sugar**	2½ **cups all-purpose flour**
1 **teaspoon salt**	1 **cup ground unblanched almonds (about ⅔ cup whole almonds)**
1 **teaspoon grated lemon zest (yellow part of rind only)**	2½ **cups raspberry jam (about 30 ounces)**
½ **teaspoon ground cinnamon**	
1 **egg**	

1. Beat together the butter, sugar, salt, lemon zest, cinnamon, egg and egg yolk in a large bowl with an electric mixer until the mixture is fluffy. Stir in the flour and the ground almonds. Shape the dough into a ball, and place it in a plastic bag. Refrigerate the dough for at least 1 hour.

2. When ready to bake, preheat the oven to moderate (350°). Press two-thirds of the dough into an even layer across the bottom and up the sides of an ungreased 15 x 10 x 1-inch baking pan. Spread the raspberry jam evenly over the dough on the bottom of the pan.

3. Roll out the remaining dough on a floured surface to a 10-inch square. Cut the dough into ½-inch-wide strips.* Arrange the strips, pieced together as needed, on top of the jam to form a diamond pattern.

4. Bake the cake in the preheated moderate oven (350°) for 30 minutes. Cool the cake in the pan on a wire rack. Cut the cake into 2 x 1¼-inch rectangles.

***Note:** Or use the palms of your hands to roll the dough, a small portion at a time, on the floured surface into ¼-inch-diameter ropes. Arrange the ropes on top of the jam to form a diamond pattern.*

Decorator Icing

Makes 3 cups.

Nutrient Value Per Serving: Not available.

1 **package meringue powder***

Using the meringue powder, prepare 1 recipe of Royal Icing following the package directions.

***Note:** We recommend using dried meringue powder for uncooked frosting, instead of making meringue from raw egg whites. Recent reports have indicated the presence of salmonella bacteria in raw eggs. To avoid this potential health risk, substitute meringue powder, which is available in stores where baking and cake decorating supplies are sold.*

Venetians

Perhaps these cookies are called Venetians because they are reminiscent of the shimmering colors of Venice, the jewel of a city by the sea.

Bake at 350° for 15 minutes.

Makes about 7⅓ dozen Venetians.

Nutrient Value Per Venetian: 76 calories, 1 g protein, 4 g fat, 9 g carbohydrate, 29 mg sodium, 18 mg cholesterol.

1 **can (8 ounces) almond paste (not marzipan)**	2 **cups all-purpose flour**
1½ **cups (3 sticks) unsalted butter, softened**	**Green food coloring**
	Red food coloring
1 **cup sugar**	1 **jar (12 ounces) apricot preserves**
4 **eggs, separated**	2½ **squares (1 ounce each) semisweet chocolate**
1 **teaspoon salt**	
1 **teaspoon almond extract**	

1. Preheat the oven to moderate (350°). Grease three 13 x 9-inch baking pans. Line the pans with wax paper, and grease the wax paper.

2. Break up the almond paste with a fork in a large bowl. Add the butter, sugar, egg yolks, salt and almond extract. Beat with an electric mixer until the almond mixture is light colored and fluffy. Mix in the flour until it is well blended.

3. Beat the egg whites in a medium-size bowl until stiff peaks form. Fold the beaten whites into the almond mixture with a wooden spoon.

4. Spread 1½ cups of the batter evenly in one prepared pan. Remove another 1½ cups of the batter to a small bowl, and tint the batter green. Spread the green batter evenly in the second prepared pan. Tint the remaining batter pink, and spread the pink batter evenly in the third prepared pan.

5. Bake all three layers in the preheated moderate oven (350°) for 15 minutes, or until the layers' edges are lightly golden; each layer will be about ¼ inch thick. Immediately remove the layers from the pans to large wire racks to cool.

6. Heat the apricot preserves in a small saucepan. and strain them through a sieve. Place the green layer on a baking sheet. Spread half the warm preserves over the green layer, spreading the preserves to the layer's edge. Place the yellow layer on top, and spread the remaining preserves on it. Place the pink layer, top side up, on the yellow layer. Cover the cake with plastic wrap. Weight down the cake with a large wooden cutting board, or a heavy, flat tray. Refrigerate the cake overnight.

7. Melt the chocolate in the top of a double boiler over hot water. Trim the edges of the cake to make them even. Spread the chocolate over the top of the cake, and let the chocolate set at room temperature.

8. Cut the cake into 1-inch squares. Store the Venetians in the refrigerator.

"The holly's up, the house is all bright, The tree is ready, The candle alight; Rejoice and be glad, all children tonight."

—*Carl August Peter Cornelius*

○ ❖ ○

QUICK TOUCHES OF KITCHEN CHEER

Don't neglect your kitchen when decorating for Christmas.

• Group kitchen plants together in a straw basket painted bright red or green. Add a perky tartan bow to the basket. If you wish, wind a string of white miniature lights around the plant pots.

• Decorate the kitchen door to look like a Christmas present. Run wide bands of ribbon vertically and horizontally across the door. Add a big bow where the ribbons meet.

• Place red, green and white pastas in glass storage jars. Tie the jar lid knobs with tartan ribbons, and add a sprig of holly or pine to each.

• Fill pretty mixing bowls with glossy wooden or real apples. Fill in with sprigs of pine or holly, and small pine cones.

• Fill an old-fashioned milk can with bunches of tree twigs sprayed with gold and silver glitter.

Christmas Eve Dinner

Mushroom Ravioli in Consommé

LOW-CHOLESTEROL

Makes 8 servings.

Nutrient Value Per Serving: 157 calories, 4 g protein, 6 g fat, 25 g carbohydrate, 452 mg sodium, 0 mg cholesterol.

Consommé:

1	large onion, thinly sliced
1	large leek (9 ounces), well washed, white and tender green parts sliced (2 cups)
3	cloves garlic, thinly sliced
1	tablespoon peeled, chopped fresh ginger
2	tablespoons olive oil
4	carrots (8 ounces), peeled and thinly sliced (1½ cups)
2	parsnips (6 ounces), peeled and thinly sliced (1 cup)
1	turnip (4 ounces), peeled and thinly sliced (1 cup)
1	can (13⅓ ounces) plum tomatoes, undrained
1	teaspoon salt
½	teaspoon dried marjoram, crumbled
8	cups water

Mushroom Ravioli:

⅓	cup finely chopped shallots
1	tablespoon olive oil
8	ounces mushrooms, finely chopped
¼	teaspoon salt
⅛	teaspoon freshly ground pepper
2	tablespoons dry port wine
12	wonton wrappers
2	carrots, peeled and finely chopped
1	parsnip, peeled and finely chopped
1	leek, washed and finely diced

1. Prepare the Consommé: Sauté the onion, leek, garlic and ginger in 1 tablespoon of the oil in a large saucepan over medium heat for 10 minutes, or until the vegetables are softened. Add the remaining tablespoon of oil, the carrot, parsnip and turnip, and cook for 5 minutes. Add the tomatoes with their liquid, the salt, marjoram and water. Bring the soup to boiling. Lower the heat and simmer, covered, for 45 minutes. Strain the soup through a fine-meshed sieve, pressing the solids to extract all the liquid. Discard the solids. Set aside the consommé.

2. Prepare the Mushroom Ravioli: Sauté the shallots in the oil in a skillet over medium-low heat for 6 minutes, or until the shallots are softened. Add the mushrooms and cook for 10 minutes, or until the mushrooms are softened and almost all the liquid has evaporated. Stir in the salt, pepper and wine, and cook over high heat for 5 minutes, or until the liquid has evaporated. Cool the mushroom mixture to room temperature.

3. Lay out the wonton wrappers on a dry work surface, and cut them in half lengthwise. Lay a scant teaspoon of the mushroom mixture on the upper part of each wrapper. Moisten each wrapper with a little water all around the mushroom mixture. Fold the dry part of the wrapper over the mushroom mixture, and press down the edges to seal them.

4. Bring the consommé to boiling in a large saucepan. Drop in the ravioli, and cook for 2 minutes. Drop in the chopped carrot, parsnip and leek, and cook for 2 minutes. Serve the consommé and ravioli hot.

Cornish Game Hens with Savory Stuffing

Half a game hen makes an ample serving for one.

Bake at 425° for 15 minutes, then at 375° for 50 minutes.
Makes 8 servings.

Nutrient Value Per Serving: 440 calories, 41 g protein, 25 g fat,
10 g carbohydrate, 950 mg sodium, 160 mg cholesterol.

Savory Stuffing:

3	**cups fresh bread crumbs**
4	**ounces fully cooked ham, finely chopped (about ¾ cup)**
¼	**cup chopped parsley**
1	**teaspoon dried marjoram, crumbled**
½	**teaspoon salt**
¼	**teaspoon freshly ground pepper**
1	**egg**
3	**tablespoons milk**
4	**Cornish game hens (about 1¼ pounds each)**

8	**teaspoons butter or margarine, softened**
½	**teaspoon salt** **Freshly ground pepper, to taste**

Pan Gravy:

¼	**cup dry white wine OR: water**
1	**tablespoon butter or margarine**
1	**tablespoon all-purpose flour**
1	**can (13¾ ounces) chicken broth** **Pinch freshly ground pepper**

1. Prepare the Savory Stuffing: Combine the bread crumbs, ham, parsley, marjoram, salt and pepper in a medium-size bowl. Mix together the egg and the milk in a small measuring cup. Add the egg mixture to the bread mixture, and stir to moisten the dry ingredients.

2. Preheat the oven to hot (425°).

3. Remove the giblets from the hens, and refrigerate the giblets for another use. Rinse the hens well inside and out with cold water. Pat the hens dry inside and out with paper toweling.

4. Stuff 1 teaspoon of the softened butter or margarine under the skin of each hen breast. Stuff each body cavity loosely with the stuffing. Tuck the wings under the bodies, and tie the legs to the tails with kitchen string. Sprinkle the outsides of the hens with the ½ teaspoon of salt and the pepper to taste. Place the hens in a flameproof roasting pan.

5. Roast the hens in the preheated hot oven (425°) for 15 minutes. Lower the oven temperature to moderate (375°), and roast the hens for 50 minutes, or until the hens are tender and the juices run clear. Remove the hens to a serving platter. Remove the strings, and keep the hens warm.

6. Prepare the Pan Gravy: Carefully pour off all the fat from the roasting pan. Place the pan over low heat. Add the wine or water, and scrape the browned bits with a wooden spoon from the bottom of the pan. Remove the pan from the heat.

7. Melt the butter or margarine in a medium-size saucepan. Stir in the flour until the mixture is smooth. Cook the flour mixture over low heat, stirring, for 3 minutes, or until the mixture is smooth and no raw flour taste remains. Add the broth, and the wine mixture from the roasting pan. Bring the gravy to boiling, stirring. Lower the heat, and simmer for 5 minutes. Add the pepper. Pour the gravy into a warmed gravy boat. Cut the hens in half, and serve the gravy on the side.

> *"Mistletoe hung from the gas brackets in all the front parlors; there was sherry and walnuts and bottled beer and crackers by the dessertspoons; and cats in their fur-abouts watched the fires; and the high-heaped fire spat, all ready for the chestnuts and the mulling pokers."*
>
> — Dylan Thomas

BROCCOLI WITH WALNUT BUTTER

Trim the outer leaves and tough ends from 4 pounds of broccoli. Separate the top half into flowerets; refrigerate the stems for another use. Steam the broccoli flowerets, or cook them in a small amount of boiling water in a medium-size saucepan, covered, for 10 minutes, or until the broccoli is crisply tender. Meanwhile, melt 1 cup (2 sticks) of butter or margarine in a small skillet over medium-low heat. Add 1½ cups of chopped walnuts and cook slowly, stirring frequently, just until the butter begins to brown; watch the butter carefully to prevent it from burning. Add 2 tablespoons of lemon juice, 1 teaspoon of salt and ¼ teaspoon of freshly ground pepper. When the broccoli is done, drain it well and place it in a serving bowl. Pour the walnut butter over the broccoli, and toss gently to coat the broccoli. Serve immediately. Makes 8 servings.

Creamy Sweet & White Potatoes

LOW-CHOLESTEROL · LOW-FAT

Makes 8 servings.

Nutrient Value Per Serving: 157 calories, 3 g protein, .37 g fat, 36 g carbohydrate, 429 mg sodium, 0 mg cholesterol.

2	pounds sweet potatoes, peeled and cubed	4	cloves garlic, crushed
1½	pounds all-purpose potatoes, peeled and cubed	4	cups water
		1½	teaspoons salt
2	parsnips (8 ounces), peeled, and thinly sliced (2 cups)	¼	teaspoon freshly ground pepper

1. Combine the sweet and all-purpose potatoes with the parsnip, garlic, water, salt and pepper in a saucepan. Bring the water to boiling. Lower the heat and simmer, covered, for 20 minutes, or until the vegetables are tender. Drain the potato mixture, reserving the cooking liquid.

2. Beat the potato mixture with an electric mixer or a potato masher, adding enough of the reserved liquid to make a thick purée. Serve hot.

Red Pepper Purée in Wedges

LOW-CALORIE · LOW-CHOLESTEROL · LOW-FAT

Broil half of red peppers for 15 minutes.

Makes 8 appetizer servings.

Nutrient Value Per Serving: 60 calories, 2 g protein, 1 g fat, 11 g carbohydrate, 139 mg sodium, 0 mg cholesterol.

4	large sweet red peppers (8 ounces each)	¼	teaspoon dried marjoram, crumbled
2	medium-size onions, halved and thinly sliced	½	cup water
1	teaspoon olive oil	2	tablespoons red wine vinegar
2	cloves garlic, thinly sliced	2	tablespoons tomato paste
½	teaspoon sugar	2	slices white bread, toasted and crumbled
¼	teaspoon salt		

1. Preheat the broiler. Place 2 of the red peppers on the broiler-pan rack. Broil the red peppers 6 inches from the heat source, turning over the peppers, until they are blackened all over, for about 15 minutes. Transfer the broiled peppers to a paper or plastic bag, and close the bag. When the peppers are cool, peel them. Remove and discard the seeds and stems. Place the peppers in the container of a food processor or electric blender.

2. Core and seed the remaining red peppers, and cut each lengthwise into 8 wedges. Blanch the pepper wedges in boiling water for 5 minutes, or until they are crisply tender. Drain the pepper wedges, and set them aside.

3. Sauté the onion in the oil in a nonstick skillet over medium-low heat for 5 minutes, or until the onion is lightly golden. Add the garlic, sugar, salt, marjoram and ½ cup of water. Cook, stirring, for 15 to 20 minutes, or until the onion is softened and the water has evaporated. Stir in the vinegar and the tomato paste, and cook for 1 minute more.

4. Add the onion mixture and bread crumbs to the peppers in the container. Whirl until the mixture is a coarse purée. Serve the purée in the wedges.

Paris Brest

Pronounced "perry-brest," this classic puff pastry ring is split and filled with luscious sweetened whipped cream.

Bake at 400° for 40 minutes.
Makes 8 servings.
Nutrient Value Per Serving: 538 calories, 6 g protein, 33 g fat, 47 g carbohydrate, 189 mg sodium, 219 mg cholesterol.

Cream Puff Dough:

1	cup water
½	cup (1 stick) unsalted butter, cut into pieces
1½	teaspoons grated orange zest (orange part of rind only)
½	teaspoon salt
1	cup all-purpose flour
4	eggs

Orange Cream Filling:

2	cups heavy cream
½	cup 10X (confectioners' powdered) sugar
2	tablespoons orange-flavored liqueur

Caramel Glaze:

1	cup granulated sugar
⅓	cup water
2	tablespoons orange juice

1. Preheat the oven to hot (400°).

2. Prepare the Cream Puff Dough: Grease and flour 2 baking sheets. Using an 8-inch round cake pan as a guide, mark an 8-inch circle in the center of 1 of the prepared baking sheets.

3. Combine the water, butter, orange zest and salt in a medium-size saucepan. Bring the mixture to boiling. Remove the saucepan from the heat. Immediately beat in the flour with a wooden spoon. Return the saucepan to low heat, and continue beating with the wooden spoon until the mixture forms a ball and leaves the side of the saucepan. Remove the saucepan from the heat.

4. Add the eggs, one at a time, beating well after each addition. Continue to beat the dough until it is shiny. Scrape the dough into a large pastry bag fitted with a ¾-inch plain tip. Holding the bag at a 45° angle, pipe a dough ring on top of the circle outline on the baking sheet. Pipe another dough ring inside and right next to the first dough ring. Pipe a third ring on top of the first two dough rings to cover the seam where they touch. With the remaining dough, pipe small puffs on the second baking sheet.

5. Bake the pastry ring and puffs in the preheated hot oven (400°) for 40 minutes, or until the tops of the ring and puffs are browned and crisp. Cut a small slit in each puff, and several slits in the ring to release the steam. Remove the ring and puffs to wire racks to cool. Cut the ring and puffs in half horizontally, and set them aside.

6. Prepare the Orange Cream Filling: Beat the heavy cream in a large bowl until soft peaks form. Gradually beat in the 10X (confectioners' powdered) sugar until firm peaks form. Gently stir in the liqueur. Cover the bowl, and refrigerate the filling.

7. Prepare the Caramel Glaze: Combine the granulated sugar, water and orange juice in a small saucepan over medium heat, and stir until the sugar is dissolved. Bring the mixture to boiling. Cook, without stirring, until the glaze is light amber and a candy thermometer inserted in the glaze registers 350°. Set the saucepan in a larger pan of cold water until the candy thermometer registers 240°.

> "*Be merry all,
> Be merry all,
> With holly dress
> the festive hall;
> Prepare the song,
> the feast, the ball,
> To welcome
> merry Christmas.*"
> — *W.R. Spencer*

o ⋅✦⋅ o

MAKING ARRANGEMENTS

Keep the following items on hand and you'll be able to create instant arrangements for your holiday dining table.

- **Candles:** Have a selection of red, green and white tapers, short and tall chunk candles and votive candles with holders.
- **Pretty bowls and baskets:** These can give your table a theme—baskets say "country," a pewter bowl is distinctly colonial, ornate china or crystal bowls are Victorian, stoneware adds a warm, homey touch.
- **Pine cones:** Large and small, thin and fat. Paint them, wire them, glue them, roll them in glitter, tie them with bows, or simply pile them in a pretty container.
- **Fruit:** Fill a ceramic or wooden bowl, or a basket, with bright green apples, red apples, or citrus fruit for a pretty and fragrant centerpiece.
- **Ball ornaments:** Use them as you would fresh fruit. They make a simple, sparkling centerpiece.
- **Mirror:** Lay it flat on the table, and place your arrangement on top. The mirror will reflect candlelight, and can give a simple arrangement more presence.

8. To assemble the Paris Brest, spoon some of the filling into the bottom half of each puff. Place the bottom half of the pastry ring on a serving plate, and spoon the remaining filling into the bottom half of the ring. Using a fork, dip the outside top half of each puff into the glaze,* and set the glazed puff tops on a wire rack to set. Place the top half of the pastry ring on the filled bottom half. Place the glazed puff tops on the filled puff bottoms. Set the filled puffs on top of the filled ring. Using a small spoon, drizzle the remaining glaze over the filled ring. Serve immediately.

***Note:** If the glaze in the saucepan hardens, reheat it briefly in a microwave oven, or in the saucepan over hot water.*

Café Supreme

Makes 8 to 10 servings.

Nutrient Value Per Tablespoon: 7 calories, 0 g protein, 0 g fat, 1 g carbohydrate, 3 mg sodium, 0 mg cholesterol.

12 **whole cloves**	2 **cinnamon sticks**
1¼ **teaspoons aniseed, crushed**	**Hot milk OR: whipped cream, for garnish**
1 **vanilla bean (2 inches long), split lengthwise**	**Natural OR: light brown sugar, for garnish (optional)**
6 **cups hot, freshly brewed strong coffee**	

1. Tie the cloves, aniseed and vanilla bean in a small cheesecloth bag. Place the coffee in a large saucepan over low heat. Or place the coffee in a thermos jug. Add the spice bag and the cinnamon sticks, and steep the spices in the coffee for at least 15 minutes.

2. Serve the coffee in small mugs or cups. Garnish each serving with the hot milk or whipped cream and, if you wish, natural or light brown sugar.

Great Gifts!
A Pot of Mustard

Give a loved one the gift of taste with one of these savory mustard blends.

Sweet & Simple Honey Mustard

LOW-CALORIE · LOW-CHOLESTEROL · LOW-SODIUM · LOW-FAT
Makes about 3 cups.
Nutrient Value Per Tablespoon: 23 calories, 0 g protein, .16 g fat,
6 g carbohydrate, 0 mg sodium, 0 mg cholesterol.

½	cup all-purpose flour	½	cup water
¼	cup sugar	½	cup honey
¼	cup mustard powder	2	cups cider vinegar
2	teaspoons ground turmeric		

1. Combine the flour, sugar, mustard powder and turmeric in a small bowl. Stir in the water. Let the flour mixture stand for 2 hours.

2. Combine the flour mixture with the honey and the vinegar in the top of a double boiler over boiling water. Cook the mustard, whisking often, for 3 minutes, or just until the mustard begins to thicken. Cook the mustard, whisking constantly, for 2 minutes more, or until the mustard is slightly thickened. Turn the mustard into a clean storage jar; the mustard will thicken completely while standing in the jar. Cover the jar, and refrigerate the mustard overnight, or for up to 1 month.

Mustard Pickle Relish:
Combine ½ cup of finely chopped dill pickles with ¼ cup of Sweet & Simple Honey Mustard in a small bowl.
Makes about ¾ cup.
Nutrient Value Per Tablespoon: 9 calories, 0 g protein, .06 g fat, 2 g carbohydrate, 83 mg sodium, 0 mg cholesterol.

Grainy Mustard

LOW-CHOLESTEROL · LOW-FAT
Makes about 1 cup.
Nutrient Value Per Tablespoon: 32 calories, 1 g protein, 1 g fat,
5 g carbohydrate, 76 mg sodium, 0 mg cholesterol.

¼	cup mustard seeds	⅓	cup white wine vinegar
2	teaspoons mustard powder	½	teaspoon salt
¼	cup water	¼	cup light corn syrup
¼	cup dry white wine		

THE MUSTARD MYSTIQUE

The peppery seeds of the mustard plant have been prized as a seasoning for 3,000 years. At one time, people would pop a mustard seed or two into their mouths while chewing meat. Most cooks today use prepared or dry mustard. The former can range from grainy to smooth, and mild to hot, with fruit, herb, wine and peppercorn varieties in between. It's also very easy to make your own homemade mustard using ground mustard seeds, a liquid (most commonly wine, cider, milk or vinegar), and salt, pepper, spices or herbs for flavoring and color.

○ ❖ ○

MUSTARD MINI-RECIPES

● Add crushed green peppercorns, shallots, herbs, or grated orange, lemon or lime zest (colored part of the rind only) to prepared mustard. Refrigerate the seasoned mustard for a few days before using it to let the flavors meld.
● Spike mustard with mayonnaise and horseradish for a pungent hit.
● Mix a bit of mustard and buttermilk into plain nonfat yogurt to make a tasty salad dressing or seafood sauce.

THE MUSTARD MARKET

- **Prepared Yellow Mustard:** Made with light mustard seeds. The American brand is smooth and mild, the English is smooth and hot.
Serve on or with hot dogs, sausages, cold cuts.
- **Brown Mustard:** Made with dark mustard seeds, or brown and yellow seeds combined, and vinegar. Pungent, hot and spicy.
Serve on or with sandwiches, cheese, baked ham.
- **Dijon-Style Mustard:** Made with brown mustard seeds and white wine. Smooth; most versions are mild, but a few are hot.
Serve on, with, or in meats, sandwiches, sauces.
- **Raspberry Mustard:** Made with yellow mustard seeds, vinegar and fresh raspberries. Slightly sweet, fruity, tangy, refreshing.
Serve on or with sliced turkey or chicken sandwiches, ham sandwiches, baked ham, roasted duck.
- **Sweet Honey Mustard:** Made with dark mustard seeds, vinegar and honey. Creamy and mellow.
Serve on, with, or in fruit salad dressings, baked ham glaze, sandwiches, hot dogs, mixed with yogurt as a dip.
- **Horseradish Mustard:** Made using various types of mustard. The horseradish flavor varies in intensity, but always has a bite.
Serve on or with corned beef, hash, pot roast, mild sausages.
- **Hickory Smoked Mustard:** Made with mustard seeds that have been smoked over hickory wood to give them a barbecued flavor.
Serve on or with chicken, turkey, flank steak, baked ham, pork chops.
- **Beer Mustard:** Made with light or dark mustard seeds and beer, creating a very robust flavor.
Serve on or with cold cuts, grilled meats, sausages.

1. Combine the mustard seeds, mustard powder and water in the container of an electric blender or food processor. Whirl for 1 minute, or until the mixture is coarsely puréed to a paste. Let the mustard paste stand at room temperature for at least 2 hours.

2. Combine the mustard paste with the wine, vinegar and salt in the top of a small double boiler over boiling water. Cook, stirring occasionally, for 10 minutes, or until the mustard-wine mixture is slightly thickened. Return the mustard-wine mixture to the blender container. Add the corn syrup. Whirl until the mustard is well mixed. Turn the mustard into a clean storage jar. Cover the jar, and refrigerate the mustard overnight, or for up to 1 month.

Grainy Raspberry Mustard:

In Step 2, above, substitute ⅓ cup of raspberry vinegar for the white wine vinegar, and ½ cup of seedless raspberry jam for the corn syrup.
Makes about 1¼ cups.
Nutrient Value Per Tablespoon: 36 calories, 1 g protein, 1 g fat, 7 g carbohydrate, 56 mg sodium, 0 mg cholesterol.

Grainy Sherry Mustard:

In Step 2, above, substitute ¼ cup of dry sherry for the white wine, and ⅓ cup of sherry wine vinegar for the white wine vinegar.
Makes about 1 cup.
Nutrient Value Per Tablespoon: 35 calories, 1 g protein, 1 g fat, 5 g carbohydrate, 76 mg sodium, 0 mg cholesterol.

Mustard Fruit Chutney

LOW-CHOLESTEROL · LOW-FAT
Makes 2 cups.
Nutrient Value Per Tablespoon: 29 calories, 0 g protein, .09 g fat, 7 g carbohydrate, 17 mg sodium, 0 mg cholesterol.

1 tablespoon water	⅓ cup dark, seedless raisins
2 teaspoons mustard powder	1 small onion, finely chopped (¼ cup)
½ cup sugar	1 clove garlic, finely chopped
½ cup cider vinegar	½ teaspoon ground ginger
2 medium-ripe pears, peeled, cored and diced	⅛ to ¼ teaspoon crushed red pepper flakes
1 ripe mango, peeled, seeded and diced	¼ teaspoon salt

1. Stir the water into the mustard powder in a small cup.

2. Combine the sugar with the vinegar in a medium-size saucepan. Bring the sugar mixture to boiling, stirring to dissolve the sugar. Boil the sugar mixture gently for 10 minutes.

3. Add the pears, mango, raisins, mustard mixture, onion, garlic, ginger, red pepper flakes and salt to the saucepan. Boil the chutney gently, stirring occasionally, for 30 minutes, or until most of the liquid has evaporated and the fruit is tender. Cool the chutney completely. Store the chutney, covered, in the refrigerator for up to 1 week. Serve the chutney cold.

Celebrate the Fourth!

Greet the anniversary of American independence with a feast fit for the Founding Fathers — and Mothers!

Clam Stuffies

Bake at 400° for 20 to 25 minutes.
Makes 12 servings.
Nutrient Value Per Serving: 130 calories, 8 g protein, 5 g fat, 13 g carbohydrate, 201 mg sodium, 24 mg cholesterol.

18	chowder clams, meat removed from shells	5	cups coarsely crumbled fresh bread (about 8 bread slices)
2	tablespoons butter	2	tablespoons Worcestershire sauce
1½	cups chopped onion		
6	ounces chorizo sausages (2 to 3 links), chopped	⅛	teaspoon freshly ground white pepper
½	teaspoon dried thyme, crumbled	24	clam shells, cleaned
		2	tablespoons chopped parsley

1. Preheat the oven to hot (400°).

2. Coarsely grind the clam meat, or chop it by hand; do not use a food processor, or the clam meat will become mushy. You should have 1½ cups of chopped clam meat.

3. Heat the butter in a large skillet over medium heat. Add the onion and cook for 6 minutes, or until the onion is softened. Add the sausages and the thyme, and cook for 3 minutes more. Remove the skillet from the heat, and carefully drain off the fat. Stir the chopped clam meat, bread crumbs, Worcestershire sauce and white pepper into the skillet.

4. Place the clam shells in 1 or 2 jelly-roll pans. Spoon the clam mixture, divided evenly, into the shells.

5. Bake the stuffed clam shells in the preheated hot oven (400°) for 20 to 25 minutes, or until the stuffing is heated through and the clam meat is opaque. Garnish the stuffed clam shells with the chopped parsley, and serve them immediately.

Sausage & Pepper Heroes

Makes 12 sandwiches.
Nutrient Value Per Sandwich: 344 calories, 16 g protein, 14 g fat, 38 g carbohydrate, 779 mg sodium, 45 mg cholesterol.

2	pounds chorizo OR: hot Italian sausages (about 12 links), cut into chunks	2	medium-size onions, cubed
		1	can (16 ounces) tomato sauce
6	sweet green peppers, cored, seeded and cubed	12	hard rolls, split in half

MENU

Clam Stuffies
(recipe, at left)

Sausage & Pepper Heroes
(recipe, bottom left)

New England Clambake
(recipe, page 129)

Hot Dogs & Buns

Banana Blueberry Muffins
(recipe, page 130)

Star-Spangled Broccoli Salad
(recipe, page 130)

Watermelon Sherbet Mold
(recipe, page 131)

Stars & Stripes Cheesecake
(recipe, page 132)

○ ❖ ○

SOME LIKE IT HOT!

Hot Italian sausages can be substituted for the chorizo sausages in Clam Stuffies (recipe, at left). Remove the casings from the hot Italian sausages. In Step 3 of the recipe, crumble the sausage into the skillet, and add the thyme. Cook the sausage for 3 minutes, or until it no longer is pink.

1. Cook the chorizo or Italian sausages in a large skillet over medium heat for 6 minutes, or until the sausages are cooked in the center; the Italian sausages no longer will be pink in the center. Remove the sausages from the skillet, and set them aside. Carefully drain off all but 1 tablespoon of the fat from the skillet.

2. Add the green peppers and the onion to the skillet. Cook for 10 minutes, or until the vegetables are softened. Stir in the tomato sauce. Return the cooked sausages to the skillet, and cook over medium-low heat, covered, for 10 minutes.

3. If you wish, preheat the oven to moderate (350°), and heat the rolls in the preheated moderate oven (350°) for 8 to 10 minutes. Spoon about ⅔ cup of the sausage mixture onto the bottom half of each roll, and top with the upper half of the roll. Serve the heroes with plenty of paper napkins.

New England Clambake

Here's an old-fashioned fun way to feed a large crowd.

LOW-CHOLESTEROL
Makes about 14 servings.
Nutrient Value Per Serving: 441 calories, 20 g protein, 30 g fat, 23 g carbohydrate, 878 mg sodium, 73 mg cholesterol.

Cheesecloth	**6 hot dogs (¾ pound), cut in half**
Kitchen string	
Empty tuna can, top and bottom removed	**1 kielbasa (1¼ pounds), cut into 6 pieces**
4 cups water	**3 dozen littleneck OR: steamer clams, scrubbed**
1 pound seaweed* OR: lettuce leaves, shredded (8 cups)	**6 ears corn, husked, and cut in half**
18 new potatoes (about 2¼ pounds)	
6 bratwurst OR: weisswurst (1¼ pounds), cut in half	

1. Cut nine 14-inch double-thickness cheesecloth squares, and nine 14-inch lengths of kitchen string.

2. Place the tuna can in a large canning or 12-quart pot with a fitted cover. Place a wire rack on top of the tuna can. Add the water to the pot. Spread the seaweed or lettuce evenly on the rack.

3. Place 6 of the potatoes in the center of a cheesecloth square. Gather the corners of the square together loosely, and tie them with a length of string. Repeat with the remaining potatoes. Tie the bratwurst or weisswurst pieces into 1 bundle the same way. Repeat with the hot dog pieces, and the kielbasa pieces. Divide the clams into 3 batches, and tie each batch loosely in a cheesecloth square, allowing enough room for the clams to open.

4. Bring the water in the pot to boiling. Place the bratwurst and potato bundles on the seaweed, and cook over medium heat, covered, for 20 minutes. Add the hot dog, kielbasa and clam bundles, and the corn. Cover the pot and cook for 15 minutes, or until the clams are opened.

5. Place the cheesecloth bundles and the corn on a large serving platter. When ready to serve, cut the strings to open the bundles.

__Note:__ Seaweed is available in some fish stores.

> "*We hold these truths to be self evident; that all men are created equal; that they are endowed by their creator with certain unalienable rights; that among these are life, liberty, and the pursuit of happiness.*"
> — *Thomas Jefferson*

Banana Blueberry Muffins

LOW-FAT

Bake at 400° for 20 to 22 minutes.

Makes 12 muffins.

Nutrient Value Per Muffin: 237 calories, 4 g protein, 7 g fat, 40 g carbohydrate, 236 mg sodium, 51 mg cholesterol.

Muffins:

2¼	cups all-purpose flour
2	teaspoons baking powder
½	teaspoon salt
½	teaspoon ground cinnamon
2	ripe bananas, quartered
2	eggs
⅔	cup firmly packed brown sugar
6	tablespoons butter, melted
1	teaspoon vanilla
1	cup fresh blueberries

Topping:

¼	cup granulated sugar
1	teaspoon grated lemon zest (yellow part of rind only)

1. Preheat the oven to hot (400°). Lightly grease twelve 2½-inch muffin-pan cups.

2. Prepare the Muffins: Combine the flour, baking powder, salt and cinnamon on wax paper.

3. Beat the bananas in a large bowl with an electric mixer until the bananas are mashed. Add the eggs, brown sugar, butter and vanilla, beating until they are blended.

4. Stir in the flour mixture with a wooden spoon until the flour mixture is almost blended. Fold in the blueberries just until they are combined. Spoon the batter into the prepared muffin-pan cups.

5. Prepare the Topping: Combine the granulated sugar with the lemon zest in a small dish. Sprinkle the topping evenly over the batter in the cups.

6. Bake the muffins in the preheated hot oven (400°) for 20 to 22 minutes, or until the muffins are golden. Remove the muffins from the pan to a wire rack. Serve the muffins hot.

Star-Spangled Broccoli Salad

For a festive summer holiday touch, cut the red pepper into stars.

LOW-CHOLESTEROL

Makes 12 servings.

Nutrient Value Per Serving: 241 calories, 2 g protein, 22 g fat, 11 g carbohydrate, 433 mg sodium, 0 mg cholesterol.

2	bottles (8 ounces each) oil and vinegar Italian salad dressing
2	cans (8 ounces each) whole water chestnuts, drained, rinsed and sliced
1	can (6 ounces) pitted large olives, drained and sliced
1	sweet red pepper, cored, seeded and cubed
2	bunches broccoli (2½ pounds), cut into small flowerets

GUIDE TO A BEAUTIFUL BUFFET

- Place the buffet table so there is plenty of room around it. Guests should be able to move around the table easily.
- Set the table to allow for easy self-service and a smooth flow of traffic: first the plates, then the entrées and accompaniments, and the tableware and napkins last.
- Wrap each place setting of tableware in its own napkin for easy carrying.
- The bread basket and the butter plate should be placed next to each other, either at the end of the buffet table or on an adjoining table. Bring the butter to room temperature.
- Place the correct serving utensils in or next to each dish.
- Be sure there is plenty of table space and seating for eating. Card tables and tray tables work well, and are disguised easily with pretty linens.
- If you choose to seat guests at the dining table, set the table with napkins, tableware and glassware so your guests won't have to pick these up at the buffet table.

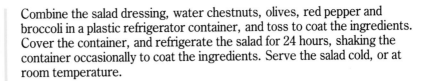

Combine the salad dressing, water chestnuts, olives, red pepper and broccoli in a plastic refrigerator container, and toss to coat the ingredients. Cover the container, and refrigerate the salad for 24 hours, shaking the container occasionally to coat the ingredients. Serve the salad cold, or at room temperature.

Watermelon Sherbet Mold

This sherbet mold looks like the real thing.

LOW-CHOLESTEROL ▪ LOW-FAT
Makes about 16 servings.
Nutrient Value Per Serving: 277 calories, 2 g protein, 6 g fat, 56 g carbohydrate, 78 mg sodium, 12 mg cholesterol.

½ **gallon raspberry sherbet**	3 **pints lemon sherbet**
¾ **cup chocolate chips**	**Green food coloring**

1. Line a baking sheet with aluminum foil. Mark a 6½ x 9-inch oval in the center of the aluminum foil.

2. Slice the raspberry sherbet, and transfer it to a large mixing bowl to soften. Stir in the chocolate chips. If the raspberry mixture is too soft to mold, place it in the freezer until it is firm enough to work with.

3. Spoon the raspberry mixture onto the marked oval, mounding the mixture in the center of the oval to form a shape similar to half a watermelon. Freeze the molded raspberry mixture until the outside of the shape is firm.

4. Scoop 1½ pints of the lemon sherbet into a medium-size bowl, and let the sherbet soften. Spread the softened lemon sherbet evenly over the molded raspberry mixture, smoothing the lemon sherbet with a spatula. Freeze the molded lemon sherbet until it is firm.

5. Scoop the remaining 1½ pints of lemon sherbet into a large electric mixer bowl. Using the lowest mixer speed, beat in enough green food coloring to give the sherbet the color of watermelon rind; beat just until the coloring and sherbet are combined. Spread the green sherbet evenly over the molded lemon sherbet, smoothing the green sherbet with a spatula. Freeze the watermelon mold until it is firm. Cover the watermelon mold with plastic wrap, and freeze the mold for at least 12 hours, or overnight.

6. To serve, cut the watermelon mold in half lengthwise. Cut the halves crosswise into 1-inch-thick slices.

Stars & Stripes Cheesecake

The perfect ending to a Fourth of July cookout.

Makes 12 servings.

Nutrient Value Per Serving: 316 calories, 9 g protein, 15 g fat, 36 g carbohydrate, 301 mg sodium, 45 mg cholesterol.

Crust:

1⅓ cups graham cracker crumbs (1 cellophane package of 12 rectangular crackers)

6 tablespoons unsalted butter, cut into pats

¼ cup sugar

1 teaspoon ground ginger

Filling:

2 envelopes unflavored gelatin

¾ cup sugar

¾ cup water

1 container (16 ounces) cottage cheese

1 package (8 ounces) Neufchâtel OR: light cream cheese

1 tablespoon grated lemon zest (yellow part of rind only)

2 tablespoons fresh lemon juice

1 cup half-and-half

½ cup blueberry preserves

Blue food coloring

Red food coloring

Whipped cream

Fresh blueberries

Fresh raspberries

1. Prepare the Crust: Combine the graham cracker crumbs with the butter, sugar and ginger in the container of a food processor or electric blender. Pulse until the butter is incorporated and the ingredients are blended. Press the crust into an even layer across the bottom of an 8½-inch springform pan. Chill the crust.

2. Prepare the Filling: Combine the gelatin with the sugar in a saucepan. Add the water and cook over medium heat, stirring to dissolve the gelatin.

3. Place the cottage cheese in the processor container. Whirl until the cottage cheese is very smooth, for about 2 minutes. Add the Neufchâtel or light cream cheese, the lemon zest and lemon juice. Whirl until the cheese mixture is smooth. With the machine running, add the gelatin mixture. Scrape the gelatin-cheese mixture into a large bowl. Stir in the half-and-half; you should have about 5 cups of cream-cheese mixture.

4. Place 1⅔ cups of the cream-cheese mixture in the processor container along with ¼ cup of the blueberry preserves. Whirl until the blueberry mixture is smooth. Add about 24 drops of blue food coloring, and whirl until the coloring is evenly blended. Pour the blue mixture over the crust. Chill the blue layer in the freezer for 10 minutes, or just until the blue layer is beginning to set.

5. Gently pour 1⅔ cups of the cream-cheese mixture over a wide rubber spatula onto the blue layer; pouring over the spatula will help retain an even layering. Chill the white layer in the freezer for 10 minutes, or just until the white layer is beginning to set on top.

6. Scrape the remaining cream-cheese mixture into the processor container along with the remaining ¼ cup of blueberry preserves. Whirl until the mixture is smooth. Add about 24 drops of red food coloring, and whirl until the coloring is evenly blended. Gently pour the red mixture over the rubber spatula onto the white layer. Cover the pan, and refrigerate the cheesecake until it is set, for up to 24 hours.

NEUFCHÂTEL

A soft, creamy cheese with a white crust, Neufchâtel originally was made in a town of the same name in the Normandy region of France. American-made Neufchâtel is similar in taste and texture to cream cheese, but has a lower butterfat content. Neufchâtel can be substituted for cream cheese in most recipes, and is particularly good in cheesecake.

◦ ❖ ◦

"I wish the bald eagle had not been chosen as the representative of our country; he is a bird of bad moral character; like those among men who live by sharping and robbing, he is generally poor, and often very lousy. The turkey is a much more respectable bird, and withal a true original native of America."

—Benjamin Franklin

7. Using a 5-inch star-shaped cookie cutter or pattern cut out of wax paper, mark a star in the center of the cheesecake; if using a wax paper pattern, place the pattern lightly on the cheesecake and score around the pattern with a knife. Fill a pastry bag fitted with a medium star tip with the whipped cream, and pipe the star's outline. Outline the star's inner edge with the blueberries. Fill the center of the star with the raspberries. Pipe 5 rosettes around the edge of the cheesecake between the points of the star. Place a raspberry on top of each rosette. Serve the cheesecake cold.

Stars & Stripes Cheesecake delivers a sweet mouthful of red, white and blue.

CHAPTER 3

Soups, Salads & Side Dishes

So often the main dish becomes the focus of our menu planning and we end up throwing together the accompaniments at the last minute, turning a potentially great meal into humdrum fare. To remedy this, we've gathered together a selection of soups, salads and side dishes that will help you turn ordinary into extraordinary.

Savory soups can play an important part in healthy, delicious eating. Vegetable Pistou makes a wonderful opening act for a meal. And Hearty Mediterranean Bean & Vegetable Soup can be served as a meal unto itself. This versatility is equally true for salads, and you'll be delighted with the variety offered at our "salad bar." This selection includes everything from simple Orange Onion Salad and Pear & Apple Slaw, to satisfying Corn & Pasta Salad and main dish Curried Chicken Salad with Nectarine Onion Salsa.

To add just the right accent to your entrée, we offer a collection of our favorite side dishes. These tasty sides include tangy Pickled Beets & Apples, crispy Zucchini Potato Pancakes and a fabulous Layered Vegetable Pâté. You'll also find recipes for rice, muffins and breads to round out any meal to perfection.

Savor this chapter for its great assortment of little treasures to serve alone, or to spice up your everyday fare.

Juicy nectarines are the sweet accent in Curried Chicken Salad with Nectarine Onion Salsa (recipe, page 143).

Soups

Starting your meal with soup can blunt the edge of your appetite, allowing you to eat less but still feel full. Soup also can be a meal in itself—full of nutrients and oh-so-satisfying!

Potato, Pepper & Corn Chowder

A colorful chowder to satisfy the soul—and the stomach!

LOW-CALORIE · LOW-CHOLESTEROL · LOW-FAT

Makes 4 servings.

Nutrient Value Per Serving: 292 calories, 11 g protein, 10 g fat, 45 g carbohydrate, 420 mg sodium, 22 mg cholesterol.

2 **cups water**	½ **cup diced sweet green pepper**
2 **large all-purpose potatoes (about 1 pound), peeled and diced**	½ **cup diced sweet red pepper**
	2 **tablespoons all-purpose flour**
2 **to 3 large ears corn**	2 **cups milk**
2 **strips bacon, chopped**	½ **teaspoon salt**
Butter or margarine (optional)	¼ **teaspoon freshly ground pepper**
1 **large onion, chopped (1 cup)**	

1. Bring the water to boiling in a large saucepan over high heat. Add the potatoes, and return the water to boiling. Reduce the heat to medium and cook the potatoes, covered, for 10 minutes.

2. Meanwhile, cut the corn kernels from the cobs with a knife into a bowl; you should have 2 to 2½ cups of kernels. Add the corn kernels to the potatoes in the saucepan. Return the mixture to boiling. Reduce the heat to medium-low, cover the saucepan, and cook for 8 minutes. Set aside the potato-corn mixture.

3. In another large saucepan, cook the bacon over medium-high heat, stirring, until the bacon is crisp. Remove the bacon with a slotted spoon to paper toweling to drain. Reduce the heat to medium. Drain off and discard all but 2 tablespoons of the bacon drippings in the saucepan. Or add butter or margarine to the saucepan to make 2 tablespoons.

4. Add the onion and the green and red peppers to the hot drippings in the saucepan. Cook, stirring, for 3 to 5 minutes, or just until the vegetables are tender. Gradually stir in the flour until it is smooth and cook, stirring constantly, for 3 to 5 minutes, or until the flour mixture is dry and thick. Gradually stir in the milk until the mixture is smooth and cook, stirring, for 3 to 5 minutes, or until the milk mixture is thickened and bubbly. Add the salt, pepper, potato-corn mixture and bacon. Gently heat the chowder through, stirring occasionally.

HISTORICAL NIBLETS

In the 19th century, America went corn-wild for the following dishes:

Scratch Backs: Corn muffins with tops so rough they scratched the top of your mouth.

Corn Dodgers: Corn sticks so hard that, if anyone threw them at you, you had to dodge them.

Hoecakes: Corn cakes baked on a hoe over a campfire.

o ❖ o

"*Lovely!*
See the cloud,
the cloud appear!
Lovely! See the rain,
the rain draw near!
Who spoke?
It was the
little corn ear
High on the
tip of the stalk."

—*Corn-grinding Song of the Zuñi*

QUICK TOMATO SOUP

● Combine 2 cups of tomato juice with 2 cups of chicken broth in a medium-size bowl. Cover the bowl, and refrigerate the soup until serving time.

● Before serving, remove any fat that has risen to the surface of the soup. Stir in any or all of the following: steamed tiny garden peas, blanched sliced celery or carrot, sautéed mushrooms, chopped blanched green beans.

● Serve the soup, hot or cold, in individual soup bowls. Garnish each serving with a dollop of plain yogurt, and a sprinkling of fresh basil. Makes 4 servings.

Vegetable Pistou

Basil pesto adds unbeatable flavor to this vegetable soup.

LOW-CALORIE ▪ LOW-CHOLESTEROL

Makes 4 servings.

Nutrient Value Per Serving: 339 calories, 12 g protein, 19 g fat, 34 g carbohydrate, 1,094 mg sodium, 3 mg cholesterol.

Pesto:

1½	cups fresh basil
¼	cup shelled sunflower seeds
2	cloves garlic, crushed
¼	cup cured ripe olives, pitted
¼	cup olive oil
¼	cup grated Parmesan cheese

Soup:

1	tablespoon olive oil
1	large onion, chopped (1 cup)
1	sweet red pepper, cored, seeded, and coarsely chopped
½	pound zucchini, sliced ¼ inch thick
½	pound yellow squash, sliced ¼ inch thick
¼	pound green beans, trimmed, and cut into 1½-inch lengths
4	new red potatoes (8 ounces), each cut into eighths
1	cup frozen lima beans
2½	cups chicken broth
2	cups water
2	tablespoons tomato paste
½	teaspoon salt
¼	teaspoon freshly ground pepper

1. Prepare the Pesto: Combine the basil, sunflower seeds, garlic, olives and oil in the container of an electric blender or small food processor. Whirl until the ingredients are blended. Stir in the Parmesan cheese. Remove ¼ cup of the pesto, and reserve it for another use; you should have ½ cup of pesto remaining.

2. Prepare the Soup: Heat the oil in a large saucepan over medium heat. Add the onion and the red pepper, and sauté for 5 minutes, or until the vegetables are tender. Add the zucchini, squash, green beans, potatoes, lima beans, broth and water to the saucepan. Bring the broth mixture to boiling. Reduce the heat to medium-low and simmer for 15 to 20 minutes, or until the vegetables are tender. Remove the saucepan from the heat. Stir in the tomato paste, pesto, salt and pepper. Serve the soup hot.

Hearty Mediterranean Bean & Vegetable Soup

LOW-CALORIE · LOW-CHOLESTEROL · LOW-FAT

Makes 4 servings.

Nutrient Value Per Serving: 297 calories, 9 g protein, 10 g fat, 49 g carbohydrate, 1,081 mg sodium, 0 mg cholesterol.

1	medium-size eggplant (1 pound)	8	ounces yellow squash, halved lengthwise, and cut crosswise into ¼-inch-thick slices
1	teaspoon salt		
2½	tablespoons olive oil	¼	pound green beans, trimmed, and cut into 1½-inch lengths
1	large onion, halved, and each half cut into 8 wedges		
3	to 4 cloves garlic, halved and thinly sliced	2½	cups tomato juice
		½	small bay leaf
1	pound ripe tomatoes, cored, quartered and seeded	¼	teaspoon freshly ground pepper
1	sweet red pepper, cored, seeded, and cut lengthwise into ½-inch-wide strips	1	can (19 ounces) cannellini beans, drained and rinsed
8	ounces zucchini, halved lengthwise, and cut crosswise into ¼-inch-thick slices	1	cup firmly packed fresh basil
		1	teaspoon chopped fresh thyme

1. Peel the eggplant, and cut it crosswise into ½-inch-thick slices. Cut the slices into ½-inch-thick cubes. Toss the eggplant with ½ teaspoon of the salt in a colander. Place the colander over a bowl or in the sink, and let the eggplant stand for about 20 minutes. Blot the eggplant dry with paper toweling.

2. Heat 2 teaspoons of the oil in a large saucepan over medium heat. Add the onion and the garlic, and sauté for 3 minutes. Add the tomatoes, and cook for 5 minutes, or until the tomatoes are softened. Remove the tomato mixture to a large bowl. Wipe out the saucepan. Heat 1½ teaspoons of the oil in the same saucepan. Add the red pepper, and sauté for 5 minutes, or until the red pepper is tender. Remove the red pepper to the bowl with the tomato mixture. Wipe out the saucepan. Heat 2 teaspoons of the oil in the same saucepan. Add the zucchini, squash and green beans, and sauté for 5 minutes, or until the squash is golden. Remove the squash mixture to the bowl with the red pepper mixture. Wipe out the saucepan. Heat the remaining 2 teaspoons of oil in the same saucepan. Add the eggplant, and sauté for 8 minutes, or just until the eggplant is tender and golden.

3. Return the red pepper-squash mixture in the bowl to the saucepan. Add the tomato juice, bay leaf, the remaining ½ teaspoon of salt and the pepper. Simmer the eggplant mixture over medium-low heat for 20 minutes. Stir in the cannellini beans, basil and thyme. Cook the soup for 5 minutes more, or until the soup is heated through.

CREAMY TOMATO & RED PEPPER SOUP

A delightfully quick and tasty soup with only 69 calories per serving!

● Combine 1 can (14½ ounces) of no-salt-added stewed tomatoes with their liquid and 1 jar (7 ounces) of roasted red peppers, drained, in the container of a food processor. Whirl until the mixture is almost smooth.

● Press the tomato mixture through a wide-mesh sieve into a medium-size saucepan. Stir in 1 can (10½ ounces) of low-sodium chicken broth, 1 thinly sliced green onion, ½ teaspoon of dried marjoram, crumbled, and ¼ teaspoon of salt.

● Bring the soup to simmering over medium heat, stirring occasionally. Stir in ½ cup of lowfat milk. Gently cook the soup until it is heated through.

Makes 4 servings.

Salads

Crisp, refreshing and surprisingly filling, salads are a wonderful accompaniment to any meal and, with a few additions, can make complete meals in themselves.

Orange Onion Salad

LOW-CALORIE · LOW-CHOLESTEROL · LOW-FAT

Makes 4 servings.

Nutrient Value Per Serving: 75 calories, 2 g protein, 2 g fat, 14 g carbohydrate, 152 mg sodium, 1 mg cholesterol.

2 **large navel oranges**	**Orange Yogurt Dressing (recipe follows)**
Lettuce leaves	
½ small red onion, cut into slivers	

Peel the oranges, and cut them into slices. Arrange the lettuce, orange slices and onion slivers on 4 individual salad plates. Pour on ⅓ cup of the Orange Yogurt Dressing; refrigerate the remaining dressing to use with any fruit salad.

Orange Yogurt Dressing:

Mix together ½ cup of plain lowfat yogurt, 2 tablespoons of thawed frozen orange juice concentrate, 1 tablespoon of vegetable oil, ½ teaspoon of sugar, ½ teaspoon of salt, ⅛ teaspoon of freshly ground pepper, and ⅛ teaspoon of cumin.
Makes ⅔ cup.

Citrus Salad with Lime Vinaigrette

LOW-CHOLESTEROL · LOW-SODIUM

Makes 4 servings.

Nutrient Value Per Serving: 163 calories, 2 g protein, 10 g fat, 19 g carbohydrate, 4 mg sodium, 0 mg cholesterol.

1 large white OR: pink grapefruit, peeled and sectioned	**3 tablespoons olive oil**
	4 teaspoons lime juice
2 large navel oranges, peeled and sectioned	**1 teaspoon honey**
	⅛ teaspoon grated lime zest (green part of rind only)
8 large leaf OR: romaine lettuce leaves, torn	**Salt and freshly ground pepper, to taste**

1. Combine the grapefruit and orange sections with the lettuce in a large serving bowl.

2. Combine the oil, lime juice, honey, lime zest, and salt and pepper in a small bowl. Pour the dressing over the salad, and toss.

Pear & Apple Slaw

A symphony of fall fruit, crisp pears and bright apples team up with shredded cabbage and a tangy orange dressing for this wonderful salad.

LOW-CHOLESTEROL
Makes 6 servings.
Nutrient Value Per Serving: 321 calories, 3 g protein, 21 g fat, 34 g carbohydrate, 115 mg sodium, 11 mg cholesterol.

2	ripe pears	⅓	cup orange juice
2	large apples	4	cups shredded cabbage
½	cup mayonnaise OR: salad dressing	½	cup chopped walnuts
		½	cup raisins

1. Quarter and core the pears. Chop the pears, and place them in a small bowl. Peel, quarter and core the apples. Chop the apples, and place them in another small bowl.

2. Combine the mayonnaise or salad dressing with the orange juice in a third small bowl. Drizzle a few tablespoons of the orange dressing over each bowl of fruit, and toss to coat the fruit well. Cover the fruit bowls tightly with plastic wrap, and refrigerate the fruits for at least 1 hour.

3. When ready to serve, layer the cabbage in the bottom of a salad bowl. Toss the chopped walnuts with the apples, and spoon the walnut mixture into the center of the bowl. Spoon the pears around the edges. Top with the raisins. To serve, pour the remaining orange dressing over the salad, and toss well to combine the ingredients. Spoon the salad onto 6 chilled individual salad plates.

Pear & Sweet Pepper Salad with Poppy Seed Dressing

Poppy Seed Dressing can be stored in a covered container in the refrigerator for up to 1 week.

LOW-CHOLESTEROL · LOW-SODIUM
Makes 4 servings.
Nutrient Value Per Serving: 153 calories, 1 g protein, 8 g fat, 21 g carbohydrate, 61 mg sodium, 0 mg cholesterol.

2	firm, ripe Anjou, Bartlett OR: Comice pears, peeled, halved, cored, and each half cut into eighths		**Poppy Seed Dressing (recipe follows)**
1	large sweet red pepper, cored, seeded, and cut lengthwise into thin slivers	4	cups mixed salad greens, such as arugula and radicchio, washed and dried

Toss together the pears and the red pepper in ¼ cup of the Poppy Seed Dressing in a medium-size bowl until the ingredients are coated. Arrange the salad greens, divided evenly, on 4 individual salad plates. Top with the pear mixture. Pass the remaining dressing.

THE PICK OF PEARS

Pears mature well off the tree, so they are picked and shipped before they ripen. Select unblemished pears.

● Let pears stand at room temperature in a covered bowl, or in a paper or plastic bag, until they are fully ripe.

● Check for ripeness by gently pressing the stem ends — when the flesh yields, the pears are ripe. Eat ripe pears immediately, or refrigerate them to prevent them from overripening.

● Pears provide a fair amount of vitamin C, and some vitamins A and B. A medium-size Bartlett pear has about 100 calories.

Poppy Seed Dressing:

Combine ⅔ cup of vegetable oil, ¼ cup of orange juice, ¼ cup of lemon juice, 3 tablespoons of sugar, 2 teaspoons of grated red onion, ½ teaspoon of dry mustard, ½ teaspoon of salt, and ¼ teaspoon of freshly ground pepper in the container of an electric blender or food processor. Whirl until the mixture is creamy. Add 2 teaspoons of poppy seeds, and whirl to combine them.

Makes 1¼ cups.

Nutrient Value Per Tablespoon: 76 calories, 0 g protein, 7 g fat, 2 g carbohydrate, 55 mg sodium, 0 mg cholesterol.

Pears are an old favorite, no matter how you serve them: tossed in salads, baked in desserts, or by their own sweet selves.

Corn & Pasta Salad

LOW-CHOLESTEROL

Makes 4 servings.

Nutrient Value Per Serving: 299 calories, 8 g protein, 12 g fat,
44 g carbohydrate, 232 mg sodium, 0 mg cholesterol.

2	to 3 large ears corn	1	tablespoon balsamic OR: red wine vinegar
½	cup water		
¾	cup small bow tie pasta, cooked and drained (1½ cups)	1	tablespoon distilled white vinegar
		2	teaspoons Dijon-style mustard
1	cup cherry tomato halves		
1	package (8 ounces) frozen sugar snap peas, thawed according to package directions, and drained	1	large clove garlic, pressed
		¼	teaspoon salt
		⅛	teaspoon freshly ground pepper
¼	cup chopped fresh basil	3	tablespoons olive oil

1. Cut the corn kernels from the cobs with a knife into a large bowl; you should have 2 to 2½ cups of kernels.

2. Bring the water to boiling in a medium-size saucepan over medium heat. Add the corn kernels. Reduce the heat to low, cover the saucepan and simmer for 4 to 5 minutes, or until the corn is tender. Drain the corn.

3. Combine the corn with the pasta, cherry tomatoes, peas and basil in the large bowl, and stir until the ingredients are well mixed. Set aside the pasta mixture.

4. Whisk the balsamic or red wine vinegar with the white vinegar, mustard, garlic, salt, pepper and oil in a small bowl. Pour the dressing over the pasta mixture, and toss to coat the ingredients. Serve the salad immediately. Or cover the bowl, and refrigerate the salad until serving time.

Waldorf Salad

For a special touch, serve this elegant salad in hollowed-out apples.

LOW-CHOLESTEROL · LOW-SODIUM

Makes 4 servings.

Nutrient Value Per Serving: 134 calories, 1 g protein, 8 g fat,
16 g carbohydrate, 49 mg sodium, 4 mg cholesterol.

2	medium-size red apples, quartered, cored and diced	2	tablespoons sliced celery
		2	tablespoons chopped walnuts
¼	cup seedless red grapes, halved		Honey Yogurt Dressing (recipe follows)

Combine the apples, grapes, celery and chopped walnuts in a medium-size bowl. Pour the Honey Yogurt Dressing on top of the salad, and stir gently to mix the ingredients well. Cover the bowl, and refrigerate the salad until serving time.

Honey Yogurt Dressing:

Stir together 2 tablespoons of plain lowfat yogurt, 2 tablespoons of mayonnaise, 2 teaspoons of lemon juice, and 2 teaspoons of honey in a small bowl until the dressing is smooth.
Makes about ⅓ cup.

HOW SWEET IT IS...

Corn is sweetest when it has just been picked. Its sweetness comes from its natural sugar, but the sugar starts turning to unsweet starch immediately after picking. The sugar-into-starch process has been slowed down in newer corn hybrids, so these varieties stay sweet longer. Three such varieties are Even Sweeter (white), Sweet Belle (yellow), and Yankee Belle (yellow). When buying corn, choose ears with fresh, green husks, moist silks, and plump, smooth, undented kernels. Avoid corn with rows of underdeveloped kernels. Refrigerate corn as soon as you get it home.

> "*Celery, raw,
> Develops the jaw,
> But celery, stewed,
> Is more quietly
> chewed.*"
>
> —*Ogden Nash*

Curried Chicken Salad with Nectarine Onion Salsa

Cooking the unskinned chicken on the bone in water produces a flavorful broth that is used in the dressing. The recipe makes extra broth, which can be used in soups, sauces or sautés.

Makes 4 servings.

Nutrient Value Per Serving: 578 calories, 33 g protein, 41 g fat, 25 g carbohydrate, 852 mg sodium, 74 mg cholesterol.

2	**whole chicken breasts (about 12 ounces each), halved**
1	**thick slice onion**
1	**leafy celery top**
1	**teaspoon salt**
	Curried Dressing (recipe follows)
6	**cups loosely packed torn summer lettuce leaves, such as Bibb, Boston, curly red leaf OR: baby romaine**

	Nectarine Onion Salsa (recipe follows)
½	**cup dry-roasted peanuts, coarsely chopped**
1	**nectarine, pitted, and cut into thin wedges, for garnish**
1	**tablespoon slivered green onion tops, for garnish**

1. Combine the chicken, onion, celery and salt in a large skillet. Pour in just enough water to barely cover the chicken. Bring the mixture to boiling. Lower the heat, cover the skillet and simmer, turning the chicken once, for 15 to 20 minutes, or until the chicken no longer is pink near the bone. Cool the chicken in the cooking liquid until the chicken is cool enough to handle. Remove and discard the skin and bones from the chicken. Cut the chicken into wide strips, and set them aside. Strain the chicken cooking liquid. Reserve 2 tablespoons of the broth for the Curried Dressing; refrigerate the remaining broth to use in soups, sauces or sautés. Discard the cooking liquid solids.

2. Combine the chicken strips with about half the dressing in a medium-size bowl. Toss the lettuce leaves with half the Nectarine Onion Salsa in another medium-size bowl. Divide the lettuce leaves among 4 individual salad plates. Mound the chicken strips, divided evenly, in the centers of the plates. Sprinkle the salads with the chopped peanuts. Garnish the salads with the nectarine wedges and the green onion. Pass the remaining dressing and salsa.

Curried Dressing:

Heat 1½ teaspoons of curry powder in a small skillet over low heat, stirring constantly, until the powder is fragrant. Add the reserved 2 tablespoons of chicken broth from Step 1 above, and cook for 30 seconds. Remove the skillet from the heat. Stir in ¼ cup of mayonnaise, ¼ cup of yogurt, 1 teaspoon of grated fresh ginger, 1 crushed small garlic clove, and a pinch of ground hot red pepper.

Nectarine Onion Salsa:

Stir together 2 cups of diced unpeeled nectarines (about 12 ounces), ½ cup of diced red onion, ⅓ cup of diced sweet red pepper, ⅓ cup of olive oil, 2 tablespoons of lime juice, ¼ teaspoon of salt, and ⅛ teaspoon of freshly ground pepper in a small bowl.

Marinated Tofu & Rice Salad

This quick-to-prepare salad takes advantage of boil-in-a-bag rice.

LOW-CHOLESTEROL

Makes 4 servings.

Nutrient Value Per Serving: 541 calories, 26 g protein, 22 g fat, 62 g carbohydrate, 858 mg sodium, 0 mg cholesterol.

⅓ cup reduced-sodium soy sauce	1 pound firm tofu, cut into bite-size pieces
2 tablespoons vegetable oil	2 boil-in bags (3½ ounces each) rice
2 tablespoons light brown sugar	¼ cup sliced green onion
1 tablespoon vinegar	1 large carrot, peeled and shredded
1 teaspoon Oriental sesame oil (see Note, page 145)	¼ cup cashews, coarsely chopped
½ teaspoon dry mustard	
¼ teaspoon crushed hot red pepper flakes	

TERRIFIC TOFU

Considered the "meat" of the Orient, tofu is soybean curd pressed into cakes. Tofu is low in fat, contains no cholesterol, and has a low ratio of calories to protein. A growing number of weight-, health- and cost-conscious people are turning to tofu as an inexpensive source of protein. Tofu is bland, so it absorbs the flavor of whatever foods it is added to or cooked with.

● Tofu is made by soaking soybeans until they are soft, then grinding them with water. The resulting purée is cooked and strained; the strained liquid is soy milk. A coagulant, such as epsom salt dissolved in water, is added to hot soy milk to separate the curds from the whey, and the soy curds are pressed into cakes.

● Tofu is made in soft and firm varieties. Soft tofu is ideal for main dishes, soups, and creamed desserts. Firm tofu is excellent for stir-fried dishes, and can be stuffed.

● Tofu is available prepackaged or sold by the piece. When sold by the piece, tofu is found in a pan of water in the refrigerated section of health food stores, Oriental food stores, and the produce section of the supermarket. When buying tofu, be sure the cake is ivory-colored, and the soaking water is clear and not sour smelling. Fresh tofu should have a bland, sweetish taste.

● To store tofu, place it in a bowl of water and refrigerate it. Change the water in the bowl daily. Tofu will keep in the refrigerator for about 1 week.

● A 4-ounce serving of tofu has 8.8 grams of protein, 1 gram of carbohydrates, and 130 calories.

The complex flavors of the Orient are captured in Marinated Tofu & Rice Salad.

1. Stir together the soy sauce, vegetable oil, brown sugar, vinegar, Oriental sesame oil, mustard and hot red pepper flakes in a pie plate. Add the tofu to the marinade in the pie plate, and stir to coat the tofu.

2. Cook the rice following the package directions. When the rice is cooked, carefully open the bags and turn the rice into a medium-size bowl. Add the green onion, carrot and chopped cashews. Pour the marinade from the pie plate over the rice mixture, and toss gently to coat the ingredients well. Top the salad with the tofu, and serve the salad immediately.

Note: Oriental sesame oil has more flavor and is darker in color than regular sesame oil. It can be found in the Oriental food section of many supermarkets, and in Oriental specialty food stores.

CRAZY ABOUT CARROTS

Hearty and inexpensive, carrots taste great raw, pickled, in crudités or salads, snacked straight from the refrigerator, baked in breads, or popped into soups. Even leafy carrot tops can be cooked deliciously with other greens.

● One carrot has only 20 calories, and is an excellent source of vitamin A.

Oriental Zucchini Carrot Slaw

LOW-CALORIE ▪ LOW-CHOLESTEROL
Makes 4 servings.
Nutrient Value Per Serving: 71 calories, 1 g protein, 4 g fat, 10 g carbohydrate, 279 mg sodium, 0 mg cholesterol.

2	tablespoons cider vinegar	3	drops liquid red pepper seasoning
1	tablespoon soy sauce		
1	tablespoon Oriental sesame OR: vegetable oil	1	large zucchini (8 ounces)
2	teaspoons sugar	4	carrots (8 ounces), peeled

1. Combine the vinegar, soy sauce, Oriental sesame or vegetable oil, sugar and liquid red pepper seasoning in the container of a food processor. Whirl until the ingredients are combined. Leave the dressing in the processor container.

2. Remove the chopping blade from the processor, and insert the shredding disk. Shred the zucchini and the carrot into the dressing. Remove the shredding disk. Using a fork, toss the slaw in the processor container to coat the ingredients.

Ripe Plum Tomato Salad

For this recipe, use the best plum tomatoes you can find.

LOW-CALORIE · LOW-CHOLESTEROL · LOW-FAT
Makes 4 servings.
Nutrient Value Per Serving: 27 calories, 1 g protein, .24 g fat,
6 g carbohydrate, 285 mg sodium, 0 mg cholesterol.

2	green onions, thinly sliced	2	cloves garlic, crushed
2	tablespoons trimmed and chopped fresh cilantro OR: 2 teaspoons ground coriander	1	pound ripe plum tomatoes, cut into 1-inch chunks
		½	teaspoon salt
2	tablespoons chopped parsley	⅛	teaspoon freshly ground pepper
1	tablespoon lime juice		

Combine the green onion, cilantro or coriander, parsley, lime juice, garlic, tomatoes, salt and pepper in a medium-size, nonreactive bowl. Let the tomato mixture stand at room temperature for ½ to 2 hours. Discard the garlic, and serve the salad.

Green Bean, Pear & Ham Salad with Honey Mustard Dressing

Makes 4 servings.
Nutrient Value Per Serving: 647 calories, 20 g protein, 46 g fat,
45 g carbohydrate, 1,165 mg sodium, 43 mg cholesterol.

8	ounces thin green beans	8	ounces honey-cured OR: wood-smoked OR: regular cured ham, cut into 3 x ¼ x ¼-inch strips
2	ripe large pears, halved and cored		
1	tablespoon lemon OR: lime juice	3	ounces Saga Blue OR: other blue cheese, cut into ¼-inch dice
6	cups torn curly red leaf and romaine lettuce leaves		
½	cup Honey Mustard Dressing (see Tip, at right)	½	cup walnut pieces, toasted

1. Cook the green beans in boiling water in a medium-size saucepan for 5 minutes, or until the green beans are crisply tender. Drain the green beans, rinse them with cold water, and drain them again.

2. Cut each pear half into 4 wedges. Place the pears in a medium-size bowl. Sprinkle the pears with the lemon or lime juice, and gently toss the pears to coat them. Set aside the pears.

3. Combine the lettuce leaves with the green beans in a large bowl. Toss the green bean mixture with the Honey Mustard Dressing until the ingredients are evenly coated. Divide the green bean mixture evenly among 4 individual salad plates. Arrange the pear wedges, like the spokes of a wheel, around the green bean mixture on each plate. Place the ham strips between the pears. Sprinkle the salads with the blue cheese and the toasted walnuts.

---

*"**I**t's a very odd thing—
As odd as can be
That whatever
Miss T. eats
Turns into Miss T. "*

— *Walter de la Mare*

HONEY MUSTARD DRESSING

● Combine ¼ cup of red wine vinegar with ¼ cup of honey, 1 teaspoon of coarse-grained Dijon-style mustard, 1 chopped small garlic clove, 1 coarsely chopped 3 x 1-inch strip of orange zest (orange part of the rind only), a pinch of salt, and ⅛ teaspoon of freshly ground pepper in the container of an electric blender or food processor. Whirl until the ingredients are well mixed.
● With the motor running, gradually pour in ½ cup of olive oil until the dressing is smooth and well blended. Makes about 1 cup.

Green Bean, Pear & Ham Salad with Honey Mustard Dressing is a wonderful combination of tastes guaranteed to please the most discerning palate.

Sliced Cucumbers in Yogurt

LOW-CALORIE ▪ LOW-CHOLESTEROL ▪ LOW-FAT

Makes 4 servings.

Nutrient Value Per Serving: 27 calories, 1 g protein, .33 g fat,
5 g carbohydrate, 290 mg sodium, 1 mg cholesterol.

2	cucumbers	⅛	teaspoon celery seeds
½	teaspoon salt	⅛	teaspoon ground cumin
¼	cup plain lowfat yogurt	⅛	teaspoon freshly
½	teaspoon sugar		ground pepper
½	teaspoon lemon juice		

1. Peel and thinly slice the cucumbers. Place the cucumbers in a small bowl. Sprinkle the cucumbers with the salt, and stir. Let the cucumbers stand for 10 minutes.

2. Stir together the yogurt, sugar, lemon juice, celery seeds, cumin and pepper in a small bowl until the ingredients are well mixed.

3. Transfer the cucumbers to a colander, and rinse them with cold running water. Squeeze the cucumbers with your hands to extract as much liquid as possible. Return the cucumbers to the bowl, and stir in the yogurt mixture. Cover the bowl, and refrigerate the cucumber mixture until serving time.

Cucumber & Romaine Salad with Cilantro Dressing

You can prepare the flavorful dressing a few days in advance, and dress the salad just before serving it.

LOW-CALORIE ▪ LOW-CHOLESTEROL

Makes 4 servings.

Nutrient Value Per Serving: 96 calories, 1 g protein, 9 g fat,
4 g carbohydrate, 146 mg sodium, 0 mg cholesterol.

½	cup firmly packed fresh cilantro leaves and tender stems	5	tablespoons olive oil
3	tablespoons rice wine vinegar OR: white wine vinegar	1	European seedless cucumber (about 12 ounces), unpeeled and thinly sliced (2½ cups)
½	teaspoon sugar	6	cups torn romaine lettuce leaves (7½ ounces), washed and dried
½	teaspoon salt		

1. Combine the cilantro, rice or white wine vinegar, sugar and salt in the container of a small food processor or electric blender. Whirl to combine the ingredients. Add the oil. Whirl until the dressing is smooth.

2. Combine the cucumber with the lettuce leaves in a salad bowl. Pour half the dressing over the cucumber mixture, and toss to coat the ingredients. Pass the remaining dressing. Or refrigerate the remaining dressing to use with another salad.

VEGETABLE HEALTH HITS

- **Carrots and Sweet Red Peppers:** Loaded with vitamin A, which maintains body cells and vision, especially night vision, and may help lower the risk of some kinds of cancer.
- **Broccoli and Brussels Sprouts:** High in vitamin C, which is needed to make collagen in bones, skin and tendons, and aids the body in healing.
- **Spinach and Greens such as Collards:** Deliver B vitamins, which provide energy and help reduce stress. Spinach also has iron, which is essential for red blood cells.
- **Lima Beans:** Supply phosphorus, which promotes bone formation.
- **Peas:** Contain potassium, which is necessary to keep body fluids in balance.

Side Dishes

A bevy of wonderful accompaniments to complete any meal.

Pickled Beets & Apples

LOW-CALORIE · LOW-CHOLESTEROL · LOW-FAT
Makes 4 servings.
Nutrient Value Per Serving: 95 calories, 1 g protein, .22 g fat,
24 g carbohydrate, 300 mg sodium, 0 mg cholesterol.

1 **jar (16 ounces) pickled beets, undrained**	1 **medium-size tart apple**
1 **teaspoon lemon juice**	**Thin lemon slices, for garnish (optional)**
⅛ **teaspoon ground cloves**	

1. Pour the beets with their liquid into a small bowl. Stir in the lemon juice and the cloves.

2. Quarter, core and peel the apple. Thinly slice the apple into the bowl with the beet mixture. Let the apple-beet mixture stand at room temperature until serving time. If you wish, garnish the apple-beet mixture with thin lemon slices.

Corn with Shallot Cumin Butter

Bake at 400° for 20 to 25 minutes.
Makes 4 servings.
Nutrient Value Per Serving: 271 calories, 6 g protein, 14 g fat,
37 g carbohydrate, 102 mg sodium, 31 mg cholesterol.

4 **large ears corn in husks**	1 **large clove garlic, pressed**
4 **tablespoons (½ stick) unsalted butter or margarine**	1 **tablespoon ground cumin**
	½ **teaspoon lemon juice**
¼ **cup finely chopped shallots OR: onion**	⅛ **teaspoon salt**
	⅛ **teaspoon freshly ground pepper**

1. Preheat the oven to hot (400°).

2. Carefully pull back the corn husks without detaching them. Remove the silk, and pull the husks back over the corn. Tie the husks closed at the top with kitchen string. Soak the corn, completely immersed, in a large pot of water for 20 minutes.

3. Roast the corn directly on an oven rack in the preheated hot oven (400°) for 20 to 25 minutes, or until the corn is tender when pierced with a fork.

4. Meanwhile, melt the butter or margarine in a small skillet over medium heat. Add the shallots or onion, the garlic and cumin. Cook, stirring occasionally, for 2 to 3 minutes, or until the vegetables are tender. Stir in the lemon juice, salt and pepper. Transfer the butter mixture to a bowl. Serve the roasted corn with the butter mixture.

CORN ON THE COB: WHAT'S YOUR BITE STYLE?

The way you eat corn on the cob says a lot about you. If you nibble neatly from end to end, you're methodical, down-to-earth, and a terrific organizer. If you munch around the cob, you have a lighthearted approach to life, and an easygoing nature. If you chomp randomly, you're a rebel—you make your own rules, and like to take the lead.

Corn Pudding

Bake at 350° for 40 minutes.

Makes 6 servings.

Nutrient Value Per Serving: 207 calories, 8 g protein, 13 g fat, 17 g carbohydrate, 352 mg sodium, 137 mg cholesterol.

2	to 3 large ears corn	1	cup milk
½	cup chopped green onion, green part only	1	cup half-and-half
½	cup chopped sweet red pepper	2	teaspoons sugar
2	tablespoons unsalted butter or margarine	¾	teaspoon salt
3	eggs	⅛	teaspoon freshly ground pepper
			Boiling water

1. Preheat the oven to moderate (350°). Grease a shallow 1½-quart or 8 x 8 x 2-inch square baking dish.

2. Cut the corn kernels from the cobs with a knife into a bowl; you should have 2 to 2½ cups of kernels. Set aside the corn kernels.

3. Sauté the green onion and the red pepper in the butter or margarine in a small skillet for 3 to 5 minutes, or until the vegetables are tender.

4. Beat the eggs slightly in a medium-size bowl. Stir in the milk, half-and-half, sugar, salt, pepper, corn kernels and green onion mixture until they are well blended. Pour the corn mixture into the prepared dish. Set the dish in a larger pan, and place the pan on a rack in the preheated oven. Pour the boiling water into the larger pan to a depth of 1 inch.

5. Bake the corn pudding in the preheated moderate oven (350°) for 40 minutes, or until a knife inserted near the center comes out clean. Remove the corn pudding from the water bath, and serve.

Orange Carrots

LOW-CALORIE ▪ LOW-CHOLESTEROL ▪ LOW-FAT

Makes 4 servings.

Nutrient Value Per Serving: 61 calories, 1 g protein, .21 g fat, 14 g carbohydrate, 173 mg sodium, 0 mg cholesterol.

½	cup orange juice	1	teaspoon grated orange zest (orange part of rind only)
¼	teaspoon salt		
6	carrots, trimmed, peeled, and cut into ¼-inch-thick slices		

1. Combine the orange juice with the salt in a medium-size saucepan, and bring the mixture to boiling. Add the carrots. Lower the heat and simmer, covered, for 5 minutes.

2. Uncover the saucepan and cook the carrot mixture for 8 to 10 minutes more, or until most of the liquid has evaporated. Stir in the orange zest, and serve.

COOKING CORN

The secret to cooking corn perfectly is to be sure you don't overcook it. To prepare corn for boiling, steaming or microwaving, remove the husks and silk, and rinse the ears gently in running water. If you have young, fresh corn, cook it for the shortest time indicated below.

● **Boiling:** Drop the corn, a few ears at a time, into a pot of boiling water. Cook for 4 to 7 minutes.

● **Steaming:** Set the corn on a rack over boiling water inside a pot. Cover the pot, and cook for 6 to 10 minutes.

● **Microwaving:** Place 4 to 6 ears of corn in a microwave-safe baking dish. Add 3 tablespoons of water, and cover the dish. Microwave at full power for 3 minutes on each side in a 600-watt oven, for 5 minutes on each side in a 400-watt oven.

● **Roasting:** Follow the directions in Corn with Shallot Cumin Butter (recipe, page 149).

● **Grilling:** Remove the silk, but leave the husks on. Cook the corn over coals for 15 to 20 minutes, turning the ears every 3 minutes.

Squash Kebabs

LOW-CALORIE ▪ LOW-CHOLESTEROL

Broil for 6 to 8 minutes.

Makes 4 servings.

Nutrient Value Per Serving: 99 calories, 2 g protein, 7 g fat, 8 g carbohydrate, 141 mg sodium, 0 mg cholesterol.

2 **tablespoons olive oil**	1 **pound zucchini (2 medium-size zucchini), sliced crosswise into 1-inch-thick chunks**
1 **tablespoon white wine vinegar**	
1 **clove garlic, finely chopped**	1 **pound yellow squash (2 medium-size squash), sliced crosswise into 1-inch-thick chunks**
½ **teaspoon dried oregano, crumbled**	
¼ **teaspoon salt**	
⅛ **teaspoon freshly ground pepper**	

1. Preheat the broiler. Lightly grease the broiler-pan rack.

2. Combine the oil, vinegar, garlic, oregano, salt and pepper in a medium-size bowl. Add the zucchini and the squash to the marinade in the bowl. Alternating colors, thread the zucchini and squash on four 8-inch skewers. Arrange the skewers on the broiler-pan rack. Reserve the marinade.

3. Broil the kebabs, with the bottom of the broiler pan 6 inches from the heat source, for 6 to 8 minutes, turning the kebabs once or twice and brushing them with the reserved marinade. Serve the kebabs hot.

Baked Stuffed Tomatoes

LOW-CHOLESTEROL ▪ LOW-FAT ▪ MICROWAVE

Bake at 425° for 10 minutes; or microwave at full power for 6 minutes, then at three quarters power for 8 minutes.

Makes 4 servings.

Nutrient Value Per Serving: 159 calories, 5 g protein, 5 g fat, 27 g carbohydrate, 255 mg sodium, 0 mg cholesterol.

4 **tomatoes (about 1½ pounds)**	**Half 6-ounce package cornbread stuffing mix (about 1 cup)**
1 **medium-size onion, chopped (½ cup)**	
¼ **pound zucchini, chopped**	**Half stuffing mix seasoning packet (about 1 tablespoon)**
2 **ounces mushrooms, chopped**	
1 **tablespoon olive oil**	

1. Preheat the oven to hot (425°).

2. Cut a thin slice from the top of each tomato, and core the tomato. Scoop out the insides of the tomatoes, reserving the juice. Place the tomato shells upside down on paper toweling to drain. Chop the tomato pulp.

3. Sauté the onion, zucchini and mushrooms in the oil in a large skillet over medium heat until the vegetables are tender. Mix in the tomato pulp, stuffing mix and seasoning. Spoon the tomato mixture into the tomato shells. Place any extra tomato mixture in a greased custard cup.

4. Bake the stuffed tomatoes and extra tomato mixture in the preheated hot oven (425°) for 10 minutes, or until the stuffed tomatoes are heated through. Serve the stuffed tomatoes hot, or at room temperature.

STUFFED TOMATOES À LA MICROWAVE

● Prepare the tomatoes following Step 2 of Baked Stuffed Tomatoes *(at right)*.

● Combine the onion, zucchini, mushrooms and oil in a microwave-safe 1½-quart casserole dish. Microwave, uncovered, at full power in a 650-watt variable power microwave oven, stirring once, for 6 minutes, or until the onion is tender. Stir in the tomato pulp, stuffing mix and seasoning. Spoon the tomato mixture into the tomato shells. Place any extra tomato mixture in a custard cup.

● Evenly space the stuffed tomatoes and custard cup around the edge of a microwave-safe 10-inch pie plate. Microwave the stuffed tomatoes and extra tomato mixture, uncovered, at three quarters power for 8 minutes, rotating the pie plate one half turn halfway through the cooking time.

Baked Shredded Sweet Potatoes

LOW-CHOLESTEROL · MICROWAVE

Bake at 375° for 20 minutes; or microwave at full power for 7 minutes.
Makes 4 servings.

Nutrient Value Per Serving: 147 calories, 1 g protein, 7 g fat,
20 g carbohydrate, 284 mg sodium, 0 mg cholesterol.

2	**tablespoons olive oil**	**½**	**teaspoon salt**
1	**large clove garlic, crushed**	**⅛**	**teaspoon freshly ground pepper**
1	**pound sweet potatoes, peeled and shredded**		

1. Preheat the oven to moderate (375°). Combine the oil with the garlic in a 9-inch pie plate. Place the pie plate in the oven while the oven is heating.

2. When the oven is heated, remove the pie plate. Add the sweet potatoes, salt and pepper to the pie plate. Stir to coat the sweet potatoes with the oil.

3. Bake the sweet potatoes in the preheated moderate oven (375°), stirring once, for 20 minutes, or until the sweet potatoes are tender.

Microwave Instructions

(for a 650-watt variable power microwave oven)

Ingredient Changes: Use a small clove of garlic.

Directions: Stir together the oil and the garlic in a microwave-safe 10-inch pie plate. Cover the pie plate with wax paper. Microwave at full power for 2 minutes. Stir in the sweet potatoes. Cover the pie plate with wax paper. Microwave at full power for 5 minutes, stirring once. Let the sweet potatoes stand for 1 minute. Stir in the salt and the pepper.

Zucchini Potato Pancakes

Makes 4 servings (12 pancakes).

Nutrient Value Per Serving: 229 calories, 6 g protein, 13 g fat,
22 g carbohydrate, 414 mg sodium, 57 mg cholesterol.

¼	**cup milk**	**2**	**cups shredded potatoes (half purchased 20-ounce refrigerated package)**
1	**egg**		
¼	**cup all-purpose flour**	**8**	**ounces zucchini, shredded**
½	**teaspoon baking powder**	**1**	**small onion, finely chopped**
½	**teaspoon salt**	**2**	**tablespoons grated Parmesan cheese**
¼	**teaspoon freshly ground pepper**		
1	**clove garlic, finely chopped**	**3**	**tablespoons vegetable oil**

1. Whisk together the milk and the egg in a medium-size bowl. Add the flour, baking powder, salt, pepper and garlic. Whisk until the mixture is smooth. Stir in the potatoes, zucchini, onion and Parmesan cheese.

2. Heat 1 tablespoon of the oil in a large, nonstick skillet over medium heat. Using ¼ cup of batter for each pancake, scoop 4 mounds of batter into the skillet. Flatten each mound into a 4-inch-diameter pancake. Cook the pancakes for 3 minutes, or until the bottoms are browned. Turn over the pancakes, and reduce the heat to medium-low. Cook the pancakes for 5 minutes more, or until they are cooked through. Stack the pancakes on a plate, and keep them warm. Repeat with the remaining oil and batter.

THE SWEET POTATO

A sweet potato is the edible tuberous, or enlarged, root of a vine related to the morning glory. The plant is indigenous to South and Central America, where the natives raised them for food long before the Europeans arrived. The terms sweet potato and yam often are used interchangeably. Although the two vegetables appear to be similar, botanically they belong to two different plant families.

● There are many varieties of sweet potatoes, and they vary in shape, color and texture. Some potatoes taper to a point; others are cylindrical or chunky. The skin color can be yellowish-tan, whitish-tan, or brownish-red. The flesh can be orange, golden yellow, or ivory. When cooked, the flesh can be dry like a regular potato, or moist like a winter squash.

● The sweet potato is an excellent source of vitamins A and C. A 3½-ounce serving of boiled sweet potato has 114 calories; when baked in its skin, it has about 141 calories.

● Sweet potatoes are available year-round, with the best supplies in the fall to spring. Sweet potato varieties cannot be distinguished by skin color. When selecting sweet potatoes, choose thick, chunky roots that are firm and unblemished. Allow 1 medium-size sweet potato per serving.

● Store sweet potatoes in a cool, dry, well ventilated place; do not refrigerate them. Use sweet potatoes within a few weeks of purchase.

Zucchini Sauté

LOW-CALORIE · LOW-CHOLESTEROL · MICROWAVE

Microwave at full power for 8 minutes.

Makes 4 servings.

Nutrient Value Per Serving: 54 calories, 2 g protein, 4 g fat, 5 g carbohydrate, 277 mg sodium, 0 mg cholesterol.

1 **pound small zucchini**	½ **teaspoon salt**
1 **tablespoon olive oil**	¼ **teaspoon dried thyme, crumbled**
1 **medium-size onion, cut into thin slivers**	¼ **teaspoon freshly ground pepper**
1 **clove garlic, finely chopped**	

1. Quarter the zucchini lengthwise, and cut it crosswise into halves or thirds. Heat the oil in a large, nonstick skillet. Add the zucchini and cook over medium-high heat, stirring, for 3 minutes, or until the zucchini is crisply tender. Remove the zucchini from the skillet with a slotted spoon, and set aside the zucchini.

2. Reduce the heat to medium. Add the onion and the garlic to the skillet, and cook for 2 minutes, stirring often. Return the zucchini to the skillet. Stir in the salt, thyme and pepper. Serve the zucchini mixture immediately.

Microwave Instructions

(for a 650-watt variable power microwave oven)

Directions: Stir together the oil, onion and garlic in a microwave-safe 2-quart casserole dish. Cover the dish, and microwave at full power for 3 minutes. Stir in the zucchini and the thyme. Cover the dish, and microwave at full power for 5 minutes, stirring once. Stir in the salt and the pepper.

Italian Green Bean Toss

LOW-CALORIE · LOW-CHOLESTEROL · MICROWAVE

Microwave at full power for 9 minutes.

Makes 4 servings.

Nutrient Value Per Serving: 80 calories, 2 g protein, 5 g fat, 8 g carbohydrate, 107 mg sodium, 0 mg cholesterol.

1 **package (9 ounces) frozen Italian green beans**	1 **tablespoon Italian salad dressing**
½ **small red onion, thinly sliced**	⅛ **teaspoon salt**
1 **carrot, peeled and shredded**	⅛ **teaspoon freshly ground pepper**
1 **tablespoon olive oil**	

1. Cook the green beans following the package directions, and drain them.

2. Sauté the onion and the carrot in the oil in a saucepan over medium heat for 3 minutes. Add the green beans, salad dressing, salt and pepper, and toss to mix the ingredients. Serve hot, or at room temperature.

Microwave Instructions

(for a 650-watt variable power microwave oven)

Directions: Combine the onion, carrot and oil in a microwave-safe 1½-quart casserole dish. Cover the dish, and microwave at full power for 3 minutes. Add the green beans. Cover, and microwave at full power for 6 minutes, stirring once. Stir in the salad dressing, salt and pepper, and serve.

> "*He that eateth well, drinketh well; he that drinketh well, sleepeth well; he that sleepeth well, sinneth not; he that sinneth not goeth straight through Purgatory to Paradise.*"
>
> — *William Lithgow*

Layered Vegetable Pâté

You can make this pâté up to 2 days in advance, and refrigerate it.

Bake at 325° for 90 minutes.
Makes 16 servings.

Nutrient Value Per Serving: 137 calories, 4 g protein, 9 g fat,
11 g carbohydrate, 325 mg sodium, 101 mg cholesterol.

Base Mixture:

6	eggs
1	cup heavy cream OR: milk

Carrot Layer:

1½	pounds plus 3 carrots, trimmed and peeled
¼	cup plain dry bread crumbs
1	teaspoon salt
½	teaspoon freshly ground pepper
¼	teaspoon freshly ground nutmeg

Spinach Layer:

1	package (10 ounces) frozen spinach, thawed
1	tablespoon olive oil
¾	cup finely chopped onion
¾	cup cooked potatoes (about 8 ounces fresh potatoes)
2	tablespoons grated Parmesan cheese
¾	teaspoon salt
¼	teaspoon freshly ground pepper

Boiling water
Cherry tomatoes (optional)
Toast (optional)

1. Prepare the Base Mixture: Combine the eggs with the cream or milk in the container of a food processor or electric blender. Whirl until the mixture is blended. Remove and reserve ¾ cup of the base mixture for the spinach layer. Remove the remaining base mixture to a small bowl, and set it aside.

2. Prepare the Carrot Layer: Cut the 1½ pounds of carrots into 1½-inch dice; leave the 3 carrots whole. Cook the diced and whole carrots in a large pot of simmering water for about 15 minutes, or until the carrots are tender but not mushy. Drain the carrots. Transfer the diced carrots to the processor container along with the bread crumbs, salt, pepper and nutmeg. Whirl for 2 minutes, or until the carrot mixture is a smooth purée. Transfer the carrot purée to a medium-size bowl. Cover the bowl, and refrigerate the carrot purée until ready to assemble the pâté. Using a sharp small knife, cut 3 thin, lengthwise slices from each whole carrot to make a 3-sided, triangular-shaped carrot. Set aside the triangular carrots.

3. Prepare the Spinach Layer: Drain the spinach, and press out the liquid. Transfer ½ cup of the spinach to the processor container; reserve the remaining spinach for another use.

4. Heat the oil in a medium-size skillet over medium-low heat. Stir in the onion and cook, covered, stirring occasionally, for 5 minutes, or until the onion is soft and transparent. Add the onion to the spinach in the processor container. Whirl to blend the ingredients. Add the reserved base mixture, the potatoes, Parmesan cheese, salt and pepper. Whirl for 1 minute, or until the spinach mixture is blended. Transfer the spinach mixture to a clean, medium-size bowl. Cover the bowl, and refrigerate the spinach mixture until ready to assemble the pâté.

5. Preheat the oven to slow (325°).

6. Line a 9¼ x 5¼ x 2¾-inch loaf pan with aluminum foil, and brush the entire surface of the foil with oil. Spoon one third of the carrot purée over the bottom of the prepared pan, and smooth the top of the layer with a rubber spatula.

PÂTÉ

The traditional definition of pâté is a well-seasoned mixture of finely minced or ground meat and/or liver baked in a pastry crust. But the word has expanded in meaning to describe a glorified meat loaf, a savory mousse, or a cocktail spread. A pâté baked in a deep oval dish is called a terrine. Today pork, veal, chicken, duck, rabbit or other game, fish, and even vegetables are used to make pâtés. The famous — and fabulous! — "pâté de foie gras" is made with goose livers and truffles.

7. Gently spoon half the spinach mixture evenly over the carrot layer in the pan, and smooth the top of the spinach layer with the rubber spatula. Rap the loaf pan gently on the work surface. Evenly space the 3 triangular carrots on top of the spinach layer so the carrots extend the length of pan; cut and fit the carrots as necessary. Spoon the remaining spinach mixture evenly over the carrots, covering them completely. Smooth the top of the spinach layer with the rubber spatula. Rap the loaf pan on the work surface.

8. Spoon the remaining carrot purée over the spinach layer, and smooth the top of the carrot layer with the rubber spatula. Rap the loaf pan on the work surface. Cover the loaf pan with oiled aluminum foil. Place the loaf pan in a roasting pan on a rack in the preheated oven. Pour enough boiling water into the roasting pan to come halfway up the sides of the loaf pan.

9. Bake the pâté in the preheated slow oven (325°) for 90 minutes, or until the pâté is firm to the touch and a knife inserted in the center comes out clean and is hot to the touch. Remove the pâté from the water bath. Cool the pâté for 10 minutes.

10. Place a same-size loaf pan on top of the pâté. Weight the empty loaf pan with three 1-pound cans, and refrigerate the pâté overnight. The next day, invert the pâté loaf pan onto a serving platter and peel away the aluminum foil. Serve the pâté chilled, but not ice cold. To serve, cut the pâté into ¼- to ⅜-inch-thick slices. If you wish, serve the pâté with cherry tomatoes and toast.

A scrumptious food fantasy, Layered Vegetable Pâté is striped with carrots and spinach, showing off the beauty — and taste — of vegetable combinations.

155

Strawberry Chutney

Serve this chutney with cold roasted meats.

LOW-CALORIE · LOW-CHOLESTEROL · LOW-SODIUM · LOW-FAT
Makes 4 cups.
Nutrient Value Per Tablespoon: 5 calories, 0 g protein, 0 g fat,
1 g carbohydrate, 2 mg sodium, 0 mg cholesterol.

1½ pints strawberries, gently rinsed and hulled	¾ cup firmly packed light brown sugar
1 large sweet red pepper, cored, seeded, and cut into ½-inch dice	2½ teaspoons peeled, chopped fresh ginger
1 large tart apple, such as Granny Smith, peeled, cored and shredded	½ teaspoon ground allspice
1 cup raisins	¼ teaspoon salt
1 cup balsamic vinegar	¼ teaspoon ground hot red pepper

1. Combine the strawberries, red pepper, apple, raisins, vinegar, brown sugar, ginger, allspice, salt and ground hot red pepper in a large, heavy, nonreactive saucepan. Bring the chutney to boiling over medium heat. Gently boil, stirring frequently, for 40 minutes, or until the chutney is glassy and thickened.

2. Pour the chutney into 4 sterilized ½-pint canning jars with screw-top lids. Cover the jars. Cool the chutney in the jars on a wire rack. Store the chutney in the refrigerator for up to 3 weeks.

Parslied Rice Pilaf

LOW-CHOLESTEROL · LOW-FAT
Makes 4 servings.
Nutrient Value Per Serving: 209 calories, 5 g protein, 4 g fat,
39 g carbohydrate, 382 mg sodium, 8 mg cholesterol.

1 cup long-grain white rice	¼ teaspoon curry powder
⅓ cup chopped onion (1 small onion)	⅛ teaspoon salt
1 tablespoon unsalted butter or margarine	⅛ teaspoon freshly ground pepper
1¼ cups chicken broth	⅓ cup chopped parsley

1. Sauté the rice and the onion in the butter or margarine in a medium-size saucepan over medium heat for 3 minutes.

2. Place the broth in a 2-cup glass measure, and add enough water to make 2 cups. Stir the broth mixture into the saucepan along with the curry powder, salt and pepper. Bring the curry mixture to boiling. Lower the heat, cover the saucepan and simmer for 20 minutes, or until the rice is tender. Remove the saucepan from the heat. Stir in the parsley, and serve.

CHAMPION CHUTNEY

This classic accompaniment to Indian curry dishes traditionally is made from a mixture of fresh fruit (often mango), dried fruit (such as raisins), and spices. The sweetness of the chutney is a perfect foil for the hot spice of a curry dish. Chutney also can be served as a relish with poultry, pork or ham.

○ ❖ ○

"Same old slippers, Same old rice, Same old glimpse of Paradise."

—William James Lampton

RICE COOKING

Gingered Rice

LOW-CHOLESTEROL · LOW-FAT · LOW-SODIUM

Makes 4 servings.
Nutrient Value Per Serving: 142 calories, 3 g protein, 0 g fat, 31 g carbohydrate, 4 mg sodium, 0 mg cholesterol.

¾	**cup rice**	**2**	**tablespoons rice wine vinegar**
1	**cup chopped onion (1 large onion)**		
1	**tablespoon peeled, chopped fresh ginger**		

Cook the rice following the package directions, adding the onion and the ginger. When the rice is cooked, stir in the vinegar. Serve the rice hot.

Moroccan Couscous

LOW-CHOLESTEROL · LOW-FAT

Makes 4 servings.
Nutrient Value Per Serving: 151 calories, 5 g protein, 1 g fat, 30 g carbohydrate, 256 mg sodium, .17 mg cholesterol.

1	**cup couscous**	**2**	**tablespoons golden raisins**
1	**envelope (.187 ounce) instant chicken broth**	**1**	**tablespoon slivered almonds**
2	**tablespoons chopped green onion**	⅛	**teaspoon ground cinnamon**
		1½	**cups boiling water**

Stir together the couscous, instant broth, green onion, raisins, slivered almonds and cinnamon in a medium-size serving bowl. Pour in the boiling water following the directions on the couscous package, and stir. Cover the serving bowl, and let the couscous stand for 5 minutes. Stir the couscous with a fork, and serve.

RICE COOKING

Here's a guide to cooking rice perfectly every time.

● **Boiling:** Combine 2 to 2½ cups of water, 1 tablespoon of butter or margarine and, if you wish, salt to taste in a medium-size, heavy saucepan. Bring the mixture to boiling. Stir in 1 cup of long-grain or processed (converted) white rice. Return the water to boiling. Lower the heat until the water is bubbling gently, and cover the saucepan with a tight-fitting lid. Following the rice package directions, simmer the rice for 14 to 25 minutes, or until the rice is tender and the water is absorbed. Fluff the rice with a fork, and serve.

● **Baking:** Preheat the oven to moderate (350°). Combine 1 cup of long-grain or processed (converted) white rice, 1 tablespoon of butter or margarine and, if you wish, salt to taste in a 4- or 6-cup baking dish. Pour in 2½ cups of boiling water, and stir. Cover the baking dish. Bake the rice in the preheated moderate oven (350°) for 1 hour, or until the rice is tender and the water is absorbed. Fluff the rice with a fork, and serve.

Basil Zucchini Muffins

Bake at 400° for 22 to 24 minutes.
Makes 12 muffins.

Nutrient Value Per Muffin: 134 calories, 4 g protein, 6 g fat,
16 g carbohydrate, 199 mg sodium, 21 mg cholesterol.

1¾ cups all-purpose flour	¾ cup milk
3 tablespoons grated Parmesan cheese	¼ cup olive oil
1 tablespoon sugar	1 cup shredded zucchini
2 teaspoons baking powder	1 tablespoon finely chopped fresh basil
½ teaspoon salt	Butter or margarine (optional)
1 egg, slightly beaten	

1. Preheat the oven to hot (400°). Lightly grease the bottoms of twelve 2½-inch muffin-pan cups.

2. Combine the flour, Parmesan cheese, sugar, baking powder and salt in a large bowl. Combine the egg, milk, oil, zucchini and basil in a small bowl. Pour the egg mixture all at once into the flour mixture, and stir quickly with a fork just until the ingredients are combined; do not overstir. The batter will look lumpy. Divide the batter evenly among the muffin-pan cups.

3. Bake the muffins in the preheated hot oven (400°) for 22 to 24 minutes, or until the tops are lightly browned and a wooden pick inserted in the centers comes out clean. Cool the muffins in the pan on a wire rack for 3 minutes. Run a small, flexible knife around the edge of each muffin, and remove the muffins from the pan. Cool the muffins on the wire rack for 6 minutes. Serve the muffins warm, with butter or margarine if you wish.

ABOUT BASIL

There are many varieties of this fragrant annual herb, but only a few are cultivated for culinary or decorative purposes. Purple basil is grown in home gardens for its beautiful foliage. Sweet basil, the variety most often used in cooking, grows in temperate regions. A native of the Mediterranean, Middle East and India, sweet basil has a spicy, clove-like flavor that complements eggs, cheese, tomatoes, fish and poultry. Basil is the main ingredient in a sauce that is known as "pesto" in Italy, and "pistou" in France.

● Basil is available fresh during the summer, and is dried for year-round use. Preserve fresh basil leaves by freezing them. Or pack the leaves in a jar, fill the jar with olive oil and store the jar in the refrigerator. Fresh basil also can be dried in the microwave.

Full of summer's best flavors, try Basil Zucchini Muffins with dinner, breakfast, or as a snack.

Prosciutto, Pear & Cheese Toasts

Bake at 500° for 6 minutes.

Makes 30 toasts.

Nutrient Value Per Toast: 78 calories, 3 g protein, 3 g fat, 10 g carbohydrate, 149 mg sodium, 6 mg cholesterol.

1	loaf (15 inches long) French OR: Italian bread	3	to 6 drops liquid red pepper seasoning
1	firm, ripe Bartlett, Anjou OR: Comice pear	1/3	cup walnut halves, toasted and chopped
1	teaspoon lemon juice	1/4	pound prosciutto OR: thinly sliced baked ham
4	ounces blue cheese		
1	package (3 ounces) cream cheese, softened		

1. Preheat the oven to extremely hot (500°).

2. Cut the bread crosswise into thirty ½-inch-thick slices. Arrange the slices on baking sheets.

3. Cut the pear in half lengthwise. Peel and core one pear half, and cut it into ¼-inch dice. Set aside the diced pear. Core the remaining pear half, and thinly slice it lengthwise. Toss the pear slices with the lemon juice in a small bowl. Set aside the pear slices.

4. Mash together the blue cheese, cream cheese, liquid red pepper seasoning and ¼ cup of the chopped walnuts in a small bowl until they are well blended. Stir in the diced pear. Set aside the cheese mixture.

5. Bake the bread slices in the preheated extremely hot oven (500°) for 3 minutes, or until the bread slices are golden. Leave the oven on.

6. Spread about 1 teaspoon of the cheese mixture on the untoasted side of each bread slice. Arrange the slices, coated side up, on the baking sheets.

7. Bake the bread slices in the preheated extremely hot oven (500°) for 3 minutes, or until the cheese mixture is bubbly and the bread is toasted. Remove the toasts from the oven. Top the toasts with the pear slices, remaining chopped walnuts and the prosciutto or baked ham, divided evenly.

Herbed Italian Bread

LOW-CHOLESTEROL · LOW-FAT

Bake at 375° for 10 minutes.

Makes 4 servings.

Nutrient Value Per Serving: 217 calories, 5 g protein, 7 g fat, 32 g carbohydrate, 332 mg sodium, 1 mg cholesterol.

½	loaf (8 ounces) Italian bread	1/4	teaspoon dried basil, crumbled
2	tablespoons olive oil		
2	tablespoons chopped parsley		

1. Preheat the oven to moderate (375°).

2. Cut the bread crosswise into 8 equal slices. Place the bread slices on a baking sheet. Brush the tops of the slices with the oil. Combine the parsley with the basil in a cup. Sprinkle the herb mixture over the bread slices.

3. Bake the bread slices in the preheated moderate oven (375°) for 10 minutes. Serve the bread slices hot.

PEARS: A SWEET SENSATION

Why are pears so sweet? Levulose, the sweetest of known sugars, is found in fresh pears to a greater extent than in any other fruit. Pear varieties to choose include:
- **Bartlett:** Bell-shaped, crimson-blushed yellow. Delicious fresh, preserved, or baked.
- **Anjou:** Egg-shaped, green or yellow green, thin-skinned, juicy. Best eaten fresh.
- **Bosc:** Slender, golden brown to russet skin, crunchy. Holds shape when cooked.
- **Comice:** Chubby, yellow green, aromatic. Excellent eaten fresh; does not hold shape when cooked.
- **Seckel:** Bite-size, all red or blushing green. Good fresh, pickled, or canned.

HERBAL ESSENCE

- When using dried herbs, crush the leaves in the palm of your hand just before adding them to the recipe.
- Herbs in dried leaf form have a fresher flavor than ground herbs.
- When substituting dried herbs for fresh, use 1 teaspoon of dried herbs for each tablespoon of fresh.

Parsley Cheese Bread

Any leftover bread can be sealed tightly in aluminum foil, and frozen. Heat the foil packet in the oven just before serving for just-baked flavor.

LOW-CHOLESTEROL
Bake at 450° for 7 minutes.
Makes 8 servings.
Nutrient Value Per Serving: 150 calories, 4 g protein, 6 g fat, 20 g carbohydrate, 231 mg sodium, 1 mg cholesterol.

3	tablespoons olive oil	2	tablespoons chopped parsley
2	cloves garlic, halved	2	tablespoons grated Parmesan cheese
1	loaf (10 ounces) Italian bread, cut into ¾-inch-thick slices		

1. Preheat the oven to hot (450°).

2. Heat the oil with the garlic in a small saucepan until the oil is hot. Remove and discard the garlic. Place the bread slices on a baking sheet. Brush the slices with the hot oil.

3. Bake the bread slices in the preheated hot oven (450°) for 5 minutes, or until the bread slices are golden brown.

4. Combine the parsley with the Parmesan cheese in a cup. Sprinkle the parsley mixture over the bread slices. Bake the bread slices for 2 minutes more. Serve the toasted bread hot.

Hot Bread with Seasoned Butter

Bake at 450° for 10 minutes.
Makes 8 servings.
Nutrient Value Per Serving: 259 calories, 5 g protein, 12 g fat, 32 g carbohydrate, 403 mg sodium, 32 mg cholesterol.

½	cup (1 stick) unsalted butter	1	tablespoon chopped parsley
1	teaspoon lime juice	1	tablespoon sliced green onion
¼	teaspoon salt	1	loaf Italian bread
4	drops liquid red pepper seasoning		

1. Preheat the oven to hot (450°).

2. Beat together the butter, lime juice, salt, liquid red pepper seasoning, parsley and green onion in a small bowl.

3. Split the bread in half lengthwise. Spread 2½ tablespoons of the butter mixture over the bread halves. Wrap the remaining butter mixture in aluminum foil, and refrigerate or freeze it for another use. Wrap the bread halves in aluminum foil.

4. Bake the bread halves in the preheated hot oven (450°) for 10 minutes. Unwrap the bread halves, and serve.

> *"There is communion of more than our bodies when bread is broken and wine is drunk. And that is my answer, when people ask me: Why do you write about hunger, and not wars or love."*
> —M.F.K. Fisher

CHAPTER 4

Out of the Microwave

Microwave ovens are one of the wonders of the modern world, and people everywhere are discovering, or rediscovering, the ease and convenience of microwave cooking. Whether you create entire meals in the microwave, or use it in tandem with a conventional stove top and oven to speed supper along, this chapter has something just for you.

Starting with seafood, which cooks up moist and flavorful in the microwave, we offer tempting dishes such as Marinated Swordfish Kebabs, Cajun Shrimp in Shells and Vermicelli with Crab & Chicken. If you're in the mood for poultry, trot out an extra-special Turkey Loaf with Spicy Citrus Sauce or Curried Chicken & Vegetable Salad.

For super soups, try our meal-in-a-dish Vegetarian Bean Soup or rich, creamy Seafood Chowder. Our Hearty Chicken Noodle Soup can practically double as a stew! And don't forget to look at our selection of snappy side dishes and sumptuous sweets.

Don't dismiss your microwave oven as just a device to defrost or heat up food. Use the recipes on the following pages to explore this modern marvel, and learn how easy and delicious microwave cooking can be.

A fast and filling main dish that will delight your family: Turkey & Vegetable Burgers (recipe, page 173).

Seafood

Fish and shellfish have a true friend in the microwave oven. These marvels microwave perfectly, retaining their moist, delicious flavors.

Marinated Swordfish Kebabs

These kebabs are marinated for 3 hours, so plan ahead!

LOW-CALORIE · LOW-CHOLESTEROL · LOW-FAT · MICROWAVE
Makes 4 servings.
Nutrient Value Per Serving: 303 calories, 35 g protein, 14 g fat,
9 g carbohydrate, 341 mg sodium, 66 mg cholesterol.

4 ounces large mushrooms, wiped clean, ends trimmed, and cut into sixteen ½-inch-thick slices	½ cup orange juice
	2 tablespoons olive oil
	3 cloves garlic, finely chopped
1½ pounds swordfish, trimmed, and cut into twenty-four 1½-inch cubes	¼ teaspoon dried oregano, crumbled
	¼ teaspoon dried basil, crumbled
1 small zucchini (about 3 ounces), cut into sixteen ¼-inch-thick slices	¼ cup freshly squeezed lemon juice
8 large basil leaves, washed and dried	½ teaspoon coarse (kosher) salt
8 cherry tomatoes, halved	¼ teaspoon freshly ground pepper

1. On a 6-inch wooden skewer, thread a mushroom slice, a fish cube, and a zucchini slice. Wrap a basil leaf around another fish cube, and thread the wrapped cube on the skewer. Add another mushroom slice, a cherry tomato half, a zucchini slice, a third fish cube, and a cherry tomato half. Repeat on seven more 6-inch wooden skewers. Arrange the kebabs in rows, without touching each other, in a microwave-safe 13 x 9 x 2-inch dish.

2. Combine the orange juice, oil, garlic, oregano and basil in a small bowl. Cover the bowl tightly with microwave-safe plastic wrap. Microwave at full power for 2 minutes. Pierce the plastic wrap with a knife to release the steam. Remove the bowl from the oven, and carefully uncover it.

3. Stir the lemon juice, salt and pepper into the bowl. Pour the lemon juice mixture over the kebabs. Cover the kebab dish tightly with microwave-safe plastic wrap, and marinate the kebabs in the refrigerator for 3 hours.

4. Remove the kebab dish from the refrigerator. Leave the dish covered. Microwave at full power for 5 minutes. Carefully pierce the plastic wrap with a knife to release the steam. Remove the dish from the oven. Carefully uncover the dish.

5. Move the kebabs in the center of the dish to the edge of the dish. Turn over all the kebabs. Re-cover the dish with plastic wrap. Microwave at full power for 1½ minutes, or until the fish is cooked through. Carefully pierce the plastic wrap with a knife to release the steam. Remove the dish from the oven, and carefully uncover it. Pour the cooking broth into a gravy boat. Serve the kebabs with the cooking broth.

FISH KEBABS
Marinated Swordfish Kebabs
Hot Cooked Rice
Poached Pears

o ⋅⋈⋅ o

DINNER FOR TWO

● To prepare Marinated Swordfish Kebabs for two, divide all the ingredients in half.
● In Step 1, thread the vegetables and fish cubes onto four 6-inch wooden skewers.
● In Step 2, microwave at full power for 1 minute.
● In Step 4, microwave at full power for 4½ minutes, or until the fish is cooked through. Carefully pierce the plastic wrap with a knife to release the steam. Remove the dish from the oven, and carefully uncover it. Serve the kebabs with their cooking broth.

Serve Marinated Swordfish Kebabs on rice, spooning the flavorful cooking broth over all.

Summer Vegetable & Shrimp Stew

LOW-CALORIE · MICROWAVE

Makes 4 servings.

Nutrient Value Per Serving: 216 calories, 22 g protein, 10 g fat, 12 g carbohydrate, 362 mg sodium, 140 mg cholesterol.

1	medium-size head broccoli (about 5 ounces), stem peeled and cut into coins, and head cut into flowerets	1	yellow squash (6 ounces), trimmed, halved lengthwise, and cut crosswise into ¼-inch-thick slices (1½ cups)
1	medium-size sweet red pepper (about 4 ounces), cored, seeded, and cut into ¼-inch-wide strips	4	green onions, cut into thin slices
1½	cups Tomato Sauce (recipe, below)		Salt and freshly ground pepper, to taste
1	pound large shrimp, peeled and deveined		Hot cooked rice

1. Combine the broccoli coins, red pepper and Tomato Sauce in a microwave-safe 3-quart glass or ceramic dish with a lid. Cover the dish. Microwave at full power for 3 minutes.

2. Remove the dish from the oven. Stir in the shrimp, broccoli flowerets and squash. Cover the dish. Microwave at full power for 2 minutes. Remove the dish from the oven. Uncover the dish, and stir well. Cover the dish. Microwave at full power for 2 minutes. Remove the dish from the oven. Add the green onion, and stir well. Cover the dish. Microwave at full power for 1 minute. Stir in the salt and pepper. Serve the stew over the hot cooked rice.

Tomato Sauce

LOW-CHOLESTEROL · MICROWAVE

Makes 2 cups.

Nutrient Value Per Serving: 61 calories, 1 g protein, 5 g fat, 4 g carbohydrate, 143 mg sodium, 0 mg cholesterol.

1½	pounds ripe plum tomatoes, cored, and cut into 1-inch pieces	½	teaspoon salt
3	tablespoons olive oil	⅛	teaspoon freshly ground pepper
2	cloves garlic, sliced		

1. Combine the tomatoes, oil and garlic in a microwave-safe 2½-quart dish. Cover the dish tightly with microwave-safe plastic wrap. Microwave at full power for 4 minutes. Pierce the plastic wrap with a knife to release the steam. Remove the dish from the oven. Carefully uncover the dish.

2. Pass the tomato mixture through a food mill into a large bowl. Discard the pulp. Return the tomato liquid to the microwave-safe dish. Microwave, uncovered, at full power for 5 minutes, or until the sauce reaches the desired consistency; the cooking time will depend on the amount of juice in the tomatoes.

3. Remove the dish from the oven. Stir in the salt and pepper. Use the sauce immediately. Or cool the sauce, and pour it into freezer containers. Cover the containers, and store them in the refrigerator or freezer.

SHRIMP FOR A SUMMER EVENING

Chilled Squash Soup with Mint
(recipe, page 182)

Summer Vegetable & Shrimp Stew

Chocolate Ice Cream with Fresh Raspberries

o ❀ o

THE SPICE IS RIGHT!

When microwaving dishes prepared from conventional recipes, the amounts of spices, and the ways in which they are added, vary.

● **Fresh Herbs:** Increase the amounts called for by about one quarter. Add fresh herbs late in the microwave cooking time, or they will be flavorless and grassy.

● **Ginger:** Fresh ginger, which adds a sharp, clean flavor, is easy to use in microwaveable dishes. For example, try grating fresh ginger over fish. Rub in the grated ginger, and let the fish stand for ½ hour before microwaving it. Or grate fresh ginger, and squeeze the grated pulp through a strainer to make ginger juice. Add the ginger juice to a soy sauce-based marinade for chicken or fish.

● **Ground Pepper & Dried Herbs:** Decrease the amounts called for by three quarters, or their flavors will overwhelm the food.

● **Spicy Dry Seasonings:** Spices such as curry, paprika, chili powder, ground hot red pepper, and all dry seasonings based on pod peppers must be cooked in a little oil for about 1 minute before adding them to a microwavable dish; otherwise, they will have a raw, powdery taste.

● **Salt:** Decrease the amount of salt usually used in a dish, because microwaving concentrates the flavor. And less added salt in foods is much better for your health.

● **Preseasoning foods:** Foods cook in the microwave for only a short time. You may want to season dishes and let them stand for a while, to allow the flavors to penetrate, before microwaving them.

o ❖ o

'TIS THE SEASONING

Like herbs and spices, the following seasonings must be varied when using a microwave.

• **Garlic:** If using a conventional recipe, and the dish will be microwaved for more than 6 minutes, double the amount of garlic called for. The flavor of garlic mellows, not sharpens, during microwave cooking.

• **Alcohol & Flavorings Containing Alcohol:** When microwaving, double the amount of alcohol and flavorings that contain alcohol, such as vanilla and almond extract, called for in a conventional recipe because alcohol evaporates quickly during microwave cooking.

• **Fat:** Adding fat to a microwavable dish rarely is necessary. Instead, think of fat as a seasoning in microwave cooking, and use the very best, such as rich, fruity olive oil. Although expensive, only a little is needed to add flavor to a dish for several people, so the cost per person is low.

Crab-Stuffed Flounder

LOW-CALORIE · MICROWAVE

Makes 4 servings.

Nutrient Value Per Serving: 256 calories, 28 g protein, 13 g fat, 49 g carbohydrate, 599 mg sodium, 114 mg cholesterol.

1 **small onion, chopped (¼ cup)**	½ **teaspoon salt**
¼ **cup chopped celery**	⅛ **teaspoon freshly ground pepper**
¼ **cup chopped sweet red pepper**	**Few drops liquid red pepper seasoning**
4 **tablespoons (½ stick) butter or margarine**	4 **small flounder fillets (about 4 ounces each)**
¼ **pound crab meat, picked over and flaked**	**Paprika**
½ **cup soft bread crumbs**	**Lemon wedges, for garnish**
3 **teaspoons lemon juice**	**Parsley sprigs, for garnish**

1. Combine the onion, celery, red pepper and 2 tablespoons of the butter or margarine in a microwave-safe shallow baking dish large enough to hold 4 rolled flounder fillets. Cover the dish tightly with microwave-safe plastic wrap. Microwave at full power for 4 minutes. Carefully pierce the plastic wrap with a knife to release the steam. Remove the dish from the oven. Carefully uncover the dish.

2. Add the crab meat, bread crumbs, 1 teaspoon of the lemon juice, the salt, pepper and liquid red pepper seasoning, and mix well.

3. Place the flounder fillets on the counter, skin side up. Mound the crab meat mixture, divided evenly, in the centers of the fillets. Bring up and overlap the ends of each fillet, and secure the ends with a wooden pick. Place the fillets in the microwave-safe dish.

4. Melt the remaining 2 tablespoons of butter in a small saucepan. Stir in the remaining 2 teaspoons of lemon juice. Pour the butter mixture over the fillets. Sprinkle the fillets with the paprika. Re-cover the dish with plastic wrap. Microwave at full power for 4 minutes. Remove the dish from the oven, and carefully uncover it.

5. Garnish the fillets with the lemon wedges and the parsley sprigs.

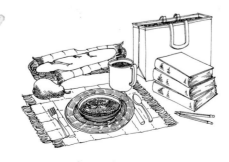

Cajun Shrimp in Shells

LOW-CALORIE ▪ LOW-FAT ▪ MICROWAVE
Makes 4 servings.
Nutrient Value Per Serving: 125 calories, 20 g protein, 2 g fat,
5 g carbohydrate, 338 mg sodium, 141 mg cholesterol.

1	tablespoon lemon juice	¼	teaspoon freshly ground pepper
¼	teaspoon dried thyme, crumbled	1¼	pounds large shrimp (30 to 35 shrimp)
¼	teaspoon celery seeds		Tangy Yogurt Sauce (recipe follows)
¼	teaspoon ground hot red pepper		
¼	teaspoon dry mustard		

1. Combine the lemon juice, thyme, celery seeds, ground hot red pepper, mustard and pepper in a microwave-safe 10-inch pie plate. Add the shrimp, and toss to mix the ingredients. Let the shrimp mixture stand for 15 minutes, tossing it once or twice.

2. Arrange the shrimp in the pie plate in a single layer, with the tails toward the center of the plate. Cover the plate with microwave-safe plastic wrap, slightly vented in one place. Microwave at full power for 3½ to 4 minutes, or until the shrimp are cooked. Remove the plate from the oven, and carefully uncover it. Remove and reserve one fifth of the shrimp to use in another dish. Serve the remaining shrimp with the Tangy Yogurt Sauce.

Tangy Yogurt Sauce:

Stir together ½ cup of plain lowfat yogurt, 1 tablespoon of catsup, ½ teaspoon of lemon juice, ¼ cup of chopped parsley, 2 chopped green onions, ¼ teaspoon of salt, and a few grains of freshly ground pepper.

Shrimp-Stuffed Fish Fillets

LOW-CALORIE ▪ LOW-FAT ▪ MICROWAVE
Makes 4 servings.
Nutrient Value Per Serving: 240 calories, 33 g protein, 8 g fat,
7 g carbohydrate, 344 mg sodium, 119 mg cholesterol.

2	green onions, trimmed and thinly sliced	¼	teaspoon salt
2	tablespoons chopped sweet red pepper	¼	teaspoon freshly ground pepper
1	tablespoon chopped celery	½	cup chopped cooked shrimp
¼	teaspoon dried thyme, crumbled	1	cup fresh bread crumbs (2 slices bread)
2	tablespoons unsalted butter or margarine	4	flounder fillets (5 ounces each)
2	tablespoons chopped parsley	⅛	teaspoon paprika
2	teaspoons lemon juice		Lemon slices (optional)

1. Combine the green onion, red pepper, celery, thyme and butter or margarine in a microwave-safe 1-quart measure. Cover the measure with wax paper. Microwave at full power for 3 minutes. Add the parsley, lemon juice, ⅛ teaspoon of the salt, ⅛ teaspoon of the pepper, the shrimp and bread crumbs. Mix gently to combine the ingredients.

SOUTHERN-STYLE SPICY SHRIMP

Cajun Shrimp in Shells

Corn on the Cob

Tomatoes & Cucumbers in Vinaigrette

Chocolate Pudding

o ❖ o

CONVENTIONAL CAJUN

● To cook the shrimp for Cajun Shrimp in Shells conventionally on the stove, bring 2 quarts of water to boiling in a medium-size saucepan.
● Add 2 tablespoons of lemon juice, ¼ teaspoon of crumbled dried thyme, ¼ teaspoon of celery seeds, 1 teaspoon of ground hot red pepper, 1 teaspoon of freshly ground black pepper, 1 teaspoon of dry mustard, and the shrimp. Bring the shrimp mixture to boiling and cook for 1 minute, or until the shrimp are cooked. Drain the shrimp, and serve with the Tangy Yogurt Sauce.

DYNAMIC DUO

Shrimp-Stuffed Fish Fillets
Parslied Rice Pilaf
(recipe, page 156)

Steamed Green Beans

Lemon Frozen Yogurt with Fresh Strawberries

o ❖ o

2. Place the flounder fillets, skin side up, on a piece of wax paper. Sprinkle the fillets with the remaining ⅛ teaspoon of salt and ⅛ teaspoon of pepper. Mound the shrimp mixture, divided evenly, across the centers of the fillets. Bring up and overlap the ends of each fillet. Place the fillets, spoke fashion and seam side down, in a microwave-safe 10-inch pie plate. Sprinkle the fillets with the paprika. Cover the plate with another same-size pie plate. Microwave at full power for 6 minutes, rotating the plate one half turn halfway through the cooking time. Serve with lemon slices, if you wish.

A delicious duo from the sea: Shrimp-Stuffed Fish Fillets.

Vermicelli with Crab & Chicken

MICROWAVE

Makes 6 servings.

Nutrient Value Per Serving: 657 calories, 39 g protein, 25 g fat, 69 g carbohydrate, 539 mg sodium, 124 mg cholesterol.

1	pound vermicelli	⅛	teaspoon freshly ground white pepper
2	cloves garlic, lightly smashed		Generous pinch ground hot red pepper
2	tablespoons butter		
1	tablespoon all-purpose flour	1	package (10 ounces) frozen peas, thawed
2	cups half-and-half		
½	cup milk	8	ounces fresh OR: thawed frozen crab meat
1	cup shredded Monterey Jack cheese (4 ounces)	2	cans (5 ounces each) chunk white chicken packed in water, drained
2	tablespoons grated Parmesan cheese		

1. Cook the vermicelli in a large pot of boiling water following the package directions until the vermicelli is al dente, tender but firm to the bite.

2. Meanwhile, place the garlic and the butter in a microwave-safe 2-quart casserole dish. Microwave, uncovered, at full power for 2 minutes. Remove and discard the garlic.

3. Stir the flour into the butter until the mixture is smooth. Add the half-and-half and the milk. Cover the dish. Microwave at full power for 5½ to 6½ minutes, or until the mixture is boiling. Whisk the mixture well.

4. Add the Monterey Jack cheese, Parmesan cheese, white pepper and ground hot red pepper. Stir until the cheeses melt.

5. Stir in the peas, crab meat and chicken. Cover the dish. Microwave at full power for 4 minutes to heat the sauce through.

6. Drain the cooked vermicelli in a colander. Transfer the vermicelli to a large serving bowl. Add the sauce, and toss until well mixed. Serve the vermicelli immediately.

Two Beans, Tomatoes & Tuna

LOW-CALORIE · LOW-CHOLESTEROL · MICROWAVE

Makes 4 servings.

Nutrient Value Per Serving: 288 calories, 14 g protein, 20 g fat, 16 g carbohydrate, 832 mg sodium, 10 mg cholesterol.

1	large onion, thinly sliced	½	pound wax beans, trimmed, and steamed until crisply tender
1	clove garlic, finely chopped		
2	tablespoons good-quality olive oil	16	black oil-cured olives
6	ripe plum tomatoes (about 1 pound), peeled, quartered and seeded	1	can (6½ ounces) tuna packed in oil, drained and flaked
		¼	teaspoon salt
½	pound green beans, trimmed, and steamed until crisply tender	¼	teaspoon freshly ground pepper
		¼	cup thinly sliced fresh basil

FASTA PASTA

Vermicelli with Crab & Chicken

Cucumber Salad

Whole Wheat Breadsticks

Honeydew Melon Slices

∘ ❖ ∘

CONCERNING CRABS

Many varieties of crab are found along the Pacific and Atlantic coasts, but only a handful are marketed commercially. In the U.S., the blue crab, from the Atlantic and Gulf coasts, comprises the bulk of the crab meat available. Each blue crab weighs from 5 to 8 ounces, and has a dark blue to brownish shell.

● Live blue crabs are available in coastal markets. Most other crabs are cooked in the shell and frozen. Crab also is available as fresh cooked crab meat, and frozen or canned meat. Fresh lump crab meat comes from the large body portion of the crab and is best used in recipes where appearance is important, such as appetizers and salads. Flake crab meat is the small bits and pieces taken from the rest of the crab's body.

TERRIFIC TUNA

Consommé

Two Beans, Tomatoes & Tuna

Rye Bread

Honeyed Fruit Compote
(recipe, page 183)

∘ ❖ ∘

1. Sprinkle the onion and the garlic over the bottom of a microwave-safe 11½ x 7½-inch baking dish. Drizzle the oil over the vegetables. Microwave, uncovered, at full power for 3 minutes, stirring once.

2. Stir the tomatoes into the dish. Arrange the green beans and the wax beans over the tomatoes in an even layer. Cover the dish tightly with microwave-safe plastic wrap. Microwave at full power for 6 minutes, stirring once. Carefully pierce the plastic wrap with a knife to release the steam. Remove the dish from the oven. Carefully uncover the dish.

3. Stir in the olives, tuna, salt and pepper. Microwave, uncovered, at full power for 30 seconds. Sprinkle the basil over the tuna mixture. Serve the tuna mixture warm.

Fusilli with Shrimp & Zucchini

LOW-CHOLESTEROL · MICROWAVE
Makes 4 servings.
Nutrient Value Per Serving: 531 calories, 20 g protein, 26 g fat, 57 g carbohydrate, 391 mg sodium, 66 mg cholesterol.

½ **pound fusilli**	2 **medium-size zucchini (12 ounces), trimmed, quartered lengthwise, and sliced ¼ inch thick**
1 **small dried red chili pepper**	
½ **pound small shrimp, shelled, deveined, and shells reserved**	½ **teaspoon dried oregano, crumbled**
3 **tablespoons olive oil**	½ **teaspoon dried thyme, crumbled**
6 **small shallots, thinly sliced**	½ **teaspoon salt**
1 **tablespoon peeled, chopped fresh ginger**	¼ **teaspoon freshly ground pepper**
2 **large cloves garlic, finely chopped**	¼ **cup coarsely chopped fresh basil**
4 **ripe large tomatoes (1½ pounds), peeled, halved, seeded and chopped**	2 **tablespoons finely chopped fresh parsley**

1. Cook the fusilli in a large pot of boiling water following the package directions until the fusilli is al dente, tender but firm to the bite. Drain the fusilli in a colander.

2. Meanwhile, combine the chili pepper, reserved shrimp shells and 2 tablespoons of the oil in a microwave-safe 12 x 8-inch baking dish. Cover the dish with microwave-safe plastic wrap vented at one corner. Microwave at full power for 1½ minutes. Remove and discard the shells and chili pepper.

3. Add the shrimp to the dish in one layer. Re-cover the dish with plastic wrap. Microwave at full power for 2 minutes, stirring once. Remove the shrimp, and chop it coarsely. Place the shrimp in a small bowl, cover the bowl, and set aside the shrimp.

4. Add the shallots, ginger and garlic to the microwave-safe dish. Re-cover the dish with plastic wrap. Microwave at full power for 3 minutes. Stir in the tomatoes. Re-cover the dish with plastic wrap. Microwave at full power for 3 minutes. Stir in the zucchini and the remaining tablespoon of oil. Re-cover the dish with plastic wrap. Microwave at full power for 4 minutes, stirring once. Remove the dish from the oven, and carefully uncover it.

5. Stir in the hot cooked fusilli, the chopped shrimp, oregano, thyme, salt, pepper, basil and parsley. Serve immediately.

FUSILLI FEAST

Fusilli with Shrimp & Zucchini
Italian Bread
**Coffee Sorbet
with Amaretti Cookies**

" *H*onest Bread *is very well — it's the butter that makes the temptation.* "

—*Jerrold*

Poultry

For fast, healthy dinners, try chicken or turkey in the microwave.

Turkey Loaf with Spicy Citrus Sauce

LOW-CALORIE · LOW-CHOLESTEROL · LOW-FAT · MICROWAVE
Makes 4 servings.
Nutrient Value Per Serving: 173 calories, 28 g protein, 2 g fat,
10 g carbohydrate, 527 mg sodium, 70 mg cholesterol.

1 **can (14½ ounces) plum tomatoes**	1 **tablespoon cornstarch** **Pinch ground ginger**
1 **small red onion (about 4 ounces), peeled and cut into chunks**	¼ **teaspoon liquid red pepper seasoning** **Juice of ½ lemon**
¼ **cup parsley**	2 **tablespoons orange juice**
1 **pound boned, skinless turkey breast cut into 1-inch cubes OR: ground turkey**	**Additional salt, to taste** **Freshly ground pepper, to taste**
½ **teaspoon salt** **Pinch ground hot red pepper**	

1. Drain the tomatoes, reserving their juice. Coarsely chop the tomatoes, and place them in a medium-size bowl.

2. Place the onion and the parsley in the container of a food processor or electric blender. Whirl until the onion mixture is coarsely chopped. Add the onion mixture to the tomatoes in the bowl.

3. If using the turkey cubes, place them in the processor container. Pulse until the meat is finely chopped. Mix the chopped or ground turkey into the tomato mixture. Add the ½ teaspoon of salt and the ground hot red pepper.

4. Shape the turkey mixture into a 2-inch-thick, 9-inch-diameter ring in a microwave-safe 10-inch pie plate; invert a microwave-safe custard cup in the center of the turkey ring. Or shape the mixture into 4 equal patties, and place them around the edges of a microwave-safe 13 x 9 x 2-inch baking dish. Cover the plate or dish tightly with microwave-safe plastic wrap.

5. Microwave at full power for 6 to 7 minutes, or until the loaf is cooked through the center. Pierce the plastic wrap with a knife to release the steam. Remove the plate from the oven, and carefully uncover it. Let the loaf stand for about 5 minutes.

6. Meanwhile, place the cornstarch in a microwave-safe 4-cup measure. Stir in the reserved tomato juice, the ginger and liquid red pepper seasoning until the cornstarch mixture is smooth. Cover the measure tightly with microwave-safe plastic wrap. Microwave at full power for 2½ minutes. Carefully pierce the plastic wrap with a knife to release the steam. Remove the measure from the oven. Carefully uncover the measure.

7. Drain off the cooking liquid from the turkey loaf. Stir the cooking liquid into the cornstarch mixture along with the lemon juice and the orange juice. Season the sauce with the additional salt and the pepper. Spoon some of the sauce over the turkey loaf, and serve. Pass the remaining sauce.

TURKEY IN THE LOAF

**Turkey Loaf
with Spicy Citrus Sauce**

Hot Cooked Rice

Tossed Green Salad

**Rice Pudding
with Sliced Strawberries**

o ❖ o

CORNSTARCH

A fine, white powder ground from the endosperm, or starchy portion, of a corn kernel, cornstarch is used as a thickener in puddings, gravies and sauces. It also is used in baking cakes and some cookies.

Low-Wattage Microwave Oven Instructions

Directions: In Step 4, place the loaf in a microwave-safe 10-inch pie plate, or the patties in a microwave-safe 9-inch square baking dish. In Step 5, microwave at full power for 8 minutes. In Step 6, microwave at full power for 5 minutes. Continue with the recipe.

Turkey & Vegetable Burgers

LOW-CALORIE · LOW-CHOLESTEROL · LOW-FAT · MICROWAVE
Makes 4 servings.
Nutrient Value Per Serving: 161 calories, 30 g protein, 2 g fat, 6 g carbohydrate, 503 mg sodium, 70 mg cholesterol.

1	pound fresh spinach, stemmed and washed (about 6 cups)	1	pound boned, skinless turkey breast cut into 1-inch cubes OR: ground turkey
8	green onions, green and white parts cut into 1-inch pieces	1	teaspoon summer savory
½	pound zucchini, halved lengthwise, and cut crosswise into ½-inch-thick slices	1	teaspoon coarse (kosher) salt
			Freshly ground pepper, to taste
			Chopped parsley (optional)
		4	hard rolls (optional)

1. Place the spinach in a microwave-safe 10-inch pie plate or quiche dish. Microwave, uncovered, at full power for 5½ minutes. Remove the plate from the oven. Drain the spinach well. When the spinach is cool enough to handle, squeeze out any remaining liquid from it.

2. Place the spinach, green onion and zucchini in the container of a food processor or electric blender. Whirl until the spinach mixture is coarsely chopped. Transfer the spinach mixture to a medium-size bowl. If using the turkey cubes, place them in the processor container and pulse until the meat is finely chopped but not smooth. Stir the chopped or ground turkey into the spinach mixture. Mix in the summer savory, salt, pepper and, if you wish, chopped parsley.

3. Shape the turkey mixture into 4 equal patties. Place the patties around the inside edge of a microwave-safe 13 x 9 x 2-inch baking dish. Or shape the turkey mixture into a 2-inch-thick ring in a microwave-safe 10-inch pie plate; invert a microwave-safe custard cup in the center of the turkey ring. Cover the dish or plate tightly with microwave-safe plastic wrap.

4. Microwave at full power for 6 minutes. Carefully pierce the plastic wrap with a knife to release the steam. Remove the dish from the oven. Carefully uncover the dish. Let the burgers stand for 5 minutes. Serve each burger on a hard roll, if you wish.

Low-Wattage Microwave Oven Instructions

Directions: In Step 1, microwave at full power for 10 minutes. In Step 3, place the patties in a microwave-safe 9-inch square baking dish, or the loaf in a microwave-safe 10-inch pie plate. In Step 4, microwave at full power for 9 to 10 minutes. Continue with the recipe.

BURGER BONANZA

Turkey & Vegetable Burgers

Parslied New Potatoes
(see Tip, page 182)

Peachy Buttermilk Shake
(recipe, page 210)

BURGER HEAVEN

To get a jump start on lunch or dinner, double the recipe for Turkey & Vegetable Burgers, shape the patties, wrap them individually in plastic wrap, and store them in the freezer. When needed, unwrap the patties, pop them in the microwave, and microwave them at full power for 6 minutes. Serve the burgers on buns.

Warm Chicken Salad

LOW-CALORIE · MICROWAVE

Makes 4 servings.

Nutrient Value Per Serving: 328 calories, 35 g protein, 19 g fat, 4 g carbohydrate, 407 mg sodium, 85 mg cholesterol.

4	boned, skinless chicken breast halves (5 ounces each)	2	green onions, trimmed and sliced
¾	cup Catalina Dressing (recipe follows)		Green leaf lettuce
2	slices bacon	½	bunch watercress, stemmed, for garnish
1	large tomato, cored and cubed		

1. Place the chicken in a microwave-safe 10-inch pie plate. Pour ½ cup of the Catalina Dressing over the chicken. Cover the plate, and marinate the chicken in the refrigerator for 20 minutes, turning over the chicken once.

2. Cut the bacon crosswise into thin strips. Scatter the bacon strips over a double thickness of paper toweling. Cover the strips with another doubled thickness of paper toweling. Microwave the bacon strips at full power for 1½ minutes, or until the bacon is crisp. Set aside the bacon strips.

3. Combine the tomato, green onion and 2 tablespoons of the dressing in a small bowl. Set aside the tomato mixture.

4. Rearrange the chicken in the marinade in the same plate, with the thicker parts of the chicken at the outside edge of the plate and the thinner parts toward the center. Cover the pie plate with another same-size pie plate. Microwave at full power for 7 minutes, or until the chicken is cooked through, rotating the plate one half turn halfway through the cooking time.

5. Place the lettuce on a serving platter. Lift the chicken from the marinade to a cutting board. Slice the chicken across the grain, and place the slices on the lettuce. Garnish with the watercress and the tomato mixture. Drizzle the salad with the remaining 2 tablespoons of dressing. Sprinkle the salad with the bacon strips.

Catalina Dressing:

Combine 6 ounces of tomato juice, ½ cup of olive oil, 2 tablespoons of red wine vinegar, ½ teaspoon of salt, ¼ teaspoon of sugar, ¼ teaspoon of freshly ground pepper, and ¼ teaspoon of Worcestershire sauce in a jar with a tight-fitting lid. Shake the jar well to mix the ingredients. Makes about 1⅓ cups.

SPEEDY CHICKEN SALAD

Warm Chicken Salad

Corn Muffins

Chocolate Ice Milk

○ ✤ ○

CLEAN GREENS

● To clean salad greens, discard any bruised, discolored or tough outer leaves. Remove the remaining leaves from the head, and trim any tough core or rib. Wash the leaves gently in a sink or large bowl filled with cool water. Drain the leaves, and rinse them well. If the leaves are very sandy, keep changing the water until the greens are clean.

● Dry the washed greens in a salad spinner. Or gently blot the greens dry with paper toweling.

Warm Chicken Salad is a taste-fully easy way to beat the suppertime rush, and has a perfect partner in corn muffins.

FAST-TRACK CHICKEN
(650-Watt Variable Power Microwave Oven)

> Coat the chicken pieces lightly with oil, and roll them in seasoned bread crumbs. Place 1 or 2 chicken pieces at a time in a microwave-safe dish, cover the dish with wax paper, and microwave.

Parts	Power	Minutes
1 Breast Half	Full	4 to 6
1 Thigh	Three Quarters	4 to 5
1 Leg/Thigh combination	Three Quarters	7 to 9
2 Breast Halves	Full	8 to 10
2 Thighs	Three Quarters	6 to 8
2 Leg/Thigh combinations	Three Quarters	9 to 13

Curried Chicken & Vegetable Salad

LOW-CALORIE · LOW-CHOLESTEROL · LOW-FAT · MICROWAVE

Makes 4 servings.

Nutrient Value Per Serving: 326 calories, 31 g protein, 11 g fat, 26 g carbohydrate, 453 mg sodium, 72 mg cholesterol.

1	tablespoon vegetable oil
1	tablespoon curry powder
4	small baking potatoes (about 4 ounces each), peeled, and cut into ¾-inch cubes (2½ cups)
2 to 3	medium-size carrots (about 3 ounces each), peeled, and cut into ¼-inch-thick slices (about 1 cup)
¼	cup chicken broth
4	boned, skinless chicken breast halves (1 pound), cut into ½-inch-wide strips
2 to 3	stalks celery, cut into ¼-inch-thick slices (about ¾ cup)
1	cup green peas, fresh OR: thawed frozen
¼	teaspoon salt
⅛	teaspoon freshly ground pepper
⅓	cup reduced-calorie mayonnaise
	Lettuce leaves (optional)
	Tomato wedges (optional)

1. Combine the oil with the curry powder in a microwave-safe 3-quart glass or ceramic dish with a lid. Microwave, uncovered, at full power for 1 minute. Remove the dish from the oven.

2. Stir in the potatoes, carrot and broth. Cover the dish. Microwave at full power for 4 minutes. Uncover the dish, and stir. Cover the dish. Microwave at full power for 4 minutes. Stir in the chicken. Cover the dish. Microwave at full power for 3½ minutes. Add the celery and the peas, and stir to combine them. Cover the dish. Microwave at full power for 3½ minutes, or until the chicken is cooked through, and the celery and peas are tender. Remove the dish from the oven.

3. Stir in the salt and pepper. Cool the chicken mixture completely.

CURRY IN A HURRY

Curried Chicken & Vegetable Salad

Mini Pita Breads

Strawberry Kissel
(recipe, page 183)

○ ❖ ○

"I don't know which is more discouraging, literature or chickens."
— *E.B. White*

4. Add the mayonnaise, and toss the ingredients until the mayonnaise is well blended. Refrigerate the salad until serving time. If you wish, serve the salad on lettuce leaves with tomato wedges.

Low-Wattage Microwave Oven Instructions

Directions: In Step 1, microwave at full power for 2 minutes. In Step 2, microwave the potatoes, carrot and broth, covered, at full power for 8 minutes. Uncover the dish, and stir. Cover the dish. Microwave at full power for 8 minutes. Stir in the chicken. Cover the dish. Microwave at full power for 6 minutes. Add the celery and the peas, and stir to combine them. Cover the dish. Microwave at full power for 6½ minutes. Continue with the recipe.

Grecian Chicken

Fan out the stuffed chicken roll slices on an earthenware platter to create an appetizing centerpiece for a buffet.

LOW-CALORIE · LOW-FAT · MICROWAVE

Makes 8 servings.

Nutrient Value Per Serving: 197 calories, 33 g protein, 5 g fat, 2 g carbohydrate, 276 mg sodium, 121 mg cholesterol.

1 **package (10 ounces) frozen chopped spinach, thawed and squeezed dry**	½ **teaspoon dried rosemary, crumbled**
4 **ounces feta cheese, drained well and crumbled (1 cup)**	½ **teaspoon dillweed, crumbled**
1 **egg, slightly beaten**	8 **small boned, skinless chicken breast halves (2¼ pounds)**
1 **teaspoon dried basil, crumbled**	**Orzo, or packaged rice mix (optional)**

1. Stir together the spinach, feta cheese, egg, basil, rosemary and dillweed in a medium-size bowl.

2. Place the chicken pieces between sheets of wax paper. Using the smooth side of a meat mallet or the bottom of a frying pan, pound the chicken pieces to a ¼-inch thickness. Lay the chicken pieces, skinned side down, on a board. Place a scant ¼ cup of the filling in the center of each chicken piece. Roll up each chicken piece starting with the narrow end. Place the chicken rolls, spoke fashion and seam side down, in a microwave-safe 10-inch pie plate. Cover the plate with wax paper. Microwave at full power for 8 minutes, or until the chicken is tender, rearranging the rolls after 4 minutes. Let the chicken rolls stand for 5 minutes.

3. Remove the chicken rolls to a cutting board, and cut the rolls crosswise into slices. Arrange the sliced chicken rolls on a serving platter. If you wish, serve the chicken rolls with orzo or a packaged rice mix.

DINNER IN ATHENS

Olives & Stuffed Grape Leaves
Grecian Chicken
Orzo or Hot Cooked Rice
Baklava

FABULOUS FETA

A chalky Greek cheese made from sheep's milk, feta is semisoft and highly salted. It originated in the area around Athens, and was called pickled cheese because it was stored in brine. Feta can be eaten as an appetizer accompanied by Greek olives, or crumbled into salads.
● Feta cheese can be found in most supermarkets. It is sold refrigerated in jars, vacuum-sealed packages, or packed in brine.

Soups, Sides & Sweets

Soup for a start, or soup as a meal—either way it can be ready fast in the microwave. Even if you don't microwave the main course, side dishes and sweets are ready in a snap when you "zap 'em!"

Vegetarian Bean Soup

LOW-CALORIE · LOW-CHOLESTEROL · LOW-FAT · MICROWAVE
Makes 8 servings.
Nutrient Value Per Serving: 275 calories, 11 g protein, 8 g fat,
43 g carbohydrate, 900 mg sodium, 0 mg cholesterol.

1½ cups dried **Great Northern beans***	5 cloves **garlic, finely chopped**
2 cans (28 ounces each) **Italian-style plum tomatoes in juice, drained and juice reserved**	¼ cup **olive oil**
	1 teaspoon dried **oregano, crumbled**
1 pound **onions (3 large onions), cut into ½-inch dice (about 3 cups)**	Pinch hot **red pepper flakes**
	1 cup chopped **parsley**
2 medium-size **sweet red peppers (about 8 ounces each), cored, seeded, and cut into ½-inch dice (about 2½ cups)**	1 tablespoon coarse **(kosher) salt**
	⅛ teaspoon freshly **ground pepper**
4 medium-size **carrots (about 3 ounces each), peeled, and cut into ½-inch dice (about 1½ cups)**	

1. Place the beans in a microwave-safe 5-quart casserole dish with a tight-fitting lid. Add 2 cups of cold water. Cover the dish. Microwave at full power for 15 minutes. Remove the dish from the oven. Let the beans stand, covered, for 5 minutes. Uncover the dish. Add 2 cups of very hot water. Re-cover the dish. Let the beans stand for 1 hour. Drain the beans.

2. Return the beans to the dish along with 2 cups of fresh water and the reserved tomato juice. Stir in the onion, red peppers and carrot. Cover the dish. Microwave at full power for 40 minutes, stirring once. Remove the dish from the oven. Uncover the dish.

3. Stir the tomatoes into the onion mixture with a wooden spoon, breaking up the tomatoes with the spoon. Stir in the garlic, oil, oregano and hot red pepper flakes. Cover the dish. Microwave at full power for 30 minutes, or until the beans are tender. Stir in the parsley, salt and pepper. Serve the soup hot.

Note: *You can substitute two 19-ounce cans of cannellini beans for the dried Great Northern beans. Omit Step 1. Drain the cannellini beans in a sieve, and rinse them quickly under cool running water. Set aside the cannellini beans. In Step 2, omit the beans. Microwave at full power for 20 minutes. In Step 3, microwave the garlic mixture at full power for 15 minutes. Stir in the cannellini beans. Microwave the bean mixture at full power for 5 minutes. Continue with the recipe.*

THE SECOND TIME AROUND

Extra soup? Save time in future meals by freezing leftover Vegetarian Bean Soup or Hearty Chicken Noodle Soup (recipe, page 181) in single-serving containers. Defrost a frozen serving for 3 minutes in a 650- or 700-watt microwave oven, for 7 minutes in a lower-wattage oven.

*"**D**ay!
Faster and more fast,
O'er night's brim,
day boils at last. "*
—Robert Browning

*From the top, clockwise:
Hearty Chicken Noodle Soup
(recipe, page 181), Vegetarian
Bean Soup and Seafood Chowder
(recipe, page 180).*

179

Seafood Chowder

LOW-CALORIE · MICROWAVE

Makes 8 servings.

Nutrient Value Per Serving: 256 calories, 24 g protein, 10 g fat, 16 g carbohydrate, 330 mg sodium, 129 mg cholesterol.

16	Littleneck clams, well scrubbed	12	ounces flounder fillets, cut into 1½-inch pieces
1	large onion (about 10 ounces), peeled and finely chopped (1½ cups)	1	cup skim milk
		1	cup water
3	large boiling potatoes (7 ounces each), peeled, and cut into ¼-inch dice (about 3 cups)	½	cup heavy cream
		1	pound large shrimp, peeled and deveined
2	tablespoons unsalted butter	1	teaspoon coarse (kosher) salt
1	tablespoon all-purpose flour	⅛	teaspoon freshly ground pepper
¼	teaspoon ground mace		
⅛	teaspoon ground hot red pepper		

1. Arrange the clams, hinge ends down, in a microwave-safe 5-quart soufflé or casserole dish. Cover the dish tightly with microwave-safe plastic wrap. Microwave at full power for 8 minutes. Carefully pierce the plastic wrap with a knife to release the steam. Remove the dish from the oven. Carefully uncover the dish.

2. Strain the clams through a sieve lined with paper toweling placed over a bowl. Reserve the clam broth. Discard any unopened clams. Remove the clam meat from the shells. Coarsely chop the clam meat, and set it aside.

3. Stir together the onion, potatoes, butter, flour, mace, ground hot red pepper and reserved clam broth in the microwave-safe dish. Re-cover the dish with plastic wrap. Microwave at full power for 14 minutes, stirring once. Carefully pierce the plastic wrap with a knife to release the steam. Remove the dish from the oven, and carefully uncover it. Transfer the onion mixture to a medium-size bowl.

4. Place the flounder pieces, milk, water and cream in the microwave-safe dish. Re-cover the dish with plastic wrap. Microwave at full power for 8 minutes, stirring once. Carefully pierce the plastic wrap with a knife to release the steam. Remove the dish from the oven, and carefully uncover it.

5. Gently stir the onion mixture into the flounder mixture so the flounder pieces do not break up completely. Arrange the shrimp around the inside edge of the dish. Place the clam meat in the center. Re-cover the dish with plastic wrap. Microwave at full power for 5 minutes. Carefully pierce the plastic wrap with a knife to release the steam. Remove the dish from the oven. Stir in the salt and the pepper. Serve the chowder hot.

CLAMMING UP

Clams are categorized as soft shell or hard shell.

● Soft shell clams have long necks, or siphons, protruding from their thin and brittle shells. Small, tender varieties are excellent steamed. Larger types, such as the Geoduck, should be chopped and cooked.

● Hard shell clams range in size from the small Littleneck and slightly bigger Cherrystone to the still larger Quahog, or Chowder, clam. Size determines the tenderness and method of preparation. Littleneck clams are used in cooking, and are served as appetizers. Cherrystones often are steamed or baked. As their name implies, Chowder clams usually are chopped and added to chowders, soups, and other cooked dishes.

● As a result of recent concern about potential health risks, eating shellfish raw is discouraged.

Hearty Chicken Noodle Soup

This soup uses chicken parts on the bone, and is so full of vegetables and noodles it can double as a stew. But don't waste any of the tasty broth!

LOW-FAT · MICROWAVE
Makes 8 servings.
Nutrient Value Per Serving: 398 calories, 40 g protein, 7 g fat, 42 g carbohydrate, 628 mg sodium, 132 mg cholesterol.

2	**broiler-fryers (2½ to 3 pounds each), skinned, and each cut into 8 serving pieces**
1	**pound yellow onions (3 to 4 large onions), cut into 1-inch chunks (about 4 cups)**
3	**medium-size carrots (3 ounces each), peeled, and cut crosswise into ½-inch-thick slices**
8	**ounces parsnips, peeled, and cut into ½-inch dice (1 cup)**
8	**ounces turnips, peeled, quartered, and cut into ¼-inch-thick slices (about 2 cups)**
5½	**cups homemade chicken broth OR: 2 cans (13¾ ounces each) chicken broth plus 2 cups water**
2	**stalks celery, peeled, and cut crosswise into ¼-inch-thick slices (about ½ cup)**
2	**teaspoons dill seeds**
8	**ounces fine egg noodles**
1	**package (10 ounces) frozen peas, thawed in sieve under warm running water**
½	**cup chopped parsley**
	Coarse (kosher) salt and freshly ground pepper, to taste

1. Arrange the chicken legs and thighs around the inside edge of a microwave-safe 5-quart soufflé or casserole dish. Arrange the chicken breasts and wings in the center of the dish. Place the onion over the breasts and wings. Place the carrot, parsnip and turnip over the legs and thighs. Add the homemade broth or canned broth and water. Cover the dish tightly with microwave-safe plastic wrap. Microwave at full power for 30 minutes. Carefully pierce the plastic wrap with a knife to release the steam. Remove the dish from the oven. Carefully uncover the dish.

2. Stir in the celery and the dill seed. Re-cover the dish with plastic wrap. Microwave at full power for 5 minutes. Carefully pierce the plastic wrap with a knife to release the steam. Remove the dish from the oven. Carefully uncover the dish, and set it aside.

3. Bring a large pot of water to boiling on top of the stove. Add the noodles, and cook them following the package directions. Just before the noodles are done, stir in the peas. Drain the noodles and peas. Stir the noodles and peas into the chicken mixture along with the parsley. Add the salt and pepper. Serve the soup hot.

Chilled Squash Soup with Mint

LOW-CALORIE · LOW-CHOLESTEROL · LOW-FAT · MICROWAVE
Makes 4 servings.
Nutrient Value Per Serving: 65 calories, 6 g protein, 1 g fat,
8 g carbohydrate, 770 mg sodium, 1 mg cholesterol.

4	medium-size yellow squash (about 5 ounces each), trimmed, halved lengthwise, and cut into ¼-inch slices	2	teaspoons chopped fresh mint
1	medium-size onion, chopped (½ cup)	12	drops liquid red pepper seasoning, or to taste
1½	cups chicken broth	½	teaspoon salt
½	cup lowfat cottage cheese	⅛	teaspoon freshly ground pepper
2	tablespoons flat-leaf Italian parsley	½	cup water

1. Combine the squash, onion and 1 cup of the broth in a microwave-safe 3-quart glass or ceramic dish with a lid. Cover the dish. Microwave at full power for 10 minutes. Remove the dish from the oven. Carefully push the cover ajar to release the steam. Carefully uncover the dish.

2. Transfer the vegetables and broth to the container of an electric blender or food processor. Add the cottage cheese, parsley, mint, liquid red pepper seasoning, salt and pepper. Whirl until the mixture is smooth.

3. Transfer the cottage cheese mixture to the microwave-safe dish. Stir in the remaining ½ cup of broth and the water. Refrigerate the soup, covered, until it is well chilled.

Spanish Rice

LOW-CHOLESTEROL · LOW-FAT · MICROWAVE
Makes 8 servings.
Nutrient Value Per Serving: 122 calories, 3 g protein, 2 g fat,
21 g carbohydrate, 373 mg sodium, 0 mg cholesterol.

1	tablespoon vegetable oil	2	tablespoons chili powder
1	cup long-grain white rice	¼	teaspoon ground cumin
1	sweet red pepper, cored and cut into 2 x ¼-inch strips	½	teaspoon salt
1	medium-size onion, chopped (½ cup)	¼	cup tomato sauce
1	clove garlic, finely chopped	1¾	cups homemade chicken broth OR: canned chicken broth

1. Stir together the oil and the rice in a microwave-safe 2-quart casserole dish. Microwave, uncovered, at full power for 2 minutes. Stir the mixture, and microwave, uncovered, at full power for 2 minutes more, or until the rice is golden brown. Remove the dish from the oven.

2. Stir in the red pepper, onion and garlic. Microwave, uncovered, at full power for 2 minutes. Remove the dish from the oven.

3. Stir in the chili powder, cumin, salt, tomato sauce and broth. Cover the dish tightly with microwave-safe plastic wrap. Microwave at full power for 10 minutes. Stir the mixture and re-cover the dish with plastic wrap. Microwave at full power for about 5 minutes more. Remove the dish from the oven. Let the rice mixture stand, covered, for 5 minutes.

PARSLIED NEW POTATOES

- Wash 12 small new potatoes very well. Cut off the ends, or peel a ½-inch strip around the middle of each potato. Place the potatoes along with ¼ cup of water in a microwave-safe 2-quart casserole dish. Cover the dish with microwave-safe plastic wrap, slightly vented in one place. Microwave at full power for 10 to 12 minutes, stirring once. Drain the potatoes, place them in a serving bowl, and let them stand.
- Combine 3 tablespoons of butter or margarine with 1 crushed garlic clove in a 1-cup glass measure. Microwave at full power for 1 minute, or until the butter is melted. Remove and discard the garlic. Stir in 1 tablespoon of finely chopped fresh parsley, and freshly ground pepper to taste.
- Pour the parsley butter over the potatoes in the bowl, and toss the potatoes very gently to coat them.

PLUM ICE

A refreshing after dinner treat with no fat or cholesterol.

- Cut 1 pound of ripe plums (6 to 8 plums) in half. Remove and discard the pits.
- Combine the plum halves with ½ cup of water and ¾ cup of sugar in a microwave-safe 1½-quart casserole dish. Cover the dish tightly with microwave-safe plastic wrap. Microwave at full power for 8 minutes. Carefully pierce the plastic wrap with a knife to release the steam. Remove the dish from the oven, and carefully uncover it. Let the plum mixture cool for 30 minutes.
- Place the plum mixture in the container of a food processor. Cover and whirl until the mixture is puréed. Add 1 can (5½ ounces) of apple juice, and whirl just to combine the ingredients.
- Scrape the plum purée into an 8 x 8 x 2-inch square metal pan. Cover the pan with plastic wrap, and place the pan in the freezer. Freeze the purée until it is frozen around the edges, for about 45 minutes.
- Stir the plum purée with a fork to break it up. Re-cover the pan, and return it to the freezer. Break up the purée again after 45 minutes.
- Return the pan to the freezer for about 20 minutes, or until the ice is firm but easy to scoop. If the ice becomes too firm, place the pan in the refrigerator to soften the ice slightly. For the best flavor and texture, serve the ice immediately. Makes 6 servings.

Strawberry Kissel

**LOW-CALORIE · LOW-CHOLESTEROL · LOW-SODIUM
LOW-FAT · MICROWAVE**
Makes 4 servings.
Nutrient Value Per Serving: 136 calories, 1 g protein, 1 g fat, 34 g carbohydrate, 4 mg sodium, 0 mg cholesterol.

2	pints (24 ounces) very ripe strawberries, washed and cored	3	tablespoons cornstarch
		½	cup cold water
⅓	cup sugar	2	tablespoons lemon juice

1. Combine the strawberries with the sugar in a microwave-safe 2½-quart glass dish. Cover the dish tightly with microwave-safe plastic wrap. Microwave at full power for 6 minutes, stirring once. Carefully pierce the plastic wrap with a knife to release the steam. Remove the dish from the oven. Carefully uncover the dish.

2. Pour the strawberries into a fine sieve set over a bowl. Using the back of a spoon, push the strawberries through until only a little pulp remains. Discard the pulp. Return the strawberry liquid to the microwave-safe dish.

3. Stir together the cornstarch and the water in a bowl until the mixture is smooth. Gradually whisk the cornstarch mixture into the strawberry liquid. Re-cover the dish with plastic wrap. Microwave at full power for 4 minutes. Pierce the plastic wrap with a knife to release the steam. Remove the dish from the oven, and carefully uncover it.

4. Stir in the lemon juice. Divide the kissel among four 3½ x 1½-inch custard cups. Place a piece of plastic wrap directly on the surface of each kissel, and refrigerate them for at least 1 hour. Serve the kissels chilled.

Honeyed Fruit Compote

LOW-CHOLESTEROL · LOW-SODIUM · LOW-FAT · MICROWAVE
Makes 8 servings.
Nutrient Value Per Serving: 250 calories, 3 g protein, 0 g fat, 64 g carbohydrate, 16 mg sodium, 0 mg cholesterol.

1	cup dried apricots (from a 6-ounce bag)	¼	cup dark raisins
1	cup dried apples	2	thin slices lemon
1	cup dried peaches	4	cups orange juice
1	cup large prunes, unpitted	1	teaspoon honey
¼	cup golden raisins	1	to 2 teaspoons superfine sugar

1. Cut the apricots, apples and peaches into bite-size pieces. Place the fruits in a microwave-safe 3- to 4-quart bowl.

2. Add the prunes, golden raisins, dark raisins, lemon slices and orange juice, and toss to mix the ingredients. Cover the bowl with a doubled piece of wax paper. Microwave at full power for 12 to 15 minutes; the liquid should barely come to a boil.

3. Reduce the power to one third, and microwave for 3 to 4 minutes, or until the fruits are soft but not mushy. Remove the bowl from the oven. Stir in the honey and the sugar. Serve the compote chilled, or at room temperature.

CHAPTER 5

Sweet Sensations

The aroma of fresh apple pie in the oven... the vision of a strawberry shortcake, filled with whipped cream and overflowing with berries... the cool dreamy delight of homemade sherbet. Dessert can bring out a childlike excitement in all of us.

Because these sweet endings are often the most anticipated part of a meal, we've carefully selected some of our favorite crowd-pleasers. Try our simple but snappy Sliced Oranges with Honey Sauce, or the more extravagant Chocolate Raspberry Torte. You'll also find Crêpes Peach Melba, Jam-Filled Pastries and a bushel of recipes using that fall favorite, apples!

For those of us who prefer something a little lighter for dessert, taste our Lemon Sponge Cake with Strawberry Sauce or our Very Berry Bread Pudding. And for the perfect summer sweet, try one of our many sherbets and ices.

Whip up one of these sweet sensations and give your friends and family dessert excitations!

Fabulous flavors of the day include Blueberry Bits Sherbet (recipe, page 205), crunchy Chunky Cherry Vanilla Sherbet (recipe, page 212), tangy Raspberry Sherbet (recipe, page 208), exotic Mango Mint Sherbet (recipe, page 208) and Piña Colada Sherbet (recipe, page 209).

*B*aked Treats

One of the great joys of eating certainly is the incomparable flavor of goodies fresh from the oven.

Strawberry Shortcake Supreme

Bake at 425° for 15 minutes.
Makes 8 servings.
Nutrient Value Per Serving: 437 calories, 7 g protein, 22 g fat, 55 g carbohydrate, 274 mg sodium, 118 mg cholesterol.

Nonstick vegetable cooking spray	¾ **cup buttermilk**
1 **package (10 ounces) frozen raspberries in light syrup**	1 **egg**
	¾ **teaspoon vanilla**
4 **cups (1 quart) small strawberries, gently washed and hulled**	**Glaze:**
	1 **egg yolk**
Shortcake:	1 **tablespoon milk**
2¼ **cups all-purpose flour**	1 **tablespoon granulated sugar**
⅓ **cup granulated sugar**	**Whipped Cream:**
2 **teaspoons baking powder**	1 **cup heavy cream**
½ **teaspoon baking soda**	1 **tablespoon 10X (confectioners' powdered) sugar**
¼ **teaspoon salt**	
6 **tablespoons unsalted butter**	¼ **teaspoon vanilla**

1. Preheat the oven to hot (425°). Spray an 8-inch and a 9-inch round layer cake pan with nonstick vegetable cooking spray. Set aside the pans.

2. Place the raspberries with their syrup in the container of a food processor. Whirl until the raspberries are puréed. Strain the purée through a fine-mesh sieve, and discard the seeds. Combine the strawberries with the raspberry purée in a bowl. Refrigerate the berry mixture.

3. Prepare the Shortcake: Sift together the flour, granulated sugar, baking powder, baking soda and salt into a large bowl. Using a pastry blender or 2 knives, cut in the butter until the mixture resembles coarse meal.

4. Stir together the buttermilk, egg and vanilla in a small bowl. Make a well in the flour mixture, and pour in the buttermilk mixture. Stir just to combine the two mixtures; do not overmix. Divide the dough in half. With lightly floured hands, pat each dough half into a prepared pan, patting down the dough until it reaches the pan sides. Smooth the tops of the dough.

5. Prepare the Glaze: Whisk together the egg yolk and the milk in a small bowl. Brush the egg yolk mixture over the top of the dough in each pan. Sprinkle the dough with the granulated sugar, divided evenly.

6. Bake the cake layers in the lower third of the preheated hot oven (425°) for 15 minutes, or until the layers are golden brown and a wooden pick inserted in the centers comes out clean. Cool the cake layers in the pans for 5 minutes. Remove the cake layers from the pans to wire racks to cool completely.

*"*W*e may say of angling as Dr. Boteler said of strawberries: 'Doubtless God could have made a better berry, but doubtless God never did.'"*

— Izaak Walton

o ❖ o

PICKING & CHOOSING STRAWBERRIES

When shopping for strawberries, look for a deep red color and a fresh, green cap. Avoid strawberries with a green or greenish-yellow tinge, or ones with white shoulders—strawberries will not ripen once they've been picked. Do not purchase juice-stained cartons; stains are a sign of damaged fruit.

7. Prepare the Whipped Cream: Beat the heavy cream in a medium-size bowl with an electric mixer at high speed until the cream is foamy. Beat in the 10X (confectioners' powdered) sugar until soft peaks form. Beat in the vanilla. Refrigerate the whipped cream.

8. To assemble the shortcake, place the 9-inch cake layer, flat side down, on a serving plate. Spoon three quarters of the whipped cream on top of the layer, smoothing the cream to the layer's edge. Using a slotted spoon, spoon half the berry mixture over the whipped cream. Cut the 8-inch cake layer into 8 wedges. Place the cake wedges on top of the berry mixture, with their outer edges just inside the outer edge of the 9-inch cake layer. Set aside 8 strawberries from the berry mixture for garnish. Spoon the remaining berry mixture into the center of the shortcake, and mound the remaining whipped cream on top of the berry mixture. Garnish the shortcake with the reserved strawberries.

A spectacular blend of tastes and textures — fresh strawberries, raspberry purée, old-fashioned biscuit shortcake and sweet whipped cream — makes Strawberry Shortcake Supreme absolutely irresistible.

187

Chocolate Raspberry Torte

LOW-FAT
Bake at 375° for 55 minutes.
Makes 16 servings.
Nutrient Value Per Serving: 219 calories, 11 g protein, 3 g fat,
38 g carbohydrate, 279 mg sodium, 46 mg cholesterol.

3   containers (16 ounces each)
     plain lowfat yogurt
    Nonstick vegetable
     cooking spray

Chocolate Cake:
1½   cups sifted cake flour
½   cup unsweetened
     cocoa powder
1   tablespoon baking powder
3   eggs, separated
¾   cup plus ½ cup
     granulated sugar
6   tablespoons water
9   egg whites

½   teaspoon salt

Raspberry Filling:
2   packages unflavored gelatin
1   can (12 ounces) evaporated
     skim milk
¼   cup granulated sugar
1   teaspoon vanilla
2   cups raspberries, cut in half

    10X (confectioners'
     powdered) sugar (optional)
    Additional raspberries,
     for garnish (optional)

1. The day before making the torte, place the yogurt in a sieve lined with a double thickness of cheesecloth and set over a bowl. Cover the sieve with plastic wrap, and refrigerate the yogurt overnight. The next day, discard the liquid in the bowl. Refrigerate the yogurt cheese until ready to use it.

2. When ready to make the torte, preheat the oven to moderate (375°). Spray an 8-inch springform pan with nonstick vegetable cooking spray. Line the bottom of the pan with wax paper, and spray the paper.

3. Prepare the Chocolate Cake: Sift together the cake flour, cocoa and baking powder onto wax paper.

4. Beat the egg yolks in a small bowl with an electric mixer at high speed for 1 to 2 minutes, or until the yolks are foamy. Gradually beat in ¾ cup of the granulated sugar, 1 tablespoon at a time, for 3 minutes, or until the mixture is very thick. Add the water, and beat well. Fold in the flour mixture in 2 additions until the flour-egg yolk mixture is smooth.

5. Using clean beaters, beat together the 12 egg whites and the salt in a large bowl until the whites are foamy. Gradually beat in the remaining ½ cup of granulated sugar until soft peaks form. Fold one third of the whites into the flour-egg yolk mixture until the mixture is lightened in color. Fold in the remaining whites until no streaks remain. Fold the batter into the prepared pan.

6. Bake the cake in the preheated moderate oven (375°) for 55 minutes, or until the center springs back when lightly pressed with your fingertip.

7. Gently loosen the cake around the edge of the pan with a knife. Remove the outside ring from the pan. Cool the cake on a wire rack for 10 minutes. Invert the cake onto the wire rack. Carefully remove the bottom of the pan and the wax paper. Turn the cake right side up, and cool it completely. Slice the cake horizontally into 3 equal layers.

8. While the cake is cooling, prepare the Raspberry Filling: Soften the gelatin in ½ cup of the milk in a small saucepan for 3 to 5 minutes. Place the saucepan over low heat, stirring occasionally, until the gelatin is completely dissolved. Transfer the gelatin mixture to a large mixing bowl. Stir in the

KEEPING & FREEZING STRAWBERRIES

For the freshest flavor, serve strawberries as soon as possible after buying or picking them.

● Store fresh strawberries, unwashed, in the refrigerator immediately after bringing them home. If you wash strawberries before refrigerating them, they will turn soft. Refrigerated strawberries will keep for 1 to 2 days.

● To freeze strawberries, wash and dry them gently. Set the strawberries, cap side down, on a baking sheet and place the baking sheet in the freezer. When the strawberries are completely frozen — in about 2 hours — transfer them to a self-sealing freezer bag.

○ ❖ ○

" *...an egg which has succeeded in being fresh has done all that can be reasonably expected of it.* "
—Henry James

remaining milk. Chill the milk mixture for about 5 minutes, or until the milk mixture is thickened.

9. Add the yogurt cheese, granulated sugar and vanilla to the milk mixture. Beat with the electric mixer at medium-low speed until the ingredients are blended and the yogurt mixture is smooth. Stir in the raspberries.

10. Place 1 cake layer on a serving plate. Spread half the filling over the top of the layer. Repeat with another cake layer and the remaining filling. Top with the remaining cake layer. If you wish, sift 10X (confectioners' powdered) sugar over the torte, and garnish with additional raspberries.

Honey Pear Spice Cake

LOW-FAT

Bake at 350° for 55 to 60 minutes.

Makes 9 servings.

Nutrient Value Per Serving: 323 calories, 4 g protein, 9 g fat, 58 g carbohydrate, 295 mg sodium, 68 mg cholesterol.

2 **firm, ripe Bosc, Bartlett OR: Anjou pears, peeled, cored, and sliced lengthwise ¼ inch thick**	1¾ **cups all-purpose flour**
2 **teaspoons lemon juice**	2 **teaspoons baking powder**
2 **tablespoons plus ¼ cup (½ stick) unsalted butter, softened**	1¾ **teaspoons ground cinnamon**
	1 **teaspoon ground ginger**
	¾ **teaspoon salt**
2 **tablespoons plus ¼ cup honey**	¾ **cup sugar**
	2 **eggs**
1 **tablespoon crystallized ginger, finely chopped (optional)**	1 **teaspoon vanilla**
	1 **teaspoon grated lemon zest (yellow part of rind only)**
	1 **can (5½ ounces) pear nectar**

1. Preheat the oven to moderate (350°). Toss the pear slices in the lemon juice in a small bowl to coat the slices. Set aside the pear slices.

2. Melt 2 tablespoons of the butter in an 8 x 8 x 2-inch square nonstick metal baking pan over medium-low heat. Stir in 2 tablespoons of the honey. Cook, stirring often, for 3 minutes, or until the honey mixture turns deep golden brown. Remove the pan from the heat. If you wish, sprinkle 1 tablespoon of crystallized ginger, finely chopped, evenly over the honey mixture. Arrange the pear slices, overlapping, in rows on top of the honey mixture. Set aside the pan.

3. Whisk together the flour, baking powder, cinnamon, ground ginger and salt in a medium-size bowl.

4. Beat together the remaining ¼ cup of butter and the sugar in a large bowl until the mixture is creamy. Beat in the eggs, the remaining ¼ cup of honey, the vanilla and lemon zest until they are blended. Add the flour mixture alternately with the pear nectar, beating after each addition, just until the ingredients are blended. Spread the batter evenly over the pear slices in the pan.

5. Bake the cake in the preheated moderate oven (350°) for 55 to 60 minutes, or until a wooden pick inserted in the center comes out clean. Let the cake stand in the pan on a wire rack for 10 minutes. Loosen the side of the cake from the pan with a thin metal spatula. Invert a serving plate over the pan, and turn out the cake onto the plate. Let the cake stand for 30 minutes. Serve the cake warm, or cool it completely before serving it.

Jam-Filled Pastries

Make a batch of these delightful pastries using one kind of jam, or use a selection of jams and preserves for variety.

LOW-CHOLESTEROL

Bake at 400° for 10 to 15 minutes.

Makes 3 dozen pastries.

Nutrient Value Per Pastry: 103 calories, 3 g protein, 2 g fat, 19 g carbohydrate, 57 mg sodium, 0 mg cholesterol.

1 **cup milk**	**Nonstick vegetable cooking spray**
¼ **cup (½ stick) butter**	1 **cup low-sugar jam**
½ **cup granulated sugar**	**OR: preserves**
½ **teaspoon salt**	2 **egg whites**
2 **packages active dry yeast**	2 **tablespoons water**
¼ **cup warm water (105° to 115°)***	½ **cup 10X (confectioners' powdered) sugar**
2 **eggs, slightly beaten**	2 **to 3 teaspoons water**
4 **to 5 cups unsifted all-purpose flour**	

1. Heat together the milk, butter, granulated sugar and salt in a medium-size saucepan until the butter is melted and the sugar is dissolved. Cool the butter mixture to lukewarm.

2. Sprinkle the yeast over the warm water in a large bowl; stir to dissolve the yeast. Add the butter mixture, beaten eggs and 3 cups of the flour, and beat until the ingredients are blended. Stir in another cup of the flour. Stir in as much of the remaining flour as necessary to make a soft dough.

3. Turn out the dough onto a lightly floured surface. Knead the dough for 8 minutes, or until the dough is smooth. Spray a medium-size bowl with nonstick vegetable cooking spray. Press the dough into the greased bowl, and turn the greased side up. Cover the bowl with plastic wrap. Let the dough rise in a warm place, away from drafts, until it is doubled in size, for 45 to 60 minutes.

4. Punch down the dough. Divide the dough into thirds. Roll out each third to a 12 x 9-inch rectangle. Cut each rectangle into 3-inch squares. Spoon about 1 teaspoon of the jam or preserves into the center of each square. Fold two opposite corners of each square toward the center until the points touch. Pinch the points together to seal them. Place the pastries on a baking sheet, and cover them lightly with plastic wrap. Let the pastries rise in a warm place, away from drafts, until they are doubled in size, for about 20 minutes.

5. Preheat the oven to hot (400°).

6. Stir together the egg whites and the 2 tablespoons of water in a small cup. Brush the tops of the pastries with the glaze.

7. Bake the pastries in the preheated hot oven (400°) for 10 to 15 minutes, or until the pastries are golden. Remove the pastries from the baking sheet to a wire rack to cool.

8. Place the 10X (confectioners' powdered) sugar in a small bowl. Stir in enough of the 2 to 3 teaspoons of water to make an icing with a good drizzling consistency. Drizzle the icing over the pastries.

Note: *Warm water should feel tepid when dropped on your wrist.*

> "*All I ask of my food is that it doesn't harm me.*"
> — *Michael Palin*

BERRY WONDERFUL!

The crown jewel of berries, strawberries have a tantalizing, fresh taste that is like nothing else. Whether eaten straight off the vine, dipped in sugar, layered in a shortcake, piled high in a pie, or smothered in clouds of whipped cream, strawberries are utterly and completely irresistible. At one time, these crimson delicacies were prized for qualities other than their flavor. People ate them for their "curative" powers, and cherished them as symbols of love. How did strawberries get their name? Perhaps from the fact that the tempting tidbits used to be strung on reeds, and sold "by the straw."

Strawberry Raspberry Tart

This tart can be prepared 1 day in advance. For a slightly sweeter taste, add a little sugar to the cooled berry filling.

LOW-CALORIE · LOW-CHOLESTEROL
Bake shell at 400° for 10 to 12 minutes.
Makes 10 servings.
Nutrient Value Per Serving: 126 calories, 1 g protein, 7 g fat, 15 g carbohydrate, 119 mg sodium, 3 mg cholesterol.

½ **of 11-ounce package pie crust mix**	5 **tablespoons low-sugar raspberry preserves OR: jam**
2 **pint baskets strawberries, hulled**	

1. Preheat the oven to hot (400°).

2. Prepare the pie crust mix following the package directions for a single 9-inch crust. Fit the dough into a 9-inch tart pan with a removable bottom. Prick the bottom of the dough all over with a fork. Refrigerate the dough in the pan for 10 minutes to set it.

3. Bake the tart shell in the preheated hot oven (400°) for 10 to 12 minutes, or until the shell is pale golden. Remove the tart shell from the oven to a wire rack to cool.

4. Reserve 1 pint of the strawberries for garnish. Halve the remaining pint of strawberries.

5. Combine the strawberry halves with the raspberry preserves or jam in a medium-size saucepan. Bring the berry mixture to boiling. Lower the heat and simmer the berry mixture, stirring occasionally, for 7 minutes, or until the strawberries are softened.

6. Strain the berry mixture over a bowl. Transfer the strawberry halves to a small bowl. Pour the berry liquid back into the saucepan. Cook the berry liquid over low heat, stirring constantly, for 5 minutes, or until the liquid has thickened to a jamlike consistency. Add the thickened berry liquid to the strawberry halves. Cool the berry filling to room temperature.

7. Spread the berry filling in the cooled tart shell. Refrigerate the tart, lightly covered, until serving time. (The tart can be prepared to this point up to 1 day in advance.)

8. To serve, remove the outside ring from the pan. Cut the reserved strawberries into ½-inch-thick slices. Garnish the tart with the sliced strawberries, and serve.

Pear & Cranberry Tart

LOW-SODIUM

Bake at 400° for 45 to 50 minutes.

Makes 8 servings.

Nutrient Value Per Serving: 346 calories, 4 g protein, 13 g fat, 57 g carbohydrate, 46 mg sodium, 58 mg cholesterol.

Sweet Pastry:

1½	cups all-purpose flour
2	tablespoons sugar
⅛	teaspoon salt
½	cup (1 stick) unsalted butter or margarine
1	egg
2	tablespoons cold water

Pear Cranberry Filling:

1	firm, ripe Bosc OR: Bartlett pear (8 ounces), peeled, cored and diced

1½	cups cranberries
½	cup sugar
½	teaspoon ground cinnamon
⅛	teaspoon ground cloves
1	teaspoon water
2	firm, ripe Bosc OR: Bartlett pears (1 pound), peeled, cored, and sliced ¼ inch thick
1	tablespoon sugar
¼	cup apricot jam

PEAR BUTTER

This creamy topping is wonderful spooned over biscuits, muffins, pancakes, ice cream, or pound cake. Pear Butter can be stored in jars in the refrigerator for up to 4 weeks.

● Combine 3½ pounds of peeled, cored and quartered, firm ripe Bartlett pears with ½ cup of sugar and ¼ cup of lemon juice in a large, heavy saucepan or Dutch oven. Bring the pear mixture to boiling over medium heat. Cover the saucepan and cook for 15 minutes, or until the pears are very tender and mushy.

● Drain the pear mixture over a small, heavy saucepan, and set aside the drained pears. Bring the liquid in the saucepan to boiling. Reduce the heat to medium and cook, stirring frequently, until the liquid is reduced to ¼ cup; do not let the liquid burn.

● Place the drained pears in the container of a food processor or electric blender. Whirl until the pears are puréed. Pour the pear purée into a large bowl, and add the reduced liquid. Add ½ cup (1 stick) of butter cut into 8 pieces, and stir until the butter is melted. Stir in 2½ teaspoons of vanilla.

Makes 4 cups.

An intriguing combination of sweet and tangy flavor: Pear & Cranberry Tart.

1. Prepare the Sweet Pastry: Whisk together the flour, sugar and salt in a small bowl. Using a pastry blender or 2 knives, cut in the butter or margarine until the mixture resembles coarse crumbs. Stir together the egg and the cold water in a small bowl. Stir the egg mixture into the flour mixture just until the flour mixture is evenly moistened. Flatten the dough into a disk, and wrap it in wax paper. Refrigerate the dough for 1 hour.

2. Prepare the Pear Cranberry Filling: Combine the pear, cranberries, sugar, cinnamon, cloves and water in a medium-size saucepan. Cover the saucepan and cook over low heat, stirring occasionally, for about 15 minutes, or until the pears are tender. Transfer the mixture to the container of a food processor or electric blender. Whirl until the mixture is puréed. Set aside the filling.

3. Ten minutes before baking, preheat the oven to hot (400°).

4. Roll out the dough with a lightly floured rolling pin on a lightly floured surface to an 11-inch round. Fit the dough into a 9-inch tart pan with a removable bottom. Fold the edge of the dough to the inside, and press it against the side of the pan. Prick the bottom of the dough all over with a fork.

5. Spread the filling evenly over the bottom of the tart shell.

6. Arrange the pear slices, overlapping, in a circular row over the top of the filling. Sprinkle the pear slices evenly with the tablespoon of sugar.

7. Bake the tart in the preheated hot oven (400°) for 45 to 50 minutes, or until the shell is golden and the pear slices are tender. Meanwhile, heat the apricot jam in a small saucepan over low heat until the jam is melted. Brush the melted jam evenly over the pear slices in the hot tart to glaze them. Cool the tart completely before serving it.

Blueberry Crunch

LOW-CHOLESTEROL · LOW-SODIUM
Bake at 375° for 30 minutes.
Makes 4 servings.
Nutrient Value Per Serving: 247 calories, 3 g protein, 10 g fat, 40 g carbohydrate, 11 mg sodium, 23 mg cholesterol.

1	pint blueberries	¼	cup firmly packed light brown sugar
2	tablespoons granulated sugar	2	tablespoons all-purpose flour
2	teaspoons lemon juice	3	tablespoons unsalted butter or margarine, softened
1	teaspoon ground cinnamon		
½	cup old-fashioned oatmeal		

1. Preheat the oven to moderate (375°).

2. Combine the blueberries, granulated sugar, lemon juice and ½ teaspoon of the cinnamon in a 1-quart baking dish.

3. Combine the oatmeal, brown sugar, flour and remaining ½ teaspoon of cinnamon in a small bowl. Using a pastry blender or 2 knives, cut in the butter or margarine until the mixture resembles coarse crumbs. Sprinkle the oatmeal mixture over the blueberry mixture.

4. Bake the crunch in the preheated moderate oven (375°) for 30 minutes, or until the topping is browned and the blueberries are bubbly. Let the crunch stand for 15 minutes before serving it.

> *"You should go to a pear tree for pears, not to an elm."*
> — *Publilius Syrus*

Individual Apple Pies

LOW-CHOLESTEROL

Bake at 375° for 30 minutes.

Makes 6 individual pies.

Nutrient Value Per Pie (1 generous serving): 587 calories, 3 g protein, 27 g fat, 84 g carbohydrate, 476 mg sodium, 21 mg cholesterol.

1	package (11 ounces) pie crust mix	2	teaspoons lemon juice
3	pounds tart apples, such as Granny Smith	½	teaspoon ground cinnamon
¾	cup sugar	¼	teaspoon salt
2	tablespoons quick-cooking tapioca		Nonstick vegetable cooking spray
1	teaspoon grated lemon zest (yellow part of rind only)	2	tablespoons unsalted butter
		2	tablespoons half-and-half OR: milk

1. Prepare the pie crust mix following the package directions. Shape the dough into a ball, and wrap it. Refrigerate the dough for at least 15 minutes.

2. Quarter, peel and core the apples. Slice the apples into a large bowl. Stir in the sugar, tapioca, lemon zest, lemon juice, cinnamon and salt.

3. Preheat the oven to moderate (375°). Coat the insides of six 4¼-inch pie plates with nonstick vegetable cooking spray.

4. Divide the dough into 6 equal pieces. Roll out each dough piece on a lightly floured surface to a 7-inch round. Spoon the apple mixture, divided evenly, into the prepared pie plates. Dot the apple mixture in each plate with small pieces of the butter. Top each filling with a dough round. Roll under the edge of each round to make a rim, and flute the edge as desired. Cut steam vents in the dough rounds. Brush the dough rounds with the half-and-half or milk. Place the pie plates on a baking sheet.

5. Bake the pies in the preheated moderate oven (375°) for 30 minutes, or until the apples are tender and the crusts are browned. Cool the pies on a wire rack. Serve the pies warm, or at room temperature.

Apple Tart

LOW-CHOLESTEROL

Bake shell at 425° for 10 to 12 minutes; bake tart at 375° for 45 minutes.

Makes 6 servings.

Nutrient Value Per Serving: 438 calories, 3 g protein, 22 g fat, 56 g carbohydrate, 385 mg sodium, 9 mg cholesterol.

1	package (11 ounces) pie crust mix	1	tablespoon all-purpose flour
¼	cup apricot preserves, heated	2	large Granny Smith apples
¼	cup sugar		Raspberries, for garnish (optional)

1. Preheat the oven to hot (425°).

2. Prepare the pie crust mix following the package directions. Roll out the dough on a lightly floured surface to an 11-inch round. Transfer the dough to a 9-inch tart pan with a removable bottom. Fold the excess dough into the pan, press it against the pan sides, and form an edge. Line the dough with aluminum foil. Fill the foil with dried beans or pie weights.

> "*I love you as New Englanders love pie!*"
>
> — Donald Robert Perry Marquis

○ ❖ ○

"A" IS FOR APPLES!

There are all sorts of ways to use uncooked apples to make dishes more interesting and appealing. Here are a few suggestions.

● Grate raw apples into coleslaw for a snappy new taste.

● Scoop out uncooked apples, dice the pulp, and mix it with tuna, diced cooked chicken, salmon, or fruit salad. Use the apple shells as bowls to hold the salad.

● Combine equal parts of uncooked apple slices and steamed carrot slices, snow pea pods and green beans. Toss the salad with French dressing, and chill it thoroughly before serving it.

● Slice uncooked apples and dip the slices in lemon juice to keep them from turning brown. Top the apple slices with cheese, pâté or cooked sausage, and serve them as snacks or hors d'oeuvres.

● Chop uncooked apples, and mix them with granola and lemon yogurt for a great snack.

3. Bake the tart shell in the preheated hot oven (425°) for 10 to 12 minutes, or until the shell begins to color. Remove the foil and beans. Lower the oven temperature to moderate (375°). Lightly brush the tart shell with 1 tablespoon of the apricot preserves. Combine 2 tablespoons of the sugar with the flour in a small bowl. Sprinkle the flour mixture over the tart shell.

4. Peel, halve and core the apples. Place the apple halves, cut side down, on a cutting board and slice them ⅜ inch thick. Fan the slices slightly on the board. Slide the knife underneath the slices. Keeping the slices together and fanned, place them in the tart shell. Sprinkle the apple slices with the remaining 2 tablespoons of sugar.

5. Bake the tart in the preheated moderate oven (375°) for 45 minutes, or until the apple slices begin to color and are fork-tender. Remove the tart from the oven to a wire rack. Brush the apple slices with the remaining 3 tablespoons of apricot preserves. Cool the tart. Serve the tart warm, or at room temperature. If you wish, garnish the tart with raspberries.

From lower left, clockwise: Country Apple Bars (recipe, page 196) have tart green apples and apricots playing a delicious counterpoint to oats, walnuts, cinnamon, nutmeg and cloves; Apple Tart (recipe, page 194) is easy and elegant; Individual Apple Pies (recipe, page 194) are a single crust twist on tradition; sweet red grapes and a smooth honey yogurt dressing update classic Waldorf Salad (recipe, page 142).

Country Apple Bars

Bake at 375° for 30 to 35 minutes.

Makes 24 bars.

Nutrient Value Per Bar: 181 calories, 3 g protein, 9 g fat, 24 g carbohydrate, 90 mg sodium, 31 mg cholesterol.

10	**tablespoons (1¼ sticks) unsalted butter, softened**
1	**cup firmly packed brown sugar**
1½	**cups old-fashioned rolled oats**
½	**cup currants**
½	**cup dried apricots, cut into quarters**
2	**eggs**
1¼	**cups all-purpose flour**
1	**teaspoon baking powder**
½	**teaspoon baking soda**
½	**teaspoon salt**
1	**teaspoon ground cinnamon**
½	**teaspoon ground nutmeg**
¼	**teaspoon ground cloves**
1	**cup chopped walnuts (4 ounces)**
1	**pound tart green cooking apples (2 large apples), peeled, cored, and cut into ¼-inch dice (about 2 cups)**

1. Position an oven rack in the center of the oven. Preheat the oven to moderate (375°). Butter a 13 x 9 x 2-inch baking pan.

2. Melt together 2 tablespoons of the butter and 1 tablespoon of the brown sugar in a small saucepan over medium heat. Remove the saucepan from the heat. Stir in ½ cup of the oats, the currants and apricots. Reserve the oat mixture.

3. Beat together the remaining 8 tablespoons of butter and the remaining brown sugar in a large bowl for 1 to 2 minutes, or until the mixture is fluffy. Beat in the eggs, one at a time, beating well after each addition.

4. Stir together the flour, baking powder, baking soda, salt, cinnamon, nutmeg and cloves in a medium-size bowl.

5. Stir the flour mixture into the egg mixture just until the flour mixture is blended. Stir in the remaining cup of oats, the chopped walnuts and diced apples. Turn the batter into the prepared pan, and spread it evenly.

6. Bake the cake in the preheated moderate oven (375°) for 25 minutes. Sprinkle the top of the cake with the reserved oat mixture. Bake the cake for 5 to 10 minutes more, or until a wooden pick inserted in the center comes out clean. Cool the cake in the pan on a wire rack to room temperature. Cut the cake into 24 bars.

EASY APPLESAUCE PARFAITS

Here's the perfect solution when you need a quick dessert.

● Evenly divide 2 cups of unsweetened applesauce among 4 individual dessert glasses.

● Gently stir together 1 cup of plain nonfat yogurt, 2 tablespoons of sugar, ⅛ teaspoon of cinnamon, and ¼ teaspoon of vanilla just until the ingredients are blended.

● Spoon the yogurt mixture, divided evenly, over the applesauce in the glasses. Chill the parfaits until serving time.

Makes 4 servings.

CUSTARD SAUCE

A luscious topping for pound or angel cake, this sauce also is perfect with Walnut Pear Torte.

● Whisk together ¼ cup of sugar, ⅛ teaspoon of salt and 3 egg yolks in a medium-sized, heavy, non-aluminum saucepan until the ingredients are well blended and the sugar is dissolved.

● Combine ¾ cup of heavy cream with ¼ cup of milk in another heavy saucepan. Cook over medium heat just until bubbles appear around the edges of the cream mixture. Remove the saucepan from the heat. Whisking vigorously and constantly, gradually add the hot cream mixture to the egg yolk mixture.

● Cook the custard over very low heat, stirring constantly, just until the custard almost boils; steam will start to appear, and the custard will be slightly thicker than heavy cream. Do not let the custard boil. Strain the custard at once into a clean bowl, and cool the custard.

● When the custard is cooled, stir in 2 tablespoons of cognac or brandy, and ½ teaspoon of vanilla.

● Store the custard sauce, covered, in the refrigerator for up to 5 days; the sauce will thicken slightly in the refrigerator.

Walnut Pear Torte

The buttery, cakelike base of this torte is poured over walnuts, covered with pears, then sprinkled with a topping of walnuts and brown sugar. Serve the torte with ice cream, frozen yogurt or a custard sauce.

Bake at 375° for 35 minutes.
Makes 10 servings.
Nutrient Value Per Serving: 432 calories, 7 g protein, 22 g fat, 52 g carbohydrate, 166 mg sodium, 116 mg cholesterol.

1 cup plus 3 tablespoons all-purpose flour	1 teaspoon vanilla
¼ teaspoon baking powder	1 cup finely chopped walnuts
½ cup (1 stick) plus 3 tablespoons butter or margarine, softened	¼ cup firmly packed light brown sugar
½ cup plus 2 tablespoons granulated sugar	3 to 4 ripe large pears, such as Bartlett or Bosc (2 pounds)
3 eggs	2 tablespoons lemon juice
	⅓ cup currant jelly

1. Preheat the oven to moderate (375°). Grease and flour an 11-inch tart pan with a removable bottom.

2. Combine 1 cup of the flour with the baking powder in a small bowl.

3. Beat ½ cup of the butter or margarine with ½ cup of the granulated sugar in a large bowl until the mixture is smooth and creamy. Beat in the eggs until the mixture is light colored and fluffy. Gradually beat in the flour mixture until the combined mixture is smooth. Beat in the vanilla.

4. Sprinkle ½ cup of the chopped walnuts on the bottom of the prepared pan. Spoon the batter over the walnuts.

5. Combine the remaining ½ cup of chopped walnuts with the brown sugar, remaining 3 tablespoons of flour and remaining 3 tablespoons of butter in a small bowl. Mix until the ingredients are well blended.

6. Peel the pears. Halve the pears lengthwise, and core them. Slice each pear half lengthwise into thirds. Toss the pear slices in the lemon juice in a bowl to coat the slices. Press the pear slices into the batter to form an attractive design. Sprinkle the remaining 2 tablespoons of granulated sugar and the walnut-brown sugar mixture over the top of the torte. Place the pan on a baking sheet.

7. Bake the torte in the preheated moderate oven (375°) for 35 minutes, or until the top springs back when lightly touched with your fingertip. Let the torte cool in the pan on a wire rack for 45 minutes. If necessary, gently loosen the torte around the edge of the pan with the tip of a pointed knife. Remove the outside ring from the pan.

8. Melt the currant jelly in a small saucepan over low heat. Carefully brush the melted jelly over the top of the cooled torte. Serve the torte warm. Or let the melted jelly cool before serving the torte.

Lemon Sponge Cake with Strawberry Sauce

A marvel of a cake that's low in calories and high in taste!

LOW-CALORIE · LOW-SODIUM · LOW-FAT
Bake at 400° for 12 to 14 minutes.
Makes 12 servings.

Nutrient Value Per Serving: 87 calories, 3 g protein, 2 g fat, 14 g carbohydrate, 47 mg sodium, 91 mg cholesterol.

Nonstick vegetable cooking spray

Lemon Sponge Cake:

4	**eggs, separated**
⅛	**teaspoon salt**
¼	**cup granulated sugar**
½	**teaspoon grated lemon zest (yellow part of rind only)**
1	**teaspoon lemon juice**
⅔	**cup sifted all-purpose flour**

Strawberry Sauce:

3	**cups fresh strawberries, washed, hulled and sliced**
¼	**cup 10X (confectioners' powdered) sugar**
1	**teaspoon raspberry brandy (optional)**
12	**whole strawberries, for garnish (optional)**

1. Preheat the oven to hot (400°). Spray the bottom of a 9 x 9 x 2-inch square baking pan with nonstick vegetable cooking spray. Line the bottom of the pan with aluminum foil, and spray the foil.

2. Prepare the Lemon Sponge Cake: Beat together the egg whites and the salt in a large bowl until the whites are fluffy. Gradually beat in the granulated sugar until stiff, but not dry, peaks form.

3. Beat together the egg yolks, lemon zest and lemon juice in another large bowl until they are well combined. Fold in ½ cup of the beaten egg whites. Fold in the remaining whites. Fold in the flour, 1 tablespoon at a time. Spread the batter evenly in the prepared pan.

4. Bake the cake in the preheated hot oven (400°) for 12 to 14 minutes, or until the top springs back when lightly pressed with your fingertip.

5. Run a knife around the edges of the pan to loosen the cake. Invert the cake onto a wire rack, and remove the pan and foil. Invert the cake again so the golden side is on top. Cool the cake completely on the wire rack.

6. Prepare the Strawberry Sauce: Combine the strawberries, 10X (confectioners' powdered) sugar and, if you wish, raspberry brandy in the container of an electric blender or food processor. Cover and whirl until the sauce is smooth. (The sauce can be prepared 1 day in advance, covered, and refrigerated.)

7. To serve, cut the cake into 12 equal squares, and set each square on an individual dessert plate. Spoon a generous 2 tablespoons of sauce over each cake square. If you wish, garnish each serving with a whole strawberry.

BAKE A CAKE

- To separate eggs easily, use cold eggs.
- To get the maximum volume of beaten egg whites, let the whites come to room temperature before beating them.
- Remember to preheat the oven to the proper temperature 10 minutes before starting to bake.
- Cakes may turn out heavy and soggy if the oven temperature is too low.
- Cakes may fall if there isn't enough flour in the batter, if the oven is too hot, or if the oven door is opened too soon.
- If you want a cake to have the best volume, shape and texture, use the ingredients, measurements and exact pan size called for in the recipe, and follow the recipe directions exactly.

o ❖ o

DONE TO PERFECTION

A cake is finished baking when
● The cake shrinks slightly from the sides of the pan.
● The cake top springs back to shape when pressed lightly with your fingertip.
● A cake tester or wooden pick inserted near the center of the cake comes out clean, with no batter or moist particles clinging to it.

Chocolate-Glazed Sponge Cake

The more gently the egg whites are folded in Step 3, the higher and lighter the cake will be. You can prepare the cake on a weekend, and store it in the refrigerator for weekday eating.

LOW-CALORIE · LOW-SODIUM
Bake at 350° for 40 to 45 minutes.
Makes 16 servings.
Nutrient Value Per Serving: 115 calories, 3 g protein, 5 g fat, 16 g carbohydrate, 46 mg sodium, 57 mg cholesterol.

Sponge Cake:
7   egg whites
⅛   teaspoon cream of tartar
¾   cup sugar
3   egg yolks
1   teaspoon almond extract
1   cup sifted cake flour

3   tablespoons butter, melted and cooled to lukewarm

Chocolate Glaze:
1½   ounces semisweet chocolate
2   tablespoons vegetable shortening
½   teaspoon almond extract

1. Preheat the oven to moderate (350°).

2. Prepare the Sponge Cake: Beat together the egg whites and the cream of tartar in a large bowl until the whites are foamy. Beat in the sugar, 1 tablespoon at a time, until stiff, but not dry, peaks form.

3. Stir together the egg yolks and the almond extract in another large bowl. Fold in one third of the beaten egg whites. Fold in the remaining whites until no streaks remain. Sprinkle the flour over the top of the egg mixture, and gently fold it in. Very gently fold in the melted butter; do not overfold. Turn the batter into a 9-inch tube pan, and spread the batter evenly.

4. Bake the cake in the preheated moderate oven (350°) for 40 to 45 minutes, or until a wooden pick inserted near the center comes out clean. Invert the pan onto a large funnel or bottle. Let the cake hang for at least 1½ hours, or until it is cooled.

5. Run a knife around the inner and outer edges of the pan. Remove the cake, crusty portion up, to a wire rack to cool completely. Refrigerate the cooled cake until serving time.

6. At serving time, prepare the Chocolate Glaze: Melt together the chocolate and the vegetable shortening in the top of a double boiler over hot but not boiling water, stirring occasionally, until the glaze is smooth. Cool the glaze slightly, and stir in the almond extract. Spoon the glaze evenly over the top of the cake, letting the excess glaze run down the sides of the cake.

Glazed Orange Carrot Cake

A classic cake with a new citrus twist.

Bake at 325° for 65 to 70 minutes.
Makes 12 servings.
Nutrient Value Per Serving: 584 calories, 8 g protein, 31 g fat,
71 g carbohydrate, 364 mg sodium, 39 mg cholesterol.

3	cups all-purpose flour		1	tablespoon grated orange zest (orange part of rind only)
2	cups sugar			
1	teaspoon baking powder		3	cups coarsely shredded carrots (about 16 carrots)
1	teaspoon baking soda			
1	teaspoon salt		1	cup coarsely chopped walnuts
1	teaspoon ground cinnamon			
1	teaspoon ground allspice			Creamy Orange Glaze (recipe follows)
3	egg whites			
2	eggs			Candied Orange Rind, for garnish (see Tip, at right)
1¼	cups vegetable oil			
½	cup orange juice			

1. Preheat the oven to slow (325°). Grease a 10-inch Bundt pan.

2. Sift together the flour, sugar, baking powder, baking soda, salt, cinnamon and allspice into a large bowl. Combine the egg whites, eggs, oil, orange juice and orange zest in a small bowl. Make a well in the center of the dry ingredients, and pour the orange juice mixture into the well. Beat with a wooden spoon until the liquid ingredients are incorporated into the dry ingredients, and the mixture is smooth. Stir in the carrot and the chopped walnuts. Pour the batter into the prepared pan.

3. Bake the cake in the preheated slow oven (325°) for 65 to 70 minutes, or until the top springs back when lightly pressed with your fingertip, and a cake tester inserted near the center comes out clean.

4. Cool the cake in the pan on a wire rack for 10 minutes. Run a thin-bladed metal knife around the inner and outer edges of the pan to loosen the cake. Invert the cake onto the wire rack to cool completely. Spoon the Creamy Orange Glaze over the cooled cake. Garnish the cake with the Candied Orange Rind.

Creamy Orange Glaze:

Beat 1 package (3 ounces) of Neufchâtel cheese with a wooden spoon in a medium-size bowl until it is creamy. Beat in ½ cup of 10X (confectioners' powdered) sugar until the mixture is blended and smooth. Stir in 2 to 4 tablespoons of strained fresh orange juice, using only as much juice as needed to thin the glaze to the consistency of very heavy cream.
Makes about ⅔ cup.

CANDIED ORANGE RIND

● Using a sharp knife, remove only the orange part of the rind (no bitter white pith) in long strips from 1 large navel orange. Cut the rind lengthwise into ⅛-inch-wide strips.

● Combine 1 cup of sugar with 1 cup of water in a small saucepan. Bring the mixture to boiling over medium-high heat. Add the orange rinds, and return the mixture to boiling. Lower the heat, and simmer over medium heat for 10 minutes. Drain the orange rinds.

● Spread the orange rinds on a small piece of wax paper, and let them dry until they feel tacky. Makes about ¾ cup.

Glazed Orange Carrot Cake, spiced with cinnamon, allspice and oranges, is crowned with Creamy Orange Glaze and Candied Orange Rind.

Fabulous Fruits

Fruit, naturally low in calories and high in vitamins and fiber, is a great starting point for dessert — and the flavor makes fruit a natural winner.

Melon with Orange Mint Sauce

LOW-CALORIE · LOW-CHOLESTEROL · LOW-SODIUM · LOW-FAT

Makes 4 servings.

Nutrient Value Per Serving: 86 calories, 2 g protein, 2 g fat, 15 g carbohydrate, 34 mg sodium, 8 mg cholesterol.

½ cup reduced-fat dairy sour cream	½ teaspoon grated orange zest (orange part of rind only)
2 tablespoons 10X (confectioners' powdered) sugar	⅛ teaspoon dried mint, crumbled
1 tablespoon orange juice	1 small cantaloupe, cut into ½-inch cubes

Combine the sour cream, 10X (confectioners' powdered) sugar, orange juice, orange zest and mint in a medium-size bowl. Add the cantaloupe cubes, and stir gently to coat them. Cover the bowl, and refrigerate the cantaloupe mixture for up to 8 hours before serving it.

Sliced Oranges with Honey Orange Sauce

The honey orange sauce also is wonderful on slices of angel or pound cake, or spooned over frozen yogurt or ice cream.

LOW-CALORIE · LOW-CHOLESTEROL · LOW-SODIUM · LOW-FAT

Makes 4 servings.

Nutrient Value Per Serving: 97 calories, 2 g protein, .13 g fat, 24 g carbohydrate, 2 mg sodium, 0 mg cholesterol.

3 large navel oranges	⅓ cup Honey Orange Sauce (recipe follows)

1. Peel the oranges, and slice them crosswise. Place the slices in a small bowl or plastic bag, and refrigerate them until serving time.

2. To serve, divide the orange slices evenly among 4 individual dessert plates. Drizzle the orange slices with the Honey Orange Sauce.

Honey Orange Sauce:

Combine ⅓ cup of thawed frozen orange juice concentrate with ⅓ cup of honey in a small bowl. Stir to blend the ingredients thoroughly. Store the sauce in the refrigerator.
Makes ⅔ cup.

STRAWBERRIES ROMANOFF

A classic — and classy — dessert that's deliciously easy to make.

● Wash, hull and slice 1 pint of fresh strawberries, and place them in a small bowl. Add 3 tablespoons of Cointreau or other orange-flavored liqueur.

● Combine ¾ cup of whipping cream with 2 tablespoons of 10X (confectioners' powdered) sugar and 1 teaspoon of Cointreau or other orange-flavored liqueur in a second small bowl. Beat the cream mixture until soft peaks form.

● Layer the strawberries and the whipped cream in 4 individual dessert glasses or wine goblets. Refrigerate the desserts for up to 1 hour before serving them.

Once you've mastered the technique of making the delightful French pancakes, you have unlimited dessert options available to you. Crêpes can be made in advance and refrigerated or frozen, so they're a perfect mid-week treat, and an elegant ending to a meal. Here are some fillings to consider.

● Spread preserves over the crêpes, roll them up, and serve them with a dusting of 10X (confectioners' powdered) sugar or dollop of whipped cream.

● Fill crêpes with sweetened ricotta cheese, and spoon some preserves over the tops.

● Toss fresh fruits in liqueur, and refrigerate them for at least 1 hour to allow the flavors to blend. Fill crêpes with frozen yogurt or ice cream, and spoon a little of the fruits in liqueur over the tops. Or fill the crêpes with the fruits in liqueur, and serve with a dusting of 10X (confectioners' powdered) sugar or dollop of whipped cream.

● Fill crêpes with custard or pudding, and serve with sliced strawberries on top.

● Fill crêpes with vanilla or coffee frozen yogurt, and drizzle chocolate sauce in a zigzag pattern down the length of each rolled crêpe.

● Sauté diced apples in a little butter or margarine, then toss them with cinnamon sugar. Fill crêpes with the apple mixture.

Crêpes Peach Melba

The peaches in orange sauce make a great topping for waffles or French toast, too. Or try spooning them over slices of angel food cake.

LOW-CALORIE · LOW-FAT
Makes 8 servings.
Nutrient Value Per Serving: 142 calories, 3 g protein, 3 g fat, 27 g carbohydrate, 68 mg sodium, 41 mg cholesterol.

1½ **cups raspberries**	¾ **cup orange juice**
1 **tablespoon raspberry brandy (optional)**	3⅓ **cups peeled, sliced peaches (1½ pounds)**
2 **teaspoons cornstarch**	8 **Dessert Crêpes (recipe follows)**
3 **tablespoons sugar**	

1. Reserve ½ cup of the raspberries for garnish. Purée the remaining raspberries, along with 1 tablespoon of raspberry brandy if you wish, in the container of a food processor or electric blender. Strain the raspberry purée into a small bowl, and discard the solids. Cover the bowl, and refrigerate the raspberry purée.

2. Combine the cornstarch with the sugar in a small saucepan. Stir in the orange juice. Bring the orange sauce to boiling over medium-high heat. Gently boil the orange sauce, stirring, for 1 minute.

3. Place the peach slices in a large bowl. Pour the orange sauce over the peach slices, and stir to combine them well. Refrigerate the peach-orange mixture, covered, for 2 hours, or until serving time.

4. To serve, use a slotted spoon to lift out and set aside 16 peach slices for garnish. Using the slotted spoon, divide the remaining peach slices evenly among the Dessert Crêpes. Roll up the crêpes, and place them on 8 individual dessert plates. Brush the crêpes with the orange sauce remaining in the bowl. Spoon the raspberry purée, divided evenly, over the crêpes. Garnish the crêpes with the reserved peach slices and raspberries.

Microwave Instructions
(for a 650-watt variable power microwave oven)

Directions: Prepare the raspberry purée following Step 1 above. Combine the cornstarch with the sugar in a microwave-safe 4-cup measure, and stir to mix them well. Stir in the orange juice. Microwave, uncovered, at full power for 2 minutes. Whisk the orange sauce well. Microwave, uncovered, at full power for 30 seconds to a full rolling boil. Stir the peach slices into the orange sauce. Continue with the recipe.

Dessert Crêpes:
Combine 1 egg, ⅔ cup of milk, ½ cup of unsifted all-purpose flour, ⅛ teaspoon of salt, and 1 tablespoon of melted butter or margarine in the container of an electric blender. Cover and whirl at medium speed for 1 minute, or until the batter is smooth. Refrigerate the batter for ½ hour. Heat a small skillet, measuring 5 to 6 inches across the bottom, over medium-high heat. Butter the skillet lightly. Pour in 2 to 3 tablespoons of the batter, and rotate the skillet quickly to coat the bottom evenly. Cook the crêpe over medium heat for 1 minute on each side, or until the crêpe is lightly browned. Slide the crêpe onto a plate to cool. Repeat with the remaining batter. Stack the cooled crêpes with 2 sheets of wax paper between them. Wrap the crêpes with plastic wrap. Refrigerate the crêpes for up to 2 days, or freeze them for up to 2 weeks.

Apple Berry Whirl

LOW-CALORIE · LOW-CHOLESTEROL · LOW-SODIUM · LOW-FAT
Makes 8 servings.
Nutrient Value Per Serving: 85 calories, 2 g protein, 1 g fat,
20 g carbohydrate, 22 mg sodium, 2 mg cholesterol.

2	cups unsweetened applesauce	¼	cup honey, or to taste
1	cup plain lowfat yogurt	1	cup frozen dry-pack raspberries, thawed

Combine the applesauce, yogurt and honey in a bowl until they are blended.
Stir in the raspberries. Cover the bowl, and refrigerate until serving time.

Very Berry Bread Pudding

*This recipe makes extra sauce to use over ice cream, pound cake, or another
dessert. Make the pudding 1 to 2 days in advance so it will firm up.*

LOW-CALORIE · LOW-CHOLESTEROL · LOW-FAT
Makes 6 servings.
Nutrient Value Per Serving: 142 calories, 3 g protein, 1 g fat,
32 g carbohydrate, 147 mg sodium, 1 mg cholesterol.

8	slices whole wheat sandwich bread	⅓	cup sugar
1	package (10 ounces) frozen raspberries in light syrup, thawed	1	tablespoon lime juice
		½	teaspoon ground allspice
1	pint strawberries	½	cup blueberries
			Whipped cream (optional)

1. Trim the crusts from the bread slices. Line the bottom of an 8 x 4 x 2-
inch loaf pan with some of the bread slices, trimming them as needed. Halve
some of the remaining bread slices. Line the sides of the pan with the half
slices, arranging them lengthwise down the pan and trimming them as
needed. Set aside the remaining bread slices.

2. Place the raspberries with their syrup in the container of an electric
blender or food processor. Whirl until the raspberries are puréed. Scrape
the raspberry purée into a liquid measure.

3. To make extra sauce, return ⅓ cup of the raspberry purée to the
blender container. Add 3 large strawberries, and 1 tablespoon of the sugar.
Whirl until the sauce is a smooth purée. Scrape the sauce into a sauceboat.
Cover the sauceboat, and refrigerate the raspberry sauce for another use.

4. Return the remaining raspberry purée to the blender container. Add the
remaining sugar, the lime juice and allspice. Cut the remaining strawberries
in half, and add them to the blender container along with the blueberries.
Pulse just until the berries are medium-chopped.

5. Scrape the berry mixture into the bread-lined pan. Cover the mixture
with the remaining bread slices, trimming the slices as needed. Cover the
top of the pudding with plastic wrap. Place a same-size loaf pan on the
plastic wrap on top of the pudding. Weight the empty loaf pan with two
1-pound cans. Refrigerate the pudding overnight.

6. To serve, remove the weighted loaf pan and plastic wrap. Invert the
pudding onto a serving plate. Slice the pudding crosswise into 1-inch-thick
slices. Serve the pudding with whipped cream, if you wish.

> "*Poetic Justice,
> with her lifted scale,
> Where, in nice
> balance, truth with
> gold she weighs,
> And solid pudding
> against empty
> praise.*"
>
> —Alexander Pope

Chilled Desserts

Gratify your sweet tooth, and take the heat off, with these frozen finales and cooling concoctions.

MIXED BERRIES IN SPICY YOGURT SAUCE

Plain yogurt is dressed to perfection and spooned over fresh berries for an easy end-of-meal.

● In a small bowl, stir together ½ cup of plain lowfat yogurt, 1 teaspoon of honey, and ½ teaspoon of ground cinnamon until they are well blended. Cover the bowl, and refrigerate the yogurt sauce until serving time. (The yogurt sauce can be made 1 to 2 days in advance, and stored in the refrigerator.)

● Just before serving, rinse and pick over 1 pint of fresh blueberries and 1 pint of fresh raspberries. Divide the mixed berries evenly among 6 individual dessert bowls. Top each serving with a dollop of the yogurt sauce.

Makes 6 servings.

Blueberry Bits Sherbet

LOW-CALORIE ▪ LOW-CHOLESTEROL ▪ LOW-FAT
Makes about 4 cups.
Nutrient Value Per ½ Cup: 86 calories, 3 g protein, 1 g fat, 18 g carbohydrate, 83 mg sodium, 3 mg cholesterol.

2 cups fresh blueberries, picked over and rinsed	**2 tablespoons lemon juice**
2½ cups buttermilk	**⅛ teaspoon ground nutmeg**
½ cup Simple Syrup (recipe, page 206)	

1. Combine the blueberries, buttermilk, Simple Syrup, lemon juice and nutmeg in the container of a food processor or electric blender. Pulse until the blueberries are coarsely chopped, and the mixture is blended.

2. Pour the blueberry mixture into an ice cream maker. Process following the ice cream maker manufacturer's directions. Pack the sherbet into a freezer container. Freeze the sherbet until it is firm, for at least 4 hours.

Blueberry Syrup

The perfect topping for Blueberry Bits Sherbet, or any of our other sherbets.

LOW-CHOLESTEROL ▪ LOW-SODIUM ▪ LOW-FAT
Makes about 1½ cups.
Nutrient Value Per Tablespoon: 15 calories, 0 g protein, .04 g fat, 4 g carbohydrate, 1 mg sodium, 0 mg cholesterol.

1 teaspoon cornstarch	**⅓ cup Simple Syrup (recipe, page 206)**
1 tablespoon cold water	
2 cups fresh blueberries, picked over and rinsed	**1 tablespoon lime juice OR: lemon juice**

1. Dissolve the cornstarch in the cold water.

2. Combine the blueberries, Simple Syrup and lime or lemon juice in the container of a food processor or electric blender. Whirl until the mixture is puréed. Strain the blueberry purée through a wire sieve.

3. Combine the blueberry purée with the cornstarch mixture in a small saucepan. Bring the combined mixture to boiling over medium heat, and boil for 1 minute. Remove the saucepan from the heat. Let the syrup cool to room temperature.

4. Refrigerate the syrup for at least 2 hours, or until the syrup thickens. Store the syrup in the refrigerator for up to 1 week.

Simple Syrup

The syrup can be stored in the refrigerator all summer.

LOW-CHOLESTEROL · LOW-SODIUM · LOW-FAT
Makes about 3½ cups.
Nutrient Value Per ¼ Cup: 138 calories, 0 g protein, 0 g fat,
36 g carbohydrate, 0 mg sodium, 0 mg cholesterol.

2½ cups sugar	**2 cups water**

Combine the sugar with the water in a medium-size saucepan. Bring the mixture to boiling over medium heat, stirring to dissolve the sugar. Boil the syrup for about 5 minutes. Remove the saucepan from the heat. Cool the syrup to room temperature. Store the syrup, covered, in the refrigerator until ready to use it.

Tri-Colored Sherbet Mold

A spectacular finish to any summer feast, as tasty as it is beautiful.
The optional fruit will add about 40 calories per serving.

LOW-CALORIE · LOW-CHOLESTEROL · LOW-SODIUM · LOW-FAT
Makes 12 servings.
Nutrient Value Per Serving: 80 calories, 2 g protein, 1 g fat,
8 g carbohydrate, 40 mg sodium, 2 mg cholesterol.

2 cups Raspberry Sherbet (recipe, page 208), freshly cranked or refrigerator-softened	**2 cups Mango Mint Sherbet (recipe, page 208), freshly cranked or refrigerator-softened**
2 cups Piña Colada Sherbet (recipe, page 209), freshly cranked or refrigerator-softened	**4 cups mixed fresh OR: thawed frozen fruit (optional)**

1. Place a 6-cup mold in the freezer for 30 minutes.

2. Spread the Raspberry Sherbet evenly over the bottom of the mold. Place the mold in the freezer for 1 hour.

3. Spread the Piña Colada Sherbet evenly over the raspberry layer. Place the mold in the freezer for 1 hour.

4. Spread the Mango Mint Sherbet evenly over the piña colada layer. Cover the mold with plastic wrap. Freeze the sherbet until it is very firm, for at least 6 hours.

5. To unmold the sherbet, let the mold sit at room temperature for 15 minutes. Remove the plastic wrap. Dip the mold into a bowl of warm water for only 10 seconds. Invert the mold onto a cutting board. Gently tap the cutting board, with the mold on it, against the counter to loosen the sherbet. Turn the mold right side up. Invert the mold onto a cold serving platter, and unmold the sherbet onto the platter. If you wish, fill and surround the sherbet with 4 cups of mixed fresh or thawed frozen fruit. Serve the sherbet at once.

PARTY PRESENTATION

Sherbet, ices, ice cream, ice milk, and frozen yogurt all make great desserts for easy entertaining.
To add a small touch of elegance to the presentation, serve the scoops in long-stemmed wine glasses. Garnish each serving with a sprig of mint, a whole berry, or a swirl of whipped cream, and tuck a small cookie or miniature pastry alongside. For an extra-special touch, tie ribbon bows around the glass stems.

A lovely and luscious finale, Tri-Colored Sherbet Mold combines layers of Raspberry Sherbet, Piña Colada Sherbet and Mango Mint Sherbet.

Mango Mint Sherbet

LOW-CALORIE · LOW-CHOLESTEROL · LOW-FAT

Makes about 4 cups.

Nutrient Value Per ½ Cup: 87 calories, 2 g protein, 1 g fat, 19 g carbohydrate, 56 mg sodium, 2 mg cholesterol.

2 **ripe mangoes (about 1¼ pounds), peeled and cubed***	½ **cup orange juice**
½ **cup Simple Syrup (recipe, page 206)**	2 **tablespoons lime juice**
2 **cups buttermilk**	1 **tablespoon chopped fresh mint OR: 1 teaspoon dried mint, crumbled**

1. Combine the mango cubes with the Simple Syrup in the container of a food processor or electric blender. Whirl until the mixture is smooth; you should have about 1½ cups. Add the buttermilk, orange juice, lime juice and mint. Whirl until the buttermilk mixture is well blended.

2. Pour the buttermilk mixture into an ice cream maker. Process following the ice cream maker manufacturer's directions. Pack the sherbet into a freezer container. Freeze the sherbet until it is firm, for at least 4 hours.

*Note: *To cube a mango, stand it on one long side. Slice down and around the pit to remove 1 whole side. Repeat to remove the other whole side. Lay the mango slices, skin side down, on the cutting surface. Score the slices lengthwise and crosswise down to the skin. Push out the fruit cubes from the skin side, and slice them off. Scrape any remaining fruit from the skins. Slice off the fruit remaining around the pit, and peel off the skins.*

Raspberry Sherbet

Add a scoop of this tangy sherbet to a glass of cranberry-raspberry juice and seltzer for a refreshing raspberry float.

LOW-CALORIE · LOW-CHOLESTEROL · LOW-FAT

Makes about 4 cups.

Nutrient Value Per ½ Cup: 74 calories, 2 g protein, 1 g fat, 16 g carbohydrate, 65 mg sodium, 2 mg cholesterol.

2 **cups fresh raspberries, rinsed**	½ **cup Simple Syrup (recipe, page 206)**
2 **cups buttermilk**	2 **tablespoons lime juice**

1. Place the raspberries in the container of a food processor or electric blender. Whirl until the raspberries are puréed. Press the purée through a wire sieve to remove the seeds. Return the raspberry purée to the processor container. Add the buttermilk, Simple Syrup and lime juice. Whirl until the buttermilk mixture is blended.

2. Pour the buttermilk mixture into an ice cream maker. Process following the ice cream maker manufacturer's directions. Pack the sherbet into a freezer container. Freeze the sherbet until it is firm, for at least 4 hours.

MINT

There are a large number of mint species and varieties, but only spearmint and peppermint are cultivated commercially. Typically, mint plants have square stems and opposite leaves that are fragrant when crushed. Mint is cultivated commercially for its oil, which is used as a flavoring in candies and medicines, and as a scent in toiletries.

● Peppermint has bright green leaves and a sharp peppery taste. The stems of the peppermint plant are tinged lightly with purple.

● Spearmint is the most common mint found in home gardens. It has dark green leaves that are slightly smaller than those of peppermint, and have a crinkled appearance. Spearmint has a delicate mint fragrance and taste.

● Mint is available fresh or dried. Use fresh mint to flavor vegetables, salads, fruit desserts, and beverages. Use dried mint in lamb stews, seafood marinades, and sauces.

"'How long does getting thin take?' Pooh asked anxiously."

—A. A. Milne

Piña Colada Sherbet

The optional coconut will add 22 calories per serving.

LOW-CALORIE ▪ LOW-CHOLESTEROL ▪ LOW-FAT
Makes about 4 cups.
Nutrient Value Per ½ Cup: 79 calories, 2 g protein, 1 g fat, 17 g carbohydrate, 58 mg sodium, 2 mg cholesterol.

2	cups 2-inch fresh pineapple cubes (half a 4-pound pineapple)	⅓	cup sweetened flaked coconut (optional)
2	cups buttermilk	2	tablespoons lime juice
½	cup Simple Syrup (recipe, page 206)		

1. Place the pineapple cubes in the container of a food processor or electric blender. Whirl until the pineapple is puréed; you should have about 1⅔ cups. Add the buttermilk, Simple Syrup, coconut if using, and lime juice. Whirl until the buttermilk mixture is well blended.

2. Pour the buttermilk mixture into an ice cream maker. Process following the ice cream maker manufacturer's directions. Pack the sherbet into a freezer container. Freeze the sherbet until it is firm, for at least 4 hours.

Mocha Banana Split

LOW-CHOLESTEROL ▪ LOW-SODIUM ▪ LOW-FAT
Makes 4 servings.
Nutrient Value Per Serving: 206 calories, 4 g protein, 1 g fat, 47 g carbohydrate, 19 mg sodium, 4 mg cholesterol.

¼	cup chocolate sauce	1	pint frozen coffee yogurt
⅛	teaspoon ground cinnamon	2	medium-size bananas

1. Stir together the chocolate sauce and the cinnamon in a small bowl until they are well blended.

2. Scoop the yogurt, divided evenly, into 4 individual dessert glasses. Peel the bananas, and diagonally slice them. Arrange the banana slices around the yogurt in the glasses. Drizzle the cinnamon-chocolate sauce over the bananas and the yogurt. Serve the banana splits immediately.

Peachy Buttermilk Shake

LOW-CALORIE · LOW-CHOLESTEROL · LOW-FAT
Makes 4 servings.
Nutrient Value Per Serving: 129 calories, 3 g protein, 1 g fat,
29 g carbohydrate, 65 mg sodium, 2 mg cholesterol.

1	ripe peach OR: nectarine	½	recipe Orange Ice (recipe, below)
1	cup buttermilk		
1	tablespoon honey	4	mint sprigs, for garnish (optional)

1. Chill 4 glasses in the freezer. Halve the peach or nectarine, and remove the pit. Cut 4 thin peach slices, and reserve them. Cut the remainder of the peach into small cubes.

2. Combine the peach cubes, buttermilk and honey in the container of an electric blender or food processor. Whirl until the mixture is smooth.

3. Cut the Orange Ice into about 2-inch squares. Add the ice squares to the blender container. Whirl until the shake is smooth, scraping down the side of the container as needed. Pour the shake into the chilled glasses. Garnish each shake with a reserved peach slice and, if you wish, a mint sprig.

Orange Ice

This recipe makes enough orange ice to make Peachy Buttermilk Shakes, too.

LOW-CALORIE · LOW-CHOLESTEROL · LOW-SODIUM · LOW-FAT
Makes 8 servings.
Nutrient Value Per Serving: 75 calories, 1 g protein, .05 g fat,
18 g carbohydrate, 1 mg sodium, 0 mg cholesterol.

1	tray ice cubes (about 4 cups)	⅓	cup sugar
2½	cups water		Additional orange zest, for garnish (optional)
2	strips (3 x ½ inch) orange zest (orange part of rind only)		
1	can (6 ounces) frozen orange juice concentrate, undiluted		

1. Chill a 13 x 9 x 2-inch metal baking pan in the freezer. Place a fine-mesh strainer over a large bowl in the sink.

2. Working in 2 batches, combine half the ice cubes with half the water in the container of an electric blender. Whirl at medium speed for about 30 seconds, or until the ice is chopped; there may be some large ice chunks. Drain the chopped ice in the strainer. Repeat with the remaining ice cubes and water. Transfer the chopped ice to a bowl; do not drain any water that collects in the bowl.

3. Combine the orange zest, orange juice concentrate and sugar in the blender container. Add the chopped ice. Cover and whirl at medium speed until the orange mixture is smooth, scraping down the sides of the container as needed. Pour the orange mixture into the chilled pan, spreading the mixture level with a spatula. Cover the pan, and freeze the orange mixture for 1 hour.

4. Scoop half the orange ice into 4 individual dessert glasses. Garnish with additional orange zest, if you wish. Reserve the remaining orange ice for Peachy Buttermilk Shakes.

ZEST FOR TASTE

Zest is the colored part of the rind of citrus fruit that contains the essential oils. If a recipe calls for both grated zest and juice, grate the zest first, then juice the fruit.

● To remove zest in strips, use a very sharp paring knife or a vegetable peeler, and work carefully to be sure you remove only the colored part of the rind, not the bitter white pith.

GELATIN

A transparent substance containing protein, gelatin is made by boiling beef and veal bones. Gelatin has the capacity to dissolve in hot water, then form a jelly when chilled. There are two types of gelatin available. One is plain, unflavored gelatin, used for savory and sweet dishes. The other is a mixture of sugar, gelatin and flavoring, used to make desserts and salads.

Ginger Pudding with Strawberries

This dessert is a good way to use up extra ricotta cheese. When strawberries are not in season, top the pudding with other fresh, frozen or canned fruit.

LOW-CALORIE ▪ LOW-CHOLESTEROL ▪ LOW-FAT
Makes 4 servings.
Nutrient Value Per Serving: 129 calories, 7 g protein, 4 g fat, 16 g carbohydrate, 80 mg sodium, 16 mg cholesterol.

1	teaspoon unflavored gelatin	2	teaspoons finely chopped crystallized ginger
2	tablespoons cold water		
¾	cup part-skim ricotta cheese	¼	teaspoon vanilla
½	cup plain nonfat yogurt	1	cup sliced strawberries
2	tablespoons sugar		

1. Sprinkle the gelatin over the cold water in a 1-cup measure. Let the gelatin mixture stand for 3 minutes. Place the measure in gently boiling water in a small skillet or pan, and heat until the gelatin dissolves.

2. Combine the ricotta cheese, yogurt, sugar, ginger and vanilla in the container of a food processor or electric blender. Whirl until the ricotta mixture is smooth. Mix in the dissolved gelatin mixture.

3. Divide the pudding evenly among 4 individual dessert glasses. Place the puddings in the freezer for 15 minutes to quick-chill. Then place the puddings in the refrigerator until serving time. To serve, top the puddings with the strawberries.

Gingered Pineapple Vanilla Pudding

LOW-CHOLESTEROL ▪ LOW-FAT
Makes 4 servings.
Nutrient Value Per Serving: 175 calories, 3 g protein, 1 g fat, 39 g carbohydrate, 428 mg sodium, 4 mg cholesterol.

1	can (8 ounces) pineapple chunks packed in juice, drained and juice reserved	1	tablespoon finely chopped crystallized ginger
1½	cups lowfat milk		Flaked coconut, for garnish (optional)
1	package (4-serving size) instant vanilla pudding		

1. Pour the reserved pineapple juice into a 2-cup measure. Add the milk to make 2 cups. Pour the milk mixture into a small bowl. Add the instant pudding. Beat with an electric mixer at low speed, or by hand with a whisk, until the pudding mixture is well blended and slightly thickened. Stir in the ginger.

2. Spoon the pudding into 4 individual dessert glasses. Refrigerate the puddings until serving time. To serve, top the puddings with the pineapple chunks. Garnish the puddings with flaked coconut, if you wish.

Frozen Strawberry Banana Cream

LOW-CALORIE · LOW-CHOLESTEROL · LOW-FAT
Makes 8 servings.
Nutrient Value Per Serving: 106 calories, 4 g protein, 1 g fat,
19 g carbohydrate, 128 mg sodium, 5 mg cholesterol.

1	pint strawberries, hulled and halved	½	cup reduced-fat dairy sour cream
1	banana, cut up	⅓	cup honey
1	cup lowfat cottage cheese	½	teaspoon vanilla

1. Combine the strawberries, banana, cottage cheese, sour cream, honey and vanilla in the container of a food processor or electric blender. Whirl for 2 minutes, or until the strawberry banana cream is very smooth, scraping down the side of the container occasionally.

2. Pour the strawberry banana cream into a 13 x 9 x 2-inch baking pan. Freeze the strawberry banana cream for about 30 minutes, or until the edges of the cream are solid. Stir the strawberry banana cream well. Freeze the strawberry banana cream, stirring occasionally to break it up, for about 2 hours, or just until the cream is solid in the center.

3. To serve, spoon the strawberry banana cream into 8 individual dessert glasses.*

***Note:** If the strawberry banana cream is frozen for several days before serving it, remove the pan from the freezer to the refrigerator for 30 minutes. Then place the strawberry banana cream in a medium-size bowl. Chop the strawberry banana cream into pieces small enough to fit into the processor container. Place the cream pieces in the processor container, and pulse quickly until the cream softens. Scoop the strawberry banana cream into 8 individual dessert glasses, and serve.*

Chunky Cherry Vanilla Sherbet

LOW-CALORIE · LOW-CHOLESTEROL · LOW-FAT
Makes about 4½ cups.
Nutrient Value Per ½ Cup: 83 calories, 3 g protein, 1 g fat,
17 g carbohydrate, 72 mg sodium, 3 mg cholesterol.

2	cups stemmed, pitted cherries (1 pound)	½	cup Simple Syrup (recipe, page 206)
2½	cups buttermilk	1	teaspoon vanilla

1. Combine the cherries, buttermilk, Simple Syrup and vanilla in the container of a food processor or electric blender. Pulse until the cherries are chopped, and the mixture is blended.

2. Pour the cherry mixture into an ice cream maker. Process following the ice cream maker manufacturer's directions. Pack the sherbet into a freezer container. Freeze the sherbet until it is firm, for at least 4 hours.

WASHING & HULLING STRAWBERRIES

Wash strawberries with their caps on to prevent them from absorbing water. Hull strawberries by giving their caps a light twist; don't slice off the caps, or you will lose some of the fruit.

"*Cherry ripe, ripe, ripe, I cry, Full and fair ones; come and buy! If so be you ask me where They do grow, I answer, there, Where my Julia's lips do smile; There's the land, or cherry-isle.*"

— Robert Herrick

Peach Marsala Ice

LOW-CALORIE · LOW-CHOLESTEROL · LOW-SODIUM · LOW-FAT
Makes about 2½ pints.
Nutrient Value Per ½ Cup: 63 calories, 0 g protein, 0 g fat, 15 g carbohydrate, 1 mg sodium, 0 mg cholesterol.

½ cup water	1 tablespoon lemon juice
⅓ cup sugar	¼ cup Marsala wine
2½ pounds ripe peaches, peeled, pitted and diced (about 4 cups)	

1. Combine the water with the sugar in a small saucepan. Bring the mixture to boiling over medium heat, stirring constantly, until the sugar is completely dissolved. Reduce the heat to low and simmer the syrup, uncovered, for 3 minutes. Remove the saucepan from the heat, and let the syrup cool completely.

2. Working in batches if necessary, place the peaches, lemon juice and syrup in the container of a food processor or electric blender. Whirl until the mixture is a smooth purée. Stir in the wine.

3. Pour the peach purée into an 8-inch square metal pan. Freeze the peach purée for 2 to 4 hours, or until it is almost frozen, stirring the purée, especially around the edges, several times during the freezing so it freezes evenly.

4. Transfer the peach ice to the processor container, and whirl just until the ice is smooth and fluffy; do not overprocess. Or transfer the ice to a chilled large bowl and beat it with an electric mixer; do not overbeat. Return the ice to the pan, and freeze it for 30 minutes. Whirl or beat the ice again until it is smooth and fluffy.

5. Place the peach ice in a bowl, and cover the bowl tightly. Freeze the peach ice for 1 to 2 hours, or until it is almost firm. If the peach ice becomes too firm to serve, soften it in the refrigerator for 30 minutes.

EMERGENCY INGREDIENT SUBSTITUTES

WHEN THE RECIPE CALLS FOR:	YOU CAN SUBSTITUTE:
1 square unsweetened chocolate	3 tablespoons unsweetened cocoa powder plus 1 tablespoon butter, margarine or vegetable shortening
1 cup sifted cake flour	⅞ cup sifted all-purpose flour (1 cup less 2 tablespoons)
2 tablespoons flour (for thickening)	1 tablespoon cornstarch
1 teaspoon baking powder	¼ teaspoon baking powder plus ⅝ teaspoon cream of tartar
1 cup corn syrup	1 cup sugar plus ¼ cup liquid used in recipe
1 cup honey	1¼ cups sugar plus ¼ cup liquid used in recipe
1 cup whole milk	½ cup evaporated milk plus ½ cup water
1 cup buttermilk	1 tablespoon vinegar plus enough whole milk to make 1 cup
1 cup sour cream (in baking)	⅞ cup buttermilk or sour milk plus 3 tablespoons butter
1 egg (for custards)	2 egg yolks plus 1 tablespoon water
1 cup brown sugar (packed)	1 cup granulated sugar, or 1 cup granulated sugar plus 2 tablespoons molasses
1 teaspoon lemon juice	¼ teaspoon vinegar
¼ cup chopped onion	1 tablespoon instant minced onion
1 clove garlic	⅛ teaspoon garlic powder
1 cup zucchini	1 cup yellow squash
1 cup tomato juice	½ cup tomato sauce plus ½ cup water
2 cups tomato sauce	¾ cup tomato paste plus 1 cup water
1 tablespoon snipped fresh herbs	1 teaspoon dried herbs
1 tablespoon prepared mustard	1 teaspoon dry mustard
½ cup (1 stick) butter or margarine	7 tablespoons vegetable shortening

EMERGENCY BAKING DISH AND PAN SUBSTITUTES

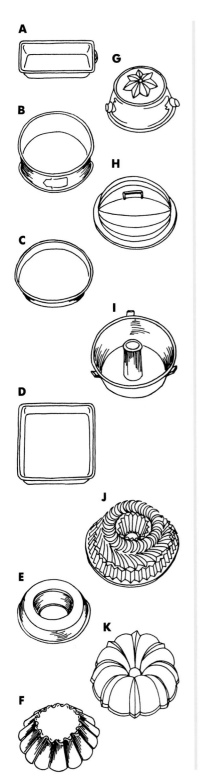

HANDY CHARTS OF KITCHEN MATH

You'll never have a cooking crisis when you use our handy charts. Need a 4- or 6-cup baking dish? Will your fancy mold be the right size for the recipe? See the charts below for the answers.

- If you do not have the specific size pan or mold called for in a recipe, substitute a pan of equal volume from the list below.
- If the pan you are substituting is made of glass, reduce the baking temperature by 25°.
- If you are substituting a pan that is shallower than the pan in the recipe, reduce the baking time by about one quarter.
- If you are substituting a pan that is deeper than the pan in the recipe, increase the baking time by one quarter.

COMMON KITCHEN PANS TO USE WHEN THE RECIPE CALLS FOR:

4-cup baking dish:
9-inch pie plate
8 x 1½-inch round layer cake pan — **C**
7⅜ x 3⅝ x 2⅝-inch loaf pan — **A**
6-cup baking dish:
10-inch pie plate
8 or 9 x 1½-inch round layer cake pan — **C**
8½ x 3⅝ x 2⅝-inch loaf pan — **A**
8-cup baking dish:
8 x 8 x 2-inch square pan — **D**
11 x 7 x 1½-inch baking pan
9 x 5 x 3-inch loaf pan — **A**
10-cup baking dish:
9 x 9 x 2-inch square pan — **D**
11¾ x 7½ x 1¾-inch baking pan
15½ x 10½ x 1-inch jelly-roll pan

12-cup baking dish and over:
13½ x 8½ x 2-inch glass baking dish (12 cups)
13 x 9 x 2-inch metal baking pan (15 cups)
14 x 10½ x 2½-inch roasting pan (19 cups)
Three 8 inch-round layer cake pans:
two 9 x 9 x 2-inch square cake pans — **D**
Two 9-inch round layer cake pans:
two 8 x 8 x 2-inch square cake pans — **D**
13 x 9 x 2-inch pan (15 cups)
9 x 5 x 3-inch loaf pan:
9 x 9 x 2-inch square cake pan — **D**
9-inch angel cake tube pan:
10 x 3¾-inch Bundt pan — **K**
9 x 3½-inch fancy tube pan — **J**

TOTAL VOLUME OF VARIOUS SPECIAL BAKING PANS

Tube Pans:

7½ x 3-inch Bundt tube pan — **K**	6 cups
9 x 3½-inch fancy tube or Bundt pan — **J** or **K**	9 cups
9 x 3½-inch angel cake or tube pan — **I**	12 cups
10 x 3¾-inch Bundt or Crownburst® pan — **K**	12 cups
9 x 3½-inch fancy tube mold — **J**	12 cups
10 x 4-inch fancy tube mold (Kugelhopf) — **J**	16 cups
10 x 4-inch angel cake or tube pan — **I**	18 cups

Melon Mold:

7 x 5½ x 4-inch mold — **H**	6 cups

Springform Pans:

8 x 3-inch pan — **B**	12 cups
9 x 3-inch pan — **B**	16 cups

Ring Molds:

8½ x 2¼-inch mold — **E**	4½ cups
9¼ x 2¾-inch mold — **E**	8 cups

Charlotte Mold:

6 x 4¼-inch mold — **G**	7½ cups

Brioche Pan:

9½ x 3¼-inch pan — **F**	8 cups

FOOD EQUIVALENTS

Berries, 1 pint	1¾ cups
Bread	
Crumbs, soft, 1 cup	2 slices
Cubes, 1 cup	2 slices
1 pound, sliced	22 slices
Broth	
Beef or Chicken, 1 cup	1 teaspoon instant bouillon or 1 envelope bouillon or 1 cube bouillon, dissolved in 1 cup boiling water
Butter or Margarine	
½ stick	¼ cup or 4 tablespoons
1 pound	4 sticks or 2 cups
Cream and Milk	
Cream, heavy, 1 cup	2 cups, whipped
Milk, evaporated, small can	⅔ cup
Milk, instant nonfat dry, 1 pound	5 quarts, liquid skim milk
Milk, sweetened condensed, 14-ounce can	1¾ cups
Cheese	
Blue, crumbled, 4 ounces	1 cup
Cheddar or Swiss, 1 pound, shredded	4 cups
Cottage, 8 ounces	1 cup
Cream, 8 ounces	1 cup
Parmesan or Romano, ¼ pound, grated	1¼ cups
Chocolate	
Semisweet pieces, 6 ounces	1 cup
Unsweetened, 1 ounce	1 square
Coconut	
Flaked, 3½-ounce can	1⅓ cups
Shredded, 4-ounce can	1⅓ cups
Cookies	
Chocolate wafers, 1 cup crumbs	19 wafers
Vanilla wafers, 1 cup fine crumbs	22 wafers
Graham crackers, 1 cup fine crumbs	14 square crackers
Dried Beans and Peas, 1 cup	2¼ cups, cooked
Eggs (large)	
Whole, 1 cup	5 to 6
Whites, 1 cup	7 to 8
Yolks, 1 cup	13 to 14
Flour	
All-purpose, sifted, 1 pound	4 cups
Cake, sifted, 1 pound	4¾ to 5 cups
Gelatin, unflavored, 1 envelope	1 tablespoon

Nuts	
Almonds, 1 pound, shelled	3½ cups
Peanuts, 1 pound, shelled	3 cups
Walnuts, 1 pound, shelled	4 cups
Pecans, 1 pound, shelled	4 cups
Pasta	
Macaroni, elbow, uncooked, 8 ounces	4 cups, cooked
Noodles, medium-width, uncooked, 8 ounces	3¾ cups, cooked
Spaghetti, uncooked, 8 ounces	4 cups, cooked
Rice	
Enriched precooked rice, uncooked, 1 cup	2 cups, cooked
Long-grain white rice, uncooked, 1 cup	3 cups, cooked
Sugar	
Brown, firmly packed, 1 pound	2¼ cups
Granulated, 1 pound	2 cups
10X (confectioners' powdered), sifted, 1 pound	3⅓ to 4 cups
Vegetables and Fruits	
Apples, 1 pound	3 medium-size
Bananas, 1 pound	3 medium-size
Cabbages, 1 pound, shredded	4 cups
Carrots, 1 pound, sliced	2½ cups
Herbs, chopped fresh, 1 tablespoon	1 teaspoon dried
Lemon, 1 medium-size, grated	2 teaspoons lemon zest
Lemon, 1 medium-size, squeezed	2 tablespoons lemon juice
Mushrooms, 1 pound, sliced	3 cups
Onions, small white silverskins, 1 pound	12 to 14
Onions, yellow cooking, 1 pound	5 to 6 medium-size
Orange, 1 medium-size, grated	2 tablespoons orange zest
Orange, 1 medium-size, squeezed	⅓ to ½ cup orange juice
Peaches, 1 pound	4 medium-size
Potatoes, all-purpose, 1 pound	3 medium-size
Tomatoes, 1 pound:	
Large	2
Medium-size	3
Small	4

MEASURING EQUIPMENT

MEASURING FLOUR

Measure all-purpose flour by spooning it from the bag or canister into a dry measuring cup, heaping the flour slightly. *(Note: The top of the measuring cup is flat; there is no spout in a dry measuring cup, as there is in a liquid measuring cup.)*

Place the heaping cup of flour over the flour bag or canister, and run the flat side of a long knife across the top to level off the cup. *(Note: Use this technique for granulated sugar, too.)*

MEASURING SHORTENING

Measure vegetable shortening by scooping it with a rubber scraper into a dry measuring cup. Run the flat blade of a long knife over the top of the cup. Scoop the shortening out of the cup with the rubber scraper into a mixing bowl. Shortening can be measured before or after it is melted.

One stick of butter or margarine equals 4 ounces; 4 sticks equal 1 pound or 2 cups.

MEASURING LIQUID

Place a liquid measuring cup on a flat surface, and stoop to be at eye level with the measuring cup. Pour the liquid to the desired measure printed on the side of the cup. *(Note: When measuring a syrup, such as molasses or honey, grease the cup with butter or margarine; the syrup will pour out easily.)*

PACKING BROWN SUGAR

Measure light or dark brown sugar by packing it into a dry measuring cup, using the back of a tablespoon.

OVEN TEMPERATURES

Very Slow	250°-275°
Slow	300°-325°
Moderate	350°-375°
Hot	400°-425°
Very Hot	450°-475°
Extremely Hot	500°+

CASSEROLE MEASUREMENT CHART

Casseroles are international dishes. Recipes are imported from all over the world, and each country has its own system for measuring. The chart below will help you convert your casserole's measurements from one system to another so you can be sure every recipe you make will turn out just right.

Cups	=	Pints	=	Quarts	=	Liters
1		½		¼		0.237
2		1*		½*		0.473
4		2*		1*		0.946
6		3		1½		1.419
8		4		2		1.892
10		5		2½		2.365
12		6		3		2.838

*In Canada, 1 pint = 2½ cups; 1 quart = 5 cups.

*G*lossary

A

À la
In the style of, as in à la francaise: French style.

Al dente
An Italian phrase used to describe pasta cooked to the perfect stage of doneness—tender, but firm enough to be felt between the teeth.

Antipasto
An Italian word meaning "before the meal." A selection of hors d'oeuvres, such as salami, marinated mushrooms, tuna or anchovies.

Au gratin
A dish, usually vegetables, cooked in a creamy sauce, topped with bread crumbs and/or cheese, and browned in the oven or broiler.

B

Blanch
To plunge food quickly into boiling water, then into cold water, to loosen the skins for easy removal. Also, a preliminary step in freezing vegetables.

Braise
To brown in fat, then to cook, covered, in a small amount of liquid.

C

Candy
A confection. Also, to cook fruit, fruit peel or ginger in a heavy syrup until it is transparent, then drain and dry it. Also, to cook vegetables, such as carrots or sweet potatoes, in a sugar syrup or honey.

Caramelize
To cook sugar over low heat until it becomes a golden brown liquid.

Chorizo
A Spanish sausage strongly flavored with paprika and garlic.

Coat the spoon
A term used to describe egg-based sauces, or liquids such as custard, when at their perfect consistency. When a metal spoon is dipped into the liquid and removed, it should be coated with a thin, jelly-like film.

Confectioners' powdered sugar
Also known as 10X sugar. The finest grind of sugar available. A small amount of cornstarch is added to the sugar to prevent it from lumping. Used for "dusting" desserts, or in uncooked icings.

Crimp
To press the edges of pastry together with the tines of a fork or your fingertips to form a decorative edging or to seal in a filling.

Cut in
To blend shortening or other solid fat with a flour mixture by working them with a pastry blender or two knives until the combined mixture resembles peas or coarse meal.

E

Egg wash
A whole egg or egg yolk that is mixed with a little water or milk brushed on bread dough before baking to create a shiny crust.

Entrée
A French term referring to the third course in a formal dinner. Also used to designate the main dish of a meal.

Evaporated milk
Canned, unsweetened milk that has been slightly thickened by the removal of some of its water.

F

Fajitas
A popular dish from the southwest. Pieces of skirt steak, usually marinated, are grilled, sliced and wrapped in flour tortillas. Fajitas also can be made from flank steak, boneless chuck, chicken or turkey.

Fillet
A thin, boneless piece of meat or fish.

Flake
To break up food, such as tuna, into smaller pieces with a fork.

Florentine
In the style of Florence, Italy—usually served on a bed of spinach, topped with a cheese sauce and browned in the oven.

Flour, Cake
Flour that is milled from soft wheat and contains less gluten-forming protein than all-purpose flour. Cake flour produces a lighter texture in cakes, cookies and pastries.

Flute
To form a ruffled edge for a pie crust with your fingers and thumb.

Fricassee
A dish consisting of meat cut into pieces, and covered by a mixture of water, vegetables and, often, wine. The meat may be browned in butter or oil first. A gravy is made from the cooking liquid, and served with the meat. Also the method by which the dish is prepared.

Frittata
An unfolded omelet often containing vegetables or meat.

G

Garnish
To decorate with colorful and/or elegantly cut pieces of food.

Glaze
To coat food with honey, syrup or other liquid to create a shiny appearance.

Gluten
The protein of wheat flour that forms the framework or structure of cakes, breads, cookies and pastries.

Ground hot red pepper
Also known as cayenne pepper.

H

Hors d'oeuvre
Any one of a variety of appetizers, such as olives, anchovies or canapés, usually served at the beginning of a meal.

Hull
To remove the caps and stems from fresh berries.

I

Ice   To cover with icing. Also, a frozen, water-based dessert.

Italienne, à l'   Served Italian style, with pasta.

J

Julienne   To cut food into uniformly long, thin slivers (1½ x ¼ inches).

K

Kasha   Buckwheat groats that are braised or cooked in liquid. Usually served as a starch in place of rice or potatoes.

Knead   To work dough with your hands until it is smooth and elastic. Kneading is necessary to develop the gluten in yeast breads, which gives them their framework and volume.

Kosher salt   A very coarse salt.

L

Liquid red pepper seasoning   The generic name for Tabasco® sauce.

M

Macerate   To let food, principally fruit, steep in wine or spirits to absorb the flavor.

Maître d'hôtel   Simply cooked dishes seasoned with finely chopped parsley, butter and lemon. Maître d'Hôtel butter is a mixture of butter or margarine, parsley, lemon juice and salt.

Marinate   To let food, principally meat, steep in an oil- or acid-based sauce before cooking. The marinade adds flavor to and tenderizes the meat.

Marzipan   A confection made from almond paste, sugar and egg whites, often colored and shaped into tiny fruit and vegetable forms.

Mask   To coat food with a sauce or aspic.

Mole   A sauce of Mexican origin containing chili peppers, onion, garlic, bitter chocolate, and other ingredients. The chocolate gives mole sauce its distinctive flavor. Usually served over poultry.

Mousse   A rich, creamy dessert. Also, a hot or cold savory dish with a velvety texture, rich with cream and bound with eggs or, if cold, with gelatin.

Mull   To heat a liquid, such as wine or cider, with whole spices added to it.

N

Niçoise   In the style of Nice, France — with tomatoes, garlic, olive oil and ripe olives.

Nouvelle Cuisine   A style of cooking developed in France that provides a lighter approach to classic French dishes and preparation techniques. The techniques have been adapted to many other cuisines.

O

Oil   To rub a pan or mold with cooking oil.

Orzo   Tiny, rice-shaped pasta.

P

Panbroil   To cook food in a small amount of fat, pouring off drippings as they accumulate.

Parboil   To cook food in boiling water until about half done; vegetables to be cooked in a casserole usually are parboiled first.

Pastry   A stiff dough made from flour, water and shortening that becomes flaky when baked. Also, a rich dough used for desserts.

Pastry bag   A cone-shaped fabric, parchment or plastic bag, with a hole at the end to which various tips are attached. Used to decorate various foods.

Pâté   A well-seasoned mixture of finely chopped or ground meats and/or liver. Pâté de foie gras is made from goose livers and truffles.

Pectin   A water-soluble fiber, obtained from certain fruits and vegetables, that is manufactured in syrup form to use in preparing jellies and jams.

Penne   A type of pasta with a short quill- or slant-cut tubular shape.

Phyllo   Also "fillo." A flaky, tissue paper-thin pastry used in Greek dishes.

Pilaf   Rice cooked in a savory broth, with herbs, spices, and often small bits of meat or vegetables.

Pinch   The amount of a dry ingredient that can be taken up between the thumb and index finger — about ⅛ teaspoon.

Pipe   To press a soft mixture through a pastry bag fitted with a decorative tip to create a garnish or fancy edging for a dish.

Plump   To soak raisins or other dried fruits in liquid until they are softened and almost returned to their natural state.

Poach   To cook food, such as fish fillets, in barely simmering liquid.

Purée   To reduce food to a smooth, velvety texture by whirling it in the container of an electric blender or food processor, or by pressing it through a sieve or food grinder. Also, the food so processed.

R

Ragoût	A stew.
Ramekin	A small, individual-size baking dish.
Reduce	To boil a liquid, uncovered, until the quantity is lessened and concentrated.
Render	To melt solid fat.
Rice	To press food through a container with small holes so the food resembles rice.
Risotto	Rice browned in fat and cooked in chicken broth or other liquid until it is tender but firm. It is creamy in texture, not dry or runny.
Roast	To cook meat or poultry in the oven by dry heat.
Rotelle	A type of pasta shaped like corkscrews.
Roulade	A slice of meat rolled around a filling. Also, a jelly-roll cake.
Roux	A cooked mixture of fat and flour used to thicken sauces and gravies.

S

Salsa	A number of sauces in Mexican and Southwestern cuisines, with flavors ranging from very spicy to very subtle. Also, an uncooked, seasoned tomato sauce served as a condiment and used to add flavor to other dishes.
Sauté	To cook food quickly in a small amount of hot fat in a skillet.
Scald	To heat a liquid just until small bubbles form around the edges of the pan, but not allow the liquid to come to a boil.
Scallop	To bake small pieces of food in a casserole, usually in a cream sauce. Also, a thin, boneless slice of meat such as veal.
Score	To make shallow, perpendicular cuts with a knife over the surface of a food.
Short	An adjective used to describe a type of bread, cake or pastry that has a high proportion of fat and an extremely tender or crisp texture.
Shortening	A solid fat, usually of vegetable origin, used to add tenderness to pastry, bread, cakes and cookies.
Simmer	To cook food in a liquid that is just below boiling.
Skewer	To thread food on a wooden or metal pin for cooking. Also, the pin itself.
Skim	To remove fat or film from the surface of a liquid or sauce.
Sliver	To cut into long, thin strips.
Steam	To cook food in a covered saucepan in a steamer basket or on a trivet over a small amount of boiling water.
Steep	To soak food, such as tea, in liquid until the liquid absorbs the food's flavor.
Stew	To cook food, covered, in simmering liquid.
Stir-fry	To cook food quickly over high heat in a small amount of oil, stirring or tossing constantly.
Stock	A liquid base for soups and sauces made by the long, slow cooking of meat, poultry or fish with their bones. Stock may be brown or white, depending on whether or not the meat and bones are browned first.

T

Terrine
A type of baking dish used to prepare dishes such as pâtés. Also, the dish so prepared.

Thicken
To make a liquid more dense by adding flour, cornstarch or a beaten egg.

Thin
To make a liquid less dense by the adding of more liquid.

Timbale
A savory meat, fish, poultry or vegetable custard baked in a small mold. Also, a pastry shell made on a special iron mold.

Torte
A very rich, multilayered cake made with eggs and, often, grated nuts. The cake usually is filled, but frequently is not frosted.

Tortilla
A thin pancake of unleavened cornmeal or wheat flour used in Mexican and Southwestern cooking. Usually served hot with a topping or filling.

Truffles
A type of underground fungi considered a delicacy. Black, dark brown or white in color, they are quite expensive because of their rarity and the method used to gather them. Also, an extremely rich, chocolate candy.

Truss
To tie food into a compact shape before roasting.

Turnover
A pastry circle or square folded over a sweet or savory filling, with the edges crimped together. Turnovers usually are baked, but sometimes are fried.

W

Whip
To beat food until frothy or stiff with an eggbeater or an electric mixer.

Wok
A large round-bottomed, bowl-shaped Chinese cooking utensil used for stir-frying.

Y

Yeast, Quick or rapid-rise
A variety of yeast that causes dough to rise in one-half to one-third less time than if using regular active dry yeast.

Z

Zest
The colored, oily, aromatic part of the rind of citrus fruits.

Index *Italicized Page Numbers Refer to Photographs*

T

Photography Credits

Antoine Bootz: Pages 141, 155, 159, 192, 201.

Steven Cohen: Page 187.

Rita Maas: Pages 162, 184.

Steven Mark Needham: Pages 195, 207.

Judd Pilossof: Page 179.

Alan Richardson: Pages 93, 95, 99, 134, 147.

Carin Riley: Pages 60, 63, 65, 72, 73, 76, 77, 78, 79, 88, 89, 133.

Jerry Simpson: Pages 81, 102.

Mark Thomas: Pages 70, 87, 108, 113, 165.

Baker Vail: Pages 6, 9, 15, 54.

René Velez: Pages 4, 19, 23, 24, 29, 32, 35, 36, 40, 43, 47, 48, 57, 145, 169, 175.

Lisa Watson: Pages 12, 91.

Contributing Food Editors

Jean Anderson: Pages 106, 107, 108, 109, 110, 111, 112, 114.

Linda Beaulieu: Pages 128-129, 130, 131, 132.

Jo Ann Brett: Pages 11, 20, 28, 30, 38-9, 50-51, 116-117, 136, 142, 149, 150.

Marlene Brown: Page 177.

Beatrice Cihak: Pages 7, 19, 21, 24, 27, 31, 34-35, 37, 42, 46-47, 52, 53, 72-73, 76-79, 88-89, 139, 144-145, 148, 151, 152, 153, 156, 160, 161, 168-169, 174, 202, 209, 211.

Sandra Rose Gluck: Pages 20, 32, 36, 40, 55, 92, 94-95, 96-97, 98, 115, 116, 118, 119, 120, 121, 122, 123, 124-125, 146, 148, 156, 157, 161, 186-187, 188.

Jean Hewitt: Page 167.

Barbara Kafka: Pages 164, 166, 172, 173, 176-177, 178, 180, 181, 182, 183.

Susan McQuillan: Pages 8-9, 10, 13, 14, 15, 16, 26, 28-29, 33, 34, 44, 49, 50, 51, 56, 74, 80, 82, 83, 86, 102-103, 104, 126-127, 137, 138, 140, 151, 154-155, 158, 160, 189, 192-193, 197, 200, 202, 204, 205, 206, 208, 209, 212.

Perla Meyers: Pages 170-171.

Diane Mogelever: Pages 170, 203.

Veronica Petta: Pages 190, 191, 198, 199.

Paul Piccuito: Pages 18, 25, 31, 39, 58, 59, 60, 61, 62, 64, 65, 66, 67, 68, 69, 105, 145, 204, 210.

Regina Ragone: Pages 8, 10, 12, 17, 22, 48, 56-57, 84-85, 90, 91, 100-101, 193.

Marie Simmons: Pages 143, 146.